DEMOCRATIC DISSENT & THE CULTURAL FICTIONS OF ANTEBELLUM AMERICA

STEPHEN JOHN HARTNETT

Democratic Dissent & the Cultural Fictions of Antebellum America

UNIVERSITY OF ILLINOIS PRESS
URBANA AND CHICAGO

Manufactured in the United States of America
c 5 4 3 2 1

This book is printed on acid-free paper.

Library of Congress Cataloging-in-Publication Data
Hartnett, Stephen J.
Democratic dissent and the cultural fictions of
antebellum America / Stephen John Hartnett.
p. cm.
Includes bibliographical references and index.
ISBN 0-252-02722-1 (cloth : alk. paper)
1. United States—Politics and government—1845–1861.
2. Rhetoric—Political aspects—United States—History—
19th century. 3. Democracy—United States—History—
19th century. 4. Propaganda—United States—History—
19th century. 5. Antislavery movements—United States—
History—19th century. 6. Capitalism—Political aspects—
United States—History—19th century. 7. Slavery—
Political aspects—United States—History—19th century.
8. United States—Territorial expansion—History—
19th century. 9. Identity (Psychology)—Political aspects—
United States—History—19th century. 10. National
characteristics, American. I. Title.
E415.7.H34 2002
973.6—dc21 2001004111

Contents

Acknowledgments

This book has been such a long time in the making that I am now, *finally,* blessed with the happy obligation of thanking a rather large number of friends and colleagues. Most recently I have benefited greatly from the editorial guidance of Dick Martin, at the University of Illinois Press. Bruce Bethell copyedited the book masterfully and deserves great thanks for helping it read more smoothly. Stephen Browne read the original 500-page manuscript closely and kindly, and pushed me toward clarity and brevity. Robert Hariman read both my original and my much-revised drafts, offering detailed and insightful suggestions on both occasions. I am deeply grateful for the opportunity to thank Dick, Bruce, Stephen, and Robert, whose contributions to this study epitomize what we all mean when we talk about constructive criticism.

I wrote the introduction, conclusion, chapter 1, and parts of chapter 4 and completed all final revising between fall 1999 and spring 2001, during which time I have had the pleasure of serving in the Department of Speech Communication at the University of Illinois. My colleagues have been uncommonly generous, particularly Cara Finnegan, who has read much of this book despite her own heavy workload in finishing a book of her own. Friends and mentors both, James Hay has provided a constant supply of world-class cooking and intellectual engagement, while Tom Conley has been an invaluable source of hard-to-find material. Joe Wenzel, Michèle Koven, Dan O'Keefe, Daena Goldsmith, Dave Tewksbury, Debbie Kemphues, Dale Brashers, Scott Althaus, Barbara Hall, John Caughlin, John Lammers, and Ken Anderson have all been models of collegiality, and my department head, David Swanson, has been incredibly generous with his support and guidance. I have also benefited from seminars and conversations with Donovan Conley, Jen Mercieca, and Jennifer Jones, all of whom will no doubt recognize some of their own ideas here.

The University of Illinois is home not only to these departmental colleagues but also to the Illinois Program for Research in the Humanities, the Unit for Criticism and Interpretation, and the American Studies Working Group, each of which has enabled me, through lectures, panels, brownbag lunches, and the lively social scene surrounding them, to learn a great deal from my colleagues. I have been happy to break bread and to share ideas with Vernon Burton, Kathy Oberdeck, Adam Sutcliffe, and Larry Ratner, from the history department; Matti Bunzl, from anthropology; Belden Fields, from political science; Barbara Mooney, from art history; Larry Schehr, from French; Dara Goldman, from Spanish; and Bill Maxwell, Trish Loughran, Julia Walker, Jed Esty, Ania Loomba, Suvir Kauhl, Matt Hurt, Debbie Hawhee, Lisa Lampert, Zohreh Sullivan, Gillen Wood, and Lori Newcomb, from English. Add to all these good people one of the nation's best libraries, complete with a world-class rare books room, and one would be hard pressed to find a place more conducive to doing good work.

Early drafts of chapters 2, 3, and 4 were produced while I was a visiting lecturer in the Department of Rhetoric at the University of California at Berkeley, from fall 1996 to spring 1999. My hallmate and skiing buddy, Will West, read those early drafts with uplifting intelligence and humor. Marianne Constable generously invited me to present a draft of chapter 2 to the department's Faculty Colloquium. My chair, Judith Butler, asked me to teach classes that enabled me to clarify my ideas about antebellum American democracy, and Mitchell Breitwieser kindly invited me to teach classes in his wonderful cross-departmental American Cultures series. Tom Sloane, Peter Dale Scott, Shadi Bartsch, Michael Mascuch, Maxine Fredericksen, Felipe Gutterriez, and James Salazar also all made my Berkeley years happier and more productive. I am particularly thankful for the friendship of Jody Lewen and Sean McPhetridge and for the efforts of the tutors, teaching assistants, and students who over the years made teaching classes in American history and speech communication at San Quentin Prison such a rewarding experience.

The material in this book has enjoyed multiple presentations before the Rhetoric Society of America, the Interdisciplinary Nineteenth-Century Studies Group, and the Radical Philosophy Association; in addition, every chapter has been aired in some form before the annual meetings of the National Communication Association. I think of the NCA as my intellectual home and attend each year's conference excited by the knowledge that Stephen Lucas, Sue Zaeske, Stephen Browne, Bonnie Dow, Robert Hariman, Jim Jasinski, Alisse Theodore, Jim Andrews, Dwight Conquergood, and Jon Rutter, among others, will provide kind, thoughtful feedback on works in progress and renew my faith in what we do as intellectuals. Perhaps more than anyone else in the field of communication, Larry Frey has championed my work and taught me how to live amid the academy with a sense of humor and perspective. Although he no longer attends the NCA, having sought communion among his fellow philosophers, Ramsey Eric Ramsey has read much of this book and for more than fifteen years has embodied what we used to talk about at Rutgers way back in the mid-1980s as loving intellectual camaraderie.

My debts to libraries, special collections, and museums are considerable. For access to printed and visual material, I would like to thank the Library of Congress, Washington, D.C.; the Newberry Library, Chicago; the Brookline Historical Society, Brookline, Mass.; the Museum of Fine Arts, Boston; the National Gallery of Art, Washington, D.C.; the Missouri Historical Society, St. Louis; the Department of Special Collections, Stanford University, Stanford, Calif.; the Peabody Museum of Archaeology and Ethnology, Harvard University, Cambridge, Mass.; the Getty Museum, Los Angeles; the Kentucky Historical Society, Frankfort; and the Bancroft Library, Berkeley, Calif. I have relied especially on the remarkable holdings of the New York Public Library; the New York Historical Society; the Pierpont Morgan Library, New York, N.Y.; and the University of Illinois Rare Book and Special Collections Library, Urbana.

Although this book mercifully bears no resemblance to the dissertation that brought me a Ph.D. from the Department of Literature at the University of California at San Diego in 1992, I nonetheless am happy to acknowledge my deep thanks to Michael Davidson, poet and teacher extraordinaire, for his many years of unflagging support. Many fine scholars and friends made UCSD a fine place to study, and I am thankful to have learned from Roy Harvey Pearce, Martin Padget, Shawn Smith, Fred Jameson, Rachel Klein, Mark Jenkins, and Andrea Slane.

Danny Postel has been a bedrock of support since the early 1990s and has been instrumental in helping me publish this book; I now look forward to returning the favor again and again. Thanks are also due to Bill Keach, David Leverenz, Aijaz Ahmad, and Stephen Bronner, each of whom inspired in me a love of the life of letters and politics.

An earlier draft of chapter 3 appeared in *American Studies* (1997); that material appears here courtesy of the American Studies Association.

Finally, along with making life just about as utopian as even a cosmos-drunk Whitman could have hoped, my darling Brett has helped me both to think and to write more clearly—she is my inspiration and joy. For a lifetime of teaching by gentle and intelligent example, this book is dedicated with more love than I can ever express to Rod and Sandy.

DEMOCRATIC DISSENT & THE CULTURAL FICTIONS OF ANTEBELLUM AMERICA

Introduction: Cultural Fictions and the Rhetorical Work of Humble Irony

This book explores the glorious and maddening paradoxes of democracy, the intertextual nature of public debate, and the curious ways in which the promises and possibilities of modernity were negotiated collectively in antebellum America. These broad themes provide the intellectual threads linking four case studies that address the rhetorics and politics of antebellum America's debates regarding abolition and capitalism (chapter 1), race and slavery (chapter 2), Manifest Destiny and empire (chapter 3), and representation and self-making (chapter 4). Some of these topics have received much attention from scholars of history and rhetoric; thus this book is in many ways a tribute to, a conversation with, and sometimes a critique of the best work of my predecessors. As a contribution to the recent explosion of interdisciplinary humanities scholarship, the work addresses a wide variety of genres of public persuasion, including speeches and debates; novels, poems, and short stories; newspaper articles, editorials, and advertisements; protest pamphlets, reform manifestos, and scientific reports; and daguerreotypes, paintings, and broadside sketches. This rich and sweeping array of textual materials is surrounded, to the best of my abilities, with thick descriptions that strive to portray antebellum America in all its stunning beauty and shocking barbarity.[1]

The title of the study, *Democratic Dissent and the Cultural Fictions of Antebellum America*, points to two assumptions. First, American democracy is most fascinating when studied through the voices of citizens engaged in critical dialogue with both the nation's founding myths and its most pressing political crises, especially when these voices slowly oscillate between dissent and assent. As Kenneth Burke argues in a 1936 *Partisan Review* symposium entitled "What Is Americanism?": "The test of a revolutionary position is not in *what one rejects*, but in *what one would put in place of the rejected* . . . A philosophy proves its value not by what new material it must *categorically reject*, but by what new material it can *assimilate*." A particularly compelling example of this strategy is found in Marion S. Barry Jr.'s 1960 speech before the Democratic Party Platform Committee, assembled in Los Angeles. Barry explains the civil rights movement as "a protest and . . . an affirmation. We protest and take direct action against conditions of discrimination. We affirm equality and brotherhood of all men, the tenets of American democracy as set forth in the Constitution, and the traditions of social justice which permeate our Judaic-Christian heritage."[2] Following the lessons of Burke and Barry, the notion of democratic dissent points toward the dialectical give and take of protest and affirmation, of dissent and assent, of critique and celebration, and is thus centrally tied to the rhetorical and political transformations that make democracy possible.[3]

The second assumption underlying the title is that our ancestors produced their own stories, norms, explanations, icons, justifications, and sustaining myths and that these coping mechanisms were often constructed and conveyed *much like fiction*, as tales that were heard, discussed, altered, debated, puzzled over, and then retold to give the world order, meaning, and purpose. The notion of cultural fictions thus suggests a humble approach: if we grant that our forebears' consciousness, habits of behavior, and modes of communication were framed—like ours—largely by their living with and by a series of such enabling and meaning-making cultural fictions, then we may proceed without the normative baggage of calling their ideas or actions *ideological* to the more interesting historical and rhetorical questions of the ways in which these cultural fictions were presented. How did they reflect, embody, or negotiate larger cultural norms and values? Why were certain cultural fictions more appealing, functional, and persuasive than other, alternative cultural fictions? And how did such cultural fictions facilitate, curtail, and otherwise complicate the practice of democratic dissent in antebellum America?[4]

Rather than lament the obvious contradictions enlivening the space between the promises of democracy and the practices of slavery, or between the rhetoric of equality and the reality of oligarchy, or between the claim to "Manifest Destiny" and the resulting imperialist genocide, my concern is to explore how, specifically in the face of such historical and political complications, Americans struggled to produce cultural fictions that could not only explain and justify their political actions but also make sense of a world that many saw as dramatically out of control. I am concerned, then, both with exploring the sheer *rhetoricality* of democratic dissent and with recognizing that although antebellum cultural fictions struggled to be politically persuasive, their more important function was to fulfill collective needs for edification and legitimation. Foregrounding the dialectical tensions between democratic dissent and cultural fictions thus indicates a move away from philosophical concerns with epistemology to the political study of rhetoric, from the accusation that others are being "ideological" to the study of their means of persuasion, from sweeping macrological surveys of epochs to detailed and multivocal explorations of specific historical situations.[5]

Chapter 1 opens with a comparative discussion of the dialectics of assent and dissent in two versions of antebellum rhetoric regarding slavery: Robert Rantoul Jr.'s nuanced anti–"Slave Power" prudence and the American Anti-Slavery Society's full-throttled abolitionist radicalism. Having established these rhetorical and political parameters, I then examine how they in turn produce different models of historical causality and political responsibility. For the purposes of rhetorical and historical illustration, I then situate Solomon Northup's *Twelve Years a Slave* alongside works wherein Theodor Adorno, Karl Marx, and Thomas Jefferson ask similar questions regarding causality and responsibility. This seemingly odd series of juxtapositions enables me to examine four models of persuasion that all hinge on the rhetorical tropes of irony and metonymy and that ask—albeit from radically different places—how individuals come to understand their roles in society. I then venture some preliminary responses to this question by returning to the dialectics of assent and dissent in Northup's novel, in Lydia Maria Child's *An Appeal in Favor of That Class of Americans called Africans,* and in Frederick Douglass's oration "What, to the Slave, is the Fourth of July?" The chapter closes by discussing how the dialectics of assent and dissent in antebellum abolitionist rhetoric played out in large part through the abolitionists' reliance on cultural fictions celebrating the custom-destroying, opportunity-making, world-changing juggernaut of modern capitalism.

Having explored the dialectics of assent and dissent with respect to some of the leading antebellum abolitionists, I move on, in chapter 2, to examine the primary texts responsible for constructing proslavery cultural fictions circa 1828–55. This dramatic shift from abolitionist to proslavery cultural fictions demonstrates my commitment throughout the study to examine issues from multiple perspectives, to hear competing claims in dialogue both with and against one another. I accordingly offer rhetorical analyses of works by David Christy, Thomas Roderick Dew, William Harper, Thomas Prentice Kettell, Edmund Ruffin, and especially George Fitzhugh. I am concerned here with two primary issues. First, how did proslavery cultural fictions manipulate white fear by hyperbolically portraying the "serious evils" of abolition? Second, how did proslavery rhetors—much like their abolitionist counterparts—base their arguments about race and slavery on arguments about modernity and capitalism? Before engaging in these rhetorical analyses, I examine the political economy of slavery, thus foregrounding the fact that much proslavery rhetoric was engaged not only in producing cultural fictions about race and region but also in responding to the political and economic crises created by the volatile mixing of slavery with capitalism, equality with oligarchy, and democracy with despotism.

The first two chapters of the study thus frame the dominant cultural fictions employed in antebellum debates about abolition and slavery while simultaneously demonstrating that both abolitionists and proslavery rhetors were deeply concerned not only with refuting each other but also with addressing the ways in which modernity and capitalism were transforming the nation. Historical factors make these changes difficult to assess, however; America changed its shapes and sizes quickly throughout the antebellum period, undermining the possibility of speaking in general terms about the political and economic developments within discrete geographical regions, let alone across the nation as a whole. Indeed, even a cursory reading of the period's newspapers demonstrates that the opening of the West left Americans reeling with a dizzy sense of both unparalleled opportunity and baffling contradiction. Chapter 3 accordingly examines the ways debates about race, slavery, modernity, and capitalism were complicated by America's ascent toward continental empire. I focus here on the Texas annexation controversy in general and the crucial role that two works by Senator Robert Walker, *Letter on Texas Annexation* and *The South in Danger,* played in that controversy. These important and understudied documents provide rich opportunities for learning a great deal about political persuasion in antebellum America, for they deftly combine cultural fictions regarding race and slavery, capitalism and modernity, and history and metaphysics. The chapter opens by discussing the genealogy of notions of empire and destiny in American political discourse, examining the dream of empire in *The Federalist Papers,* Tocqueville's bleak premonitions in *Democracy in America,*

John O'Sullivan's polemics in *The United States Magazine and Democratic Review,* and Whig congressman Robert Winthrop's eloquent critique of imperialism. The chapter thus situates Walker's propaganda within a series of surrounding arguments, hence exploring how antebellum Americans both constructed and contested the parameters of the controversial claim to Manifest Destiny.

Chapter 4 traces how the previously addressed public debates—regarding abolition and capitalism, race and slavery, and empire and Manifest Destiny—are all conflated in the rhetoric of *representation.* I italicize the term here to indicate its central importance to yet problematic status within rhetorical, historical, and political studies. Indeed, one is never sure whether the term designates the rhetorical process of making meaning through cultural fictions, the political process of making meaning through organized political bodies, the physical process of making meaning through embodied choices, or some slippery combination thereof. This confusion regarding the very notion of representation is perhaps nowhere more complete and wondrous than in the 1855 version of Walt Whitman's *Leaves of Grass,* where politics, poetry, history, and sexuality are slammed together in a wild frenzy of contradictions. My rhetorical analysis of Whitman is layered against the fact that he was obsessed with daguerreotypes, "image studios," and the intricacies of the blossoming political economy of art production, all of which complicated, commodified, and infinitely enriched both his and our concepts of what it means to represent something or someone. I am particularly interested in considering how the daguerreotype enabled Americans to produce a series of cultural fictions regarding the politics and poetics of self-making. As is often the case with such innovations, the new poetics of self-making enabled by daguerreotypes also entailed a simultaneous drive to problematize and portray social "others." This chapter thus examines not only the relationships among Whitman's poetry and the new visual art of the daguerreotype but also the ways in which the period's new means of representation and self-making intertwined with the rise of phrenology and criminology, two popular antebellum discourses purporting to represent different and dangerous others.

Taken as a whole, these four case studies both illustrate the various ways Americans responded to the paradoxes of modernity and demonstrate the intertextual and endlessly dialectical nature of their public debates. While explicitly about abolition and capitalism, race and slavery, Manifest Destiny and empire, and representation and self-making, these debates were also *always* about the promises and possibilities of democracy. Indeed, considered as representative parts of the larger whole, each case study demonstrates the curious and complicated ways in which the promises and possibilities of democracy and modernity were negotiated collectively in antebellum America.[6] This book's persuasive power thus rests in large part on its ability to recreate the tenor and feel of the period by enabling readers to hear the voices of our ancestors. This strategy necessarily forces me to look beyond tightly defined academic genres and disciplines and to consider a broad sweep of persuasive materials. This commitment to consider as many of the available means of persuasion as possible, to wonder about the ways they influenced one another, and to situate them within richly detailed historical, political, and economic contexts follows from two simple premises. First, we historians enhance and enliven our understanding of the past when we recognize the conflictual and intertextual nature of democratic dissent. We can do so by broadening the scope of materials we are willing to consider as historical evidence and then striving to understand how these alternative materials spoke to, through, and against one another in profoundly productive ways. In short, my first guiding premise obliges me to write rhetorical history that is both interdisciplinary and comparativist.[7]

My second guiding premise is that we historians writing about this period need to contextualize more thoroughly our rhetorical analyses within the period's roiling public culture and its roaring, rapidly modernizing capitalist economy. This may be accomplished in two ways. First, we need to supplement our attention to cultural and political elites with a broader, more truly representative sense of other Americans' statements regarding a given issue. This is an appeal for scholars of the democratic process to take a more democratic approach to the period's many voices. Second, we need to explore the complicated interrelationships among public rhetorics and the simultaneous structural transformations occurring in the realms of transportation and consumerism, technologies of production and distribution, and class formation and conflict. This is an appeal for scholars of modernity to take a more materialist approach to the period's political and economic changes. In short, my second guiding premise obliges me to recognize that the multivocal histories of democratic dissent in the antebellum period cannot be told without also studying the rise of modern capitalism.[8]

Thus, as an interdisciplinary and comparativist analysis of the politics of public culture in antebellum America, this book examines how certain cultural fictions were rhetorically structured and disseminated to the public, how the public responded to these persuasive appeals, how ever-changing notions of publics and parties and participation were transformed through such exchanges, and ultimately, how these intertextual negotiations created the discursive conditions of American democracy. As a contextualist and materialist analysis of the paradoxes of modernity, this book simultaneously looks at the ways in which the new discursive possibilities of the period were enabled, compromised, and otherwise entangled in the myriad economic and political transformations that were slowly but surely propelling the once loosely confederated states into a nationally orchestrated capitalist empire. The vast archive of materials regarding these questions necessitates my condensing what could be long excursions into internecine academic debates into lengthy narrative endnotes; I hope readers find them helpful.[9]

Ideally, then, this interdisciplinary and comparativist attention to democratic dissent will enable me to move beyond both the insular tendencies of traditional rhetorical criticism and the high-handed generalizations of ideological criticism. I thus hope to approach what Kenneth Burke calls "humble irony." For example, in "Four Master Tropes," in *A Grammar of Motives,* when discussing irony as an interpretive attitude that recognizes the necessity of considering an issue from multiple and even conflicting perspectives, Burke writes that "true irony, humble irony, is based upon a sense of fundamental kinship with the enemy, as one *needs* him, is *indebted* to him, is not merely outside him as an observer but contains him *within.*"[10] Burke's argument points to the fact that much rhetorical criticism and historical scholarship is written about the past while privileging the expectations and norms of the present, hence treating the past as if it were alien, other, the "enemy." Humble irony, however, recognizes that our present is indeed indebted to the past our forebears created and lived and that this past was structured by cultural fictions that, although perhaps strange to us, must surely have been enabling in some way for them. Burke is asking us, then, to be humble regarding our rush to judge the past.[11]

Irony is crucial to this humble attitude, for it encourages us to consider carefully the fact that one person's liberty was another's slavery and yet another's confusion, that one person's necessary yet unsavory tariff was another's elitist extortion and yet another's economic salvation, that one person's scientific discovery was another's dehumanization and yet another's quackery, that one person's manifest destiny was another's extension of slavery and yet another's threat to crop prices, and so on, with complications and contradictions multiplying in every direction. In short, thinking ironically obliges one to grapple with the fact that any given political question may be addressed from a variety of perspectives and that no one of these perspectives is entirely right or wrong; rather, they are simply productive of more perspectives.[12]

This is not a call for a value-free liberal pluralism but rather an appeal to recognize that the awesome political force of cultural fictions is often based on subtle rhetorical nuances so dependent on specific time, place, and lexicon that heavy-handed ideological criticism, in its rush to level judgment, misunderstands how and why one argument is more persuasive than another. A story from the 1935 American Writers' Congress illustrates my point. In a speech entitled "Revolutionary Symbolism in America," Kenneth Burke offers the thesis that "myths may be wrong, or they may be used to bad ends—but they cannot be dispensed with. In the last analysis, they are our basic psychological tools for working together." This thesis led Burke to suggest that the congress abandon its use of "the worker" as a foundational cultural fiction in favor of the less class-specific term "the people." According to Burke, the latter term was more likely to appeal to moderate and middle-class Americans than was the former because it was less obviously indebted to the then-frightening specter of communism and more affirmative of the unifying premises that underlay the congress's activities. In the discussion following the speech, Burke was relentlessly attacked by dogmatists unwilling or simply incapable of seeing the efficacy of his simple suggestion. One critic accused him of attempting to inject "petty-bourgeois" rhetoric into the movement; another declaimed, "We must not encourage such myths. We are not interested in the myth. We are interested in revealing the reality."[13] But Burke was not asking his fellow Writers' Congress delegates to ignore reality; rather, he was asking them to analyze the rhetorical construction of "reality" more astutely. This does not mean that social critics should not study the economic and political agendas driving certain cultural fictions; rather, it suggests that even the most insightful critique of class privilege needs to be sensitive to the rhetorical traditions enabling understanding and belonging.

One may address the politics of such rhetorical traditions by engaging in three related steps. First, one may offer detailed rhetorical analyses of primary texts and use these analyses as opportunities for considering not only how arguments are made—and made persuasive—but also how historical, political, and cultural assumptions are both *worked into* and *hidden by* a given text's rhetorical structures.[14] Second, one may offer enough detailed rhetorical analyses of enough primary documents to make the claim that the cultural fictions addressed stand as *synecdochic* representatives of larger cultural norms. Third, one may then trace the genealogy of these representative cultural fictions back through the specific politico-economic agendas of their authors, supporters, and consumers. Again, these steps depend on interpretive practices that are simultaneously interdisciplinary, comparative, contextualist, and materialist.

I will not belabor these methodological points any further here; instead, I illustrate their efficacy in the following four case studies. Before I conclude this introduction, however, I must frame the rhetorical and historical attitude that drives my study. I turn, then, to Thomas Benson's preface to his *American Rhetoric,* where, while listing "convictions" regarding the practice of rhetorical history, Benson observes that "the study of a rhetorical text or communicative event is a multifaceted and open-ended affair, seeking in part for judgment but, even more importantly, for understanding." Benson then cautions that "to understand a rhetorical text, we must see not only its form and its details, but also its relation to its context, especially as that context is perceived by the participants."[15] *Democratic Dissent* seeks to honor such convictions while simultaneously pushing them toward a stronger sense both of the intertextual, conflictual, and interdisciplinary nature of public debate in the antebellum period and of the powerful influences on the period's public debates exerted by the complex material transformations in economics and politics that have since come to be recognized as the foundational moments of American modernity. I hope that this study thus contributes to the ongoing interdisciplinary attempt to advance our understanding of the ways in which our antebellum ancestors argued about the promises and possibilities of democracy and modernity.

1 *The Dialectics of Assent and Dissent, Yankee Ingenuity, and the Rhetorical Politics of Abolitionism*

> Interwoven with every fiber of my heart is the love of my country; but freedom is the charm which endears and consecrates her; and if the spirit of liberty should take her flight from my native land, my love and worship are not due to brute clods and rocks, to her prairies, or her mountains; but where liberty dwells, *there* is my country, and there *only* is my country!
>
> —Robert Rantoul, *Memoirs, Speeches, and Writings*

Thus Robert Rantoul Jr., the four-term state representative, anti–death penalty activist, liberal social reformer, and lifelong Democrat, assailed the 1850 Fugitive Slave Act in his 3 April 1851 speech before the Grand Massachusetts Convention. As did many Northern Democrats, Rantoul found the Fugitive Slave Act put him in an awkward position, for he definitely was not an abolitionist, yet he chaffed at the idea of imperious Southern interests dictating compromised Northern policies. Indeed, while the mantra of "free trade, no bank, no debt, light taxes, and an economical government" clearly placed him in the comfortable center of Jacksonian rhetoric, these principles of inviolable states' rights and limited federal intervention also placed him squarely at odds with many of his party's more aggressive proslavery leaders. Along with confronting these party problems, Rantoul faced an ornery Massachusetts electorate that clung tenaciously to its revolutionary heritage and hence was aghast at the prospect of catching runaway slaves for the South's aristocratic lords. These same sons and daughters of the Revolution also manifested the deep fear of abolition that permeated much of the North and hence were equally aghast at the prospect of prompting legal, political, and sometimes physical confrontations with fellow white Americans over blacks, who were considered decidedly less than equal. Meeting a few days before the district's congressional elections, the Grand Massachusetts Convention thus offered Rantoul one last chance to garner votes by restating accepted principles but also, in the event of speaking poorly, to lose votes by muddying principles. Rantoul, then, was in a pickle.[1]

As his fellow Americans often did when confronted with the paradoxes of democracy, Rantoul opted for the tried-and-true rhetorical move of speaking less about the specifics and details of the crisis at hand than about the generalities and truisms of the nation. *When in a pickle, invoke freedom or liberty,* for few Americans would dare express opposition to such grand concepts. The comments in the opening epigraph are nonetheless confusing, for Rantoul clearly argues that freedom and liberty are not simply linked to geographically defined regions—as seen in his reference to "brute clods and rocks," "prairies," "mountains," and so on—rather, they constitute higher ideals that transcend both physical space and the dumb realities of political compromise. Considering the context of his speech, this is a seriously curious claim, for the debates over the Fugitive Slave Act were explicitly about the extent to which one set of Americans could impose its cultural fiction (that slaves are property and retrievable as such) on the lands, lives, and liberties of another set. Thus the practical and life-threatening aspects of the act, which essentially turned all Americans into slave catchers and extended the rights of slavers into the Northerners' clods, rocks, prairies, and mountains, were buried beneath the specificity-evading chant of *freedom, liberty, freedom, liberty.*

In fact, rhetorically reinforcing this strategy of eliding the hardball politics of the moment in favor of nationally sanctioned cultural fictions, Rantoul goes on to invoke the "invaluable legacy of practical sagacity" bestowed on the nation by Washington, whom Rantoul "venerates, and clings to, as to the ark of our political salvation" (732). This invocation comes at little cost while bearing easy rhetorical fruit, for Washington was still revered at the time as the great warrior, founder, and first leader of the nation. As Gustave de Beaumont observed in 1835, "Washington, in America, is not a man but a god."[2] Like John Quincy Adams (to whom I turn in chapter 2), Rantoul balances the votes he can garner by attacking the South for overstepping the bounds of the Constitution against the votes he can lose by appearing to be too cozy with abolitionism. Invoking the "god" Washington, then, like invoking freedom and liberty, is one way of rhetorically demonstrating that this balancing act is fundamentally patriotic and centrist. Rantoul emphasizes this point by stating bluntly his dislike for "such new-fangled doctrines" as "fanaticism or abolitionism" (733).

Rantoul's Grand Massachusetts Convention speech therefore attacks slavery not as a vicious practice that condemns millions of Americans to drudgery and brutality but rather as an affront to moderate and Washington-loving Northern whites' notions of freedom and liberty. This explains why Rantoul spends much of his speech invoking the Constitution, for it stands not only as the specific legal document put into question by the Fugitive Slave Act but also, and more important, as the rhetorical bedrock underlying the moderate compromises that frame the nation, what Rantoul begins his speech by calling the source of our "fundamental principles" (729). Rantoul's driving rhetorical strategy, then, is not so much *to dissent from* the immediate political crisis at hand as *to assent to* the nation's founding cultural fictions: *Washington, the Constitution, freedom,* and *liberty.*

One may measure the prudence of this assent-based strategy by comparing it to the rhetorics of dissent employed by Solomon Northup, Lydia Maria Child, and Frederick Douglass. In terms of situating these abolitionists within their historical milieu, it is instructive first to listen to the passionate scream of dissent launched by the American Anti-Slavery Society (AASS) on its founding in Philadelphia, 14 December 1833:

> Fidelity to the cause of human freedom, hatred of oppression, sympathy for those who are held in chains and slavery in the republic, and allegiance to God, require that the existing national compact should be instantly dissolved; that secession from the government is a religious and political duty; that the motto inscribed on the banner of Freedom should be, NO UNION WITH SLAVEHOLDERS; . . . and that revolutionary ground should be occupied by all those who abhor the thought of doing evil that good may come, and who do not mean to compromise the principles of Justice and Humanity.[3]

These words provoke trembling before their awesome, righteous, slightly crazy courage. For example, the early 1830s witnessed widespread political violence, when claiming "revolutionary ground" and "sympathy for those who are held in chains and slavery" was less likely to persuade fellow citizens to change their minds than to provoke a drunken tar-and-feather festival. Thus John Greenleaf Whittier, one of the courageous activists present at the founding of the AASS, recalled that "to onlookers our endeavor to undo the evil work of two centuries . . . must have seemed absurd in the last degree. . . . We could look for no response but laughs of derision or the missiles of the mob."[4] Greenleaf is not exaggerating the danger, for the period's newspapers report that violent mobs of drunken thugs frequently broke up abolitionist meetings. One such meeting in Utica, New York, in October 1835, less than two years after the founding of the AASS, was assaulted by a mob that local elites had whipped into a frenzy. According to William Thomas's chilling pamphlet *The Enemies of the Constitution Discovered; or, An Inquiry into the Origin and Tendency of Popular Violence,* the local paper warned that the abolitionists were hell-bent on nothing less than "perpetuating mischief, disturbing the peace of society, exciting civil commotion, promoting insurrection among the slaves, producing anarchy and bloodshed, and dissolving the union."[5] Even twenty-five years later, after a full generation of abolitionists had inundated the nation with an unprecedented tidal wave of propaganda and after regional tensions had reached the boiling point, Lincoln was hailed as the nation's savior specifically because he positioned himself on the moderate, prudent, Union-at-all-costs middle ground against which talk of dissolving the existing national compact sounded like nothing less than madness.

In fact, despite his nuanced rhetoric of assent to Washington, the Constitution, freedom, and liberty, Southerners painted Rantoul as dangerously radical, leading him to lament in Congress: "I have been tainted on the floor of this house with being an agitator."[6] Clearly, then, proslavery and antiabolitionist forces did not hesitate to employ hyperbole and *argumentum ad absurdum* to escalate even moderate antislavery positions into wicked calls for anarchy and bloodshed.[7] Given this rhetorical pattern of escalating even moderates such as Rantoul into agitators, it comes as no surprise to learn that in 1833 the gentlemen from the South laid bounties on the heads of AASS organizers—$100,000 for Arthur Tappan alone. Thus, although the previously quoted abolitionists were uncommonly courageous and dedicated to a truly world-changing cause, the passion and depth of their dissent not only placed them outside the scope of mainstream national politics but also made them targets, both rhetorically and physically, of mobbing Northerners and irate Southerners. As William Miller puts it, they were "not just a minority, but a very small minority that was despised, scorned, and actively opposed."[8] They were, in a word, radicals.

They were also successful radicals, for by 1838 the AASS claimed some 1,350 affiliated societies with a membership close to 250,000. In fact, radical abolitionist activism was so prevalent, particularly in flooding Congress with abolitionist petitions, that it goaded the more aggressive elements of the proslavery movement to shoot themselves in the foot by passing the 1836 "Gag Rule," which ordered Congress to table (and hence not to consider) antislavery petitions. This egregious limit on speech made abolitionists look less like extremists plotting to dissolve the Union and more like fellow Americans whose constitutional rights were being trampled by Southern despots. The bounties placed on abolitionists' heads, as well as the ongoing use of "Judge Lynch" to intimidate, injure, and sometimes kill abolitionists, reinforced this perception.[9] Thus Aileen Kraditor observes that "many Americans who did not feel strongly about slavery began to feel that if abolitionists could be mobbed with impunity and prevented from having their petitions even considered by Congress, the rights of all Americans were in danger."[10]

Abolitionists were astute in encouraging this change in public perception. *The American Anti-Slavery Almanac* of 1839, for example, features an image of a mob destroying an abolitionist printing press, complete with the charge "A PRINTING PRESS DEMOLISHED AT SLAVERY'S BIDDING" (figure 1). Text beneath the image tells readers not only about sim-

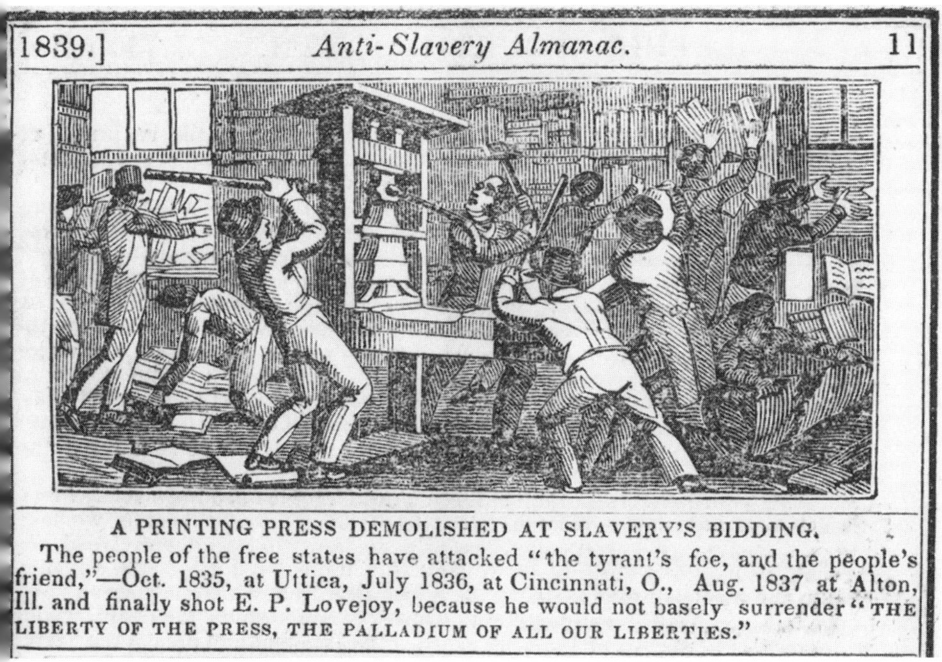
1839.] *Anti-Slavery Almanac.* 11

A PRINTING PRESS DEMOLISHED AT SLAVERY'S BIDDING.

The people of the free states have attacked "the tyrant's foe, and the people's friend,"—Oct. 1835, at Uttica, July 1836, at Cincinnati, O., Aug. 1837 at Alton, Ill. and finally shot E. P. Lovejoy, because he would not basely surrender "THE LIBERTY OF THE PRESS, THE PALLADIUM OF ALL OUR LIBERTIES."

Figure 1. "A PRINTING PRESS DEMOLISHED AT SLAVERY'S BIDDING," from the 1839 *American Anti-Slavery Almanac.* (Reproduced courtesy of the Gilder Lehrman Collection, Pierpont Morgan Library, New York City, GLC 5826.)

ilar incidents in Utica and Cincinnati but also about the recent murder of Elijah Lovejoy in Alton, Illinois. In each case murder or mayhem occurred because the abolitionists "would not basely surrender THE LIBERTY OF THE FREE PRESS, THE PALLADIUM OF ALL OUR LIBERTIES."[11] Thomas's *Enemies of the Constitution* pursues this same rhetorical strategy of portraying antiabolitionist violence as an attack on the constitutionally protected right of free speech. For example, Thomas depicts a mob's invasion of the Utica Anti-Slavery Convention as "a scene of low scurrility, horrid blasphemy, and contempt of all law, decency, and virtue." "It was," Thomas concludes, "a blow leveled at the root of liberty, which demolished the bulwarks that defend the rights of citizens. O my country!" (95). According to both these texts, then, antiabolitionist violence was not so much an issue-specific mobilization of grassroots support as a democracy-threatening assault on the very foundation of liberty. The abolitionists thus realized, as Stephen Browne has argued, "that violence could be constitutive of discourse itself," for it "gave to the abolitionists a repertoire of images, arguments, and appeals" they could manipulate in their favor. In short, the abolitionists "allowed violence to testify against itself by awakening in others the capacity to see it for what it was."[12]

The dialectics of dissent in antebellum America thus worked in a wondrously ironic way: radical Northern abolitionists forced Southerners who had previously tried to appear moderate to reveal just how radically committed to slavery they really were—even at the cost of trampling the Constitution or killing fellow white Americans—which made abolitionists look less radical and more moderate. In short, Northern abolitionist radicals goaded Southern proslavery radicals to persuade democracy-loving moderates everywhere that slavery was destroying the Union. Following this thesis, my concern in this chapter is to tease out some of the political implications of these abolitionist strategies, with Rantoul's gentle-touch prudence and the AASS's uncompromising radicalism serving as two extreme poles of rhetorical possibility. As I will show, Solomon Northup's novel *Twelve Years a Slave,* Lydia Maria Child's manifesto *An Appeal in Favor of That Class of Americans Called Africans,* and Frederick Douglass's oration "What, to the Slave, is the Fourth of July?" all fall somewhere between these two extremes. Curiously, these abolitionists derived much of their persuasive rhetorical power by positioning themselves not only as *dissenters against slavery* but also as *assenters to* one of the period's dominant cultural fictions: specifically, the notion that Northern capitalism was modernizing the world, trailing enlightenment, justice, and unprecedented opportunity in its churning wake. I am concerned, then, with exploring not only the dialectics of dissent but also the way radical abolitionist dissent against slavery simultaneously assents to the Yankee ingenuity that drives modern capitalism.

Ultimately, then, analyzing the dialectics of dissent and assent points toward the nuanced relationship between a sense of political agency and the ability to appropriate available cultural fictions for specific political goals. Before addressing this question, however, I examine how dissenters, from Thomas Jefferson through Solomon Northup, Karl Marx, and Theodor Adorno, have relied on the tropes of irony and metonymy to articulate the political and rhetorical relationships linking individuals to societies. Put differently, my goal in the following section is to understand how cultural fictions enable citizens to believe not only that their society makes sense but that this sense-making carries an obligation to reproduce itself. Addressing these complex theoretical questions about rhetorical competence and political agency establishes the foreground necessary for understanding both the specific historical paradoxes involved when abolitionists spoke to their fellow Americans regarding slavery and capitalism and the more general methodological benefits of moving away from ideological criticism to the rhetorical study of the manner in which cultural fictions persuade.

From Ideological Criticism to the Rhetorics of Persuasion

I begin with two authors who, although they differ dramatically in terms of rhetorical styles and historical situations, are inextricably linked not only by their shared reliance on irony and metonymy but also by their mutual concern with life-and-death questions regarding how to represent, remember, and reconsider the possibilities and tragedies of modernity. Specifically, in this section I address Solomon Northup's *Twelve Years a Slave* (1853), an autobiographical novel detailing modernity's founding in the blood of American slavery, and Theodor Adorno's *Negative Dialectics* (1966), a philosophical meditation on the possibility of maintaining hope in the face of modernity's culminating catastrophe, the European Holocaust. Despite the obvious rhetorical differences between Adorno's melancholy philosophical irony and Northup's compassionate novelistic forgiveness, and despite the obvious historical differences between Adorno's post-Holocaust critique of capitalism and Northup's antebellum critique of slavery and celebration of capitalism, both authors employ metonymy to address the same fundamental questions: how can one explain the relationships among individuals, their "influences," and the "systems" that make up a culture, and where, within these relationships, may one attribute the historical responsibility of causality? Adorno and Northup thus invite readers to explore the possibilities of persuasion, the means of resistance, and the structures of rhetoric available to authors concerned with representing history in its baffling splendor and cruelty. By approaching these texts humbly and ironically, and by recognizing their persuasive paradoxes as openings for creative interpretation rather than frustration, we may move beyond our own personal and presentist responses and toward something closer to historical understanding.[13]

Consider the following claim from Adorno:

> What is called communication nowadays is but the noise that drowns out the silence of the spellbound. . . . and so the categories of consciousness produced by society, including the most enlightened, inevitably grow delusive under the spell. Society and individual harmonize here as nowhere else. With society, ideology has so advanced that it no longer evolves into a socially required semblance and thus to an independent form, however brittle. All that it turns into is a kind of glue: the false identity of subject and object. . . . Spell and ideology are one and the same.[14]

Thus Adorno laments a series of startling historical transformations, including the decline of communication into noise, the decay of consciousness into a spell, and the collapse of the productive tensions between society and individual into a false identity. Adorno's tone is so pessimistic, so apparently devoid of hope, that one wonders whether this incendiary generalization is intended to prompt readers to attack it. Indeed, readers unwilling to see themselves as spellbound are clearly compelled to disagree with Adorno, lest their acquiescence demonstrate the efficacy of his thesis. At a rhetorical level, it seems fair to observe that such aggressive challenges—*are you a spellbound moron, or perhaps a storm trooper, or can you actually think for yourself?*—manifest a profound sense of hostility. Given Adorno's experiences with the Holocaust, however, such anger toward readers and doubts regarding their abilities to think and act critically make some sense; after all, he had recently witnessed history's most concentrated and streamlined machinery of death carving a mass grave across much of Europe. Humble irony asks the reader to grant Adorno the solace of his anger and then to move beyond it, to search for the historical wisdom obscured by the dogmatic rhetoric.

Having made this step, we can observe how clearly Adorno's argument illustrates the possibilities of irony, for although he claims bitterly that society and individual have become seamlessly unified by the glue of ideology, the sheer fact of his critique demonstrates that not everyone is spellbound. Likewise, even while viciously castigating the public for succumbing to the spell of capitalist ideology, the simple act of publishing such a claim implies that Adorno knows otherwise, that he counts on finding an audience with readers capable of thinking and acting critically. In short, the charge's content stands at loggerheads with its form. This contradiction appears most evidently in the tension between the claim that "the world spirit . . . would have to be defined as permanent catastrophe" (320) and the simple fact that Adorno's book illustrates the persistence of hope and hence the impermanence of catastrophe. One may speculate about the sources of Adorno's despair—duly noting, for example, that the author foregrounds his guilt for surviving the Holocaust early in the book's introduction (5)—yet by focusing instead on the ironic tension between the claim about permanent catastrophe and the fact that the book's form illustrates the anticatastrophic persistence of hope and beauty, one can recognize that such hostile claims not only fulfill Adorno's own cathartic needs but also attempt to prod the reader to begin his or her own interpretive process and thus to engage in the critical thinking that stands as the shining hope of *Negative Dialectics.* Hence, by engaging in a humbly ironic reading of the tensions between content and form, one is able to reclaim Adorno's hope despite his despair.[15]

In contrast to Adorno's text, with its angry irony, Solomon Northup's *Twelve Years a Slave* reaches out to readers on the basis of their assumed ability to understand even the worst. A free citizen kidnapped from upstate New York and sold into slavery in 1841, Northup had every reason to be screaming mad, yet his attitude regarding slavers is kind, even sympathetic. This emerges most obviously in his portrayal of William Ford, whom Northrup tells us was a Christian, a good man. In fact, in the context of the constant butchery he saw all around him, Northup viewed him as exemplary: "There never was a more kind, noble, candid, Christian man than William Ford." Northup's generous rhetoric reflects his belief that "the influences and association that had always surrounded him [Ford], blinded him to the inherent wrong at the bottom of the system of Slavery."[16] Unlike the usual portrayal of slave masters as brutal tyrants, then, this depiction shows Ford not so much as a synecdochic symbol for the Legree-like madness of slavers but more as a poignant example of the way even a kind and observant Christian may be blinded by his surrounding influences and associations.[17] In short, whereas Adorno's aggressive rhetoric challenges readers to account for their own beliefs and actions, Northup's sympathetic and explanatory rhetoric encourages readers to try to understand the beliefs and actions of others.

The specificity of genre is important here. Adorno's organizationally complicated and rhetorically angry *Negative Dialectics* no doubt leaves many readers awash in both confusion and resentment, whereas Northup's *Twelve Years a Slave* is written in a familiar narrative format with accessible prose driven by the thick (and sometimes almost clinical) description of personal experiences.[18] Sweeping generalizations, which litter Adorno's book, appear in Northup's work only as attempts to make sense of such personal experiences. As Sam Worley observes, "Northup's identity consists not of his allegiance to a fixed transcendent order, but in his creative powers, his ability to search out and even author a new moral stance in each changing situation."[19] Hence, even while struggling to make sense of the system of slavery, Northup recognizes the contingency of choices and the malleability of commitments. The novel is accordingly patterned around the telling of detailed stories that in turn, because of their ambiguous relationship to slavery as a whole, lead both Northup and the reader to wonder about the subtle factors bridging individual consciousness, systemic spells, and historically specific means of political action.

For example, after recounting the story of a "bloody and fearful battle" between two Southern "gentlemen" over some trifling matter of parlor-room honor (155–56), Northup comments:

> Such occurrences . . . are frequent on the bayou, and pass without notice, and almost without comment. Every man carries his bowie knife, and when two fall out, they set to work hacking and thrusting at each other, more like savages than civilized and enlightened beings.
>
> The existence of Slavery in its most cruel form among them has a tendency to brutalize the humane and finer feelings of their nature. . . . it cannot otherwise be expected, than that they should become brutified and reckless of human life. . . . It is not the fault of the slaveholder that he is cruel, so much as it is the fault of the system under which he lives. (157)

Northup thus argues that the system of slavery is so totalizing, so omnipotent in socializing citizens (and slaves) into accepting the necessity and benefits of brutality, that the individual acts without significant choice. This passage is a fine example of metonymy, for in arguing that the whole determines the part, and hence in clouding relationships of cause and effect (who is responsible for this system? what makes it run?), it renders each individual's actions as little more than fragments of a larger, all-engulfing yet curiously vague system. Given the (then) unprecedented butchery of antebellum slavery, one may approach Northup's metonymic perspective as the logical outcome of struggling to survive in a world apparently devoid of feasible alternative modes of existence.

It should not be surprising, then, to realize that Northup's chilling argument regarding the absolute absorption of individual consciousness into the antebellum system of slavery bears remarkable similarity to Adorno's paralyzing post-Holocaust despair. Indeed, Adorno—surveying the wreckage of World War II and the dual horrors of technocratic capitalism in America and totalitarian "communism" in the Soviet Union—essentially echoes Northup's metonymic thesis when he writes that "the reality principle, which the prudent heed in order to survive . . . , captures them as black magic; they are unable and unwilling to cast off the burden, for the magic hides from them and *makes them think it is life*" (347, emphasis added). *Negative Dialectics* is deeply concerned with understanding how this capturing happens, how ideology insinuates itself so completely into consciousness that one loses the ability to recognize it as anything other than common sense—indeed, as other than life itself. But much as Northup does, Adorno responds to this question with metonymy, for he attributes this all-pervasive "ideology" (the implied whole of life) to forces so vast, so immeasurable, so unspecific ("the reality principle") that readers walk away believing ideology to be a determinative, generative cause rather than an effect of specific human actions.

The key to understanding this metonymic perspective is to foreground Adorno's loathing of modern capitalism's omnivorous powers. Indeed, Adorno repeatedly portrays capitalism as the absent cause that determines all local effects, as the global colossus that encircles every particular, thus producing spell and ideology. Apprehending the world in such terms leads to a paradoxical sense of *disempowered radicalism*: you want to attack the mechanistic, determining powers lurking behind every action, yet because this metonymic perspective clouds agency, you cannot identify the particular causes that drive oppressive historical effects. I am arguing, then, that the explanatory function of metonymy, which Adorno uses to compress the inexplicable forces of history into effects of capitalism, contrasts with the disempowering political implications of seeing both consciousness in general and politics in particular as entirely beyond one's control—*it is life*—let alone comprehension. Adorno's version of metonymy is thus radical in its rhetorical tone, for it is uncompromising, ironic, and relentlessly critical, yet also disempowering in its political implications, for it portrays individuals as little more than lost in the cosmos of capitalism's spell. The metonymy of *Negative Dialectics* therefore embodies the paradoxes of disempowered radicalism.

Although driven by a dramatically different set of political assumptions, Northup's critique of slavery, too, largely relies on, and hence is compromised by, the rhetorical structure of metonymy. For example, even while loosely arguing that the magical, spell-like system of slavery (the whole) absorbs individual consciousness (parts), Northup attempts to illustrate the slow, daily, praxis-based mechanics of socialization through which individuals build their senses of belonging and purpose. The following exemplifies how Northup dialectically moves from small personal experiences (parts) to grand historical generalizations (whole) by describing the subtle processes socializing the plantation boss's son into the culture of slavery:

> Epps' oldest son is an intelligent lad of ten or twelve years of age. It is pitiable, sometimes, to see him chastising, for instance, the venerable Uncle Abram. He will call the old man to account, and if in his childish judgment it is necessary, sentences him to a certain number of lashes, which he proceeds to inflict with much gravity and deliberation. Mounted on his pony, he often rides into the field with his whip, playing the overseer, greatly to his father's delight. . . . Young Master Epps possessed some noble qualities, yet no process of reasoning could lead him to comprehend, that in the eye of the Almighty there is no distinction of color. (201)

No process of reasoning could have persuaded young Master Epps to behave otherwise: his entire life was a series of influences and associations that had led to his riding his pony proudly into the field, marshaling the whip to discipline unruly slaves. Hence, even when describing the minutiae of daily life, Northup portrays a world where parts and wholes are apprehended not as dialectically related causes and effects but rather as simultaneous, coterminous, mutually and reciprocally supporting forces in an all-pervasive cultural fiction from which there is almost no way out.

Northup's argument here regarding slavery calls to mind the equally metonymic indignation of another great critic of modernity, Karl Marx. Addressing an imaginary bourgeois interlocutor in part 2 of *The Communist Manifesto,* Marx levels the following accusation: "Your very ideas are but the outgrowth of the conditions of your bourgeois production and bourgeois property, just as your jurisprudence is but the will of your class made into a law for all, a will whose essential character and direction are determined by the economical conditions of existence of your class."[20] Northup observes that no process of reason could shake young Master Epps from the cultural fictions shaping his consciousness, for the blind fate of chance dictates that the child simply believes what his culture enables him to believe. Marx appears to say much the same thing in the passage just quoted, yet in the sentence following this accusation he argues that the bourgeoisie's "transform[ing] into eternal laws of nature and of reason the social forms springing from [their] present mode of production and form of property" amounts to a "selfish misconception." As Marx sees it, then, bourgeois consciousness is a willful, intentional, self-serving bending of the facts to suit one's desires. The tone here, much as in Adorno's *Negative Dialectics,* is accusatory, harsh, and condescending. Northup, however, appears to be both more forgiving toward his "enemies" and less hopeful regarding historical change, for whereas Marx and Adorno appear to cling to the notion that ideology is a product of willful misconception, and hence open to the transformations enabled by proper conception, Northup sees it simply as what life is, as what cultures produce and support in the infinite ways that make everyday life meaningful.

One response to this claustrophobic perspective is to ask the following question: if you grant that a culture's associations and influences are so powerful, so overwhelming, and so taken for granted as to dictate people's ideas, the law, and all the other forms of activity and consciousness that reinforce the status quo, then how can you account for historical change, political dissent, or even simple alienation? The implied critique lurking behind this question is that if one assents to the metonymic perspectives forwarded by Northup, the young Marx, and Adorno (and perhaps the Frankfurt school in general),[21] then one is obliged to postulate that *ideology is culture* and that *culture is ideology.* This formula in turn suggests that your world enables you to behave in certain ways, and because your culture molds you so effectively, those ways can appear as "ideology" only to someone from a culture other than your own who has learned differently and for whom your world appears cockeyed.[22]

Sure enough, as a free man who has lived most of his life as an independent entrepreneur and craftsman in New York, Northup is able to perceive the ideology behind the system of slavery because he brings to the South those norms and values of his previous life in the North. Likewise, as elite European refugees awash in the cultural banality and cowboy capitalism of postwar America, Adorno and his colleagues in the Frankfurt school offer a critique of capitalism that, so their argument would have us believe, they are qualified to make because of their perspective as outsiders, as thinkers who (in addition to being trained in Marxist dialectics) possess forms of consciousness not colonized by the ideology they intend to expose. On this reading, ideology is simply what one attributes to someone else whose values are different from her or his own. Appraising the implications of such thinking, however, Terry Eagleton observes somewhat caustically that "nobody would claim that their own thinking was ideological, just like nobody would habitually refer to themselves as Fatso. Ideology, like halitosis, is in this sense what the other person [or culture] has." Writing in a more somber tone in his award-winning treatise on contemporary critical theory, *Postmodernism; or, The Cultural Logic of Late Capitalism,* Fredric Jameson repeats this same argument when he admonishes us to recognize that "the luxury of the old-fashioned ideological critique, the indignant moral denunciation of the other, [has] become unavailable."[23]

It is hard not to conclude, then, that if ideology is simply a pejorative word used to describe actions or thoughts that strike one as unfamiliar or different from one's own (with the caveat that these actions can be recognized as ideological only by someone from outside the system under consideration), then it has no interpretive or pedagogical ability to explain either rhetorical patterns of meaning making or political methods of persuasion. That is why I focus on *cultural fictions,* for my sense is that calling something ideological simply is not explanatory. Instead I argue that it is more productive to ask detailed rhetorical and historical questions regarding specific cases of democratic dissent, hence enabling us to consider how and why some cultural fictions were more persuasive than others at a given time. In this sense, calling young Master Epps's actions ideological would be both foolish and unhelpful, for of course the boy's behavior appears strange or even inexplicable to those of us who were not raised on an antebellum plantation in the Deep South. Rather than condescend toward historical actors who appear from the critic's privileged historical perspective to be drowning in ideology and gagged by "the silence of the spellbound," the notion of cultural fictions suggests instead that we strive to reconstruct the historical contexts and rhetorical patterns of their political communications, hence moving toward a humbly ironic understanding of the complicated ways our forebears exercised agency.[24]

In the case of young Epps and his fellow slaveholders, such humbly ironic reconstructions of rhetorical and political agency are possible only by bracketing certain assumptions long enough to understand how and why slaveholders saw the world through the prism of white supremacy. As William Freehling observes in *The Road to Disunion,* "undeserved empathy for the white victimizer is a prerequisite for understanding this regime."[25] The notion of cultural fictions asks that such empathy be extended humbly and ironically, with the hope that the rich and detailed rhetorical and historical reconstructions enabled by this stance may in turn enable us to comprehend more clearly how our forebears explained and justified their actions, why they found certain cultural fictions more persuasive than others, and ultimately, how they struggled to make sense of their obligations and opportunities within the paradoxes of democracy. As I have already shown, locating the deep rhetorical structure of a given argument is an important first step in this process of historical reconstruction, for such structures illuminate the subtle paradoxes lingering within a given author's assumptions regarding causality and responsibility.

Causality, Responsibility, and Paradox in Abolitionist Rhetoric

The following two interwoven case studies of the dialectics of assent and dissent in antebellum America illustrate some of the broad methodological claims I raised earlier regarding my proposed shift from ideological criticism to the rhetorical study of cultural fictions. I begin with an excursus on the politics of metonymy as illustrated in Northup's *Twelve Years a Slave* and in Jefferson's much earlier "Draft of Instructions," both of which address the fundamental paradox of the nation in its earlier years: the coexistence of democracy and slavery. Having framed this paradox, I then turn to the responses to it offered in a humbly ironic mode by Northup, in the "scorching ironic" mode of Frederick Douglass's "What, to the Slave, is the Fourth of July?" and in the sarcastic mode of Lydia Maria Child's *Appeal in Favor of That Class of Americans Called Africans.* My first task, however, is to demonstrate how the rhetorical trope of metonymy functions as a thesis regarding historical causality and personal responsibility.

Richard Lanham has observed that whereas metonymy is traditionally understood simply as a reversal of cause and effect, its postmodern version, following Burke, "involves an affair finally of scale-manipulation." Lanham's summary is astute, for in a passage that appears to assimilate prosopopoeia to metonymy, Burke describes the latter as a form of "reduction" that strives "to convey some incorporeal or intangible state in terms of the corporeal or tangible." Metonymy, then, using the Lanham-Burke definition, amounts to a form of representational conflation in which essentially inexpressible concepts are reduced or condensed into a more recognizable object or category of perception. This explanatory function has been addressed as well by Hayden White, who observes that metonymy enables a form of "mechanistic" historiography that is "inclined to be reductive rather than synthetic," that "turns upon the search for the causal laws that determine the outcomes of processes," and that "considers individual entities to be less important as evidence than the classes of phenomena to which they can be shown to belong." Metonymy thus involves a convertibility of cause and effect in which, by reversing agent or cause and act or effect (for example, switching from "the thunder roars" to "the roar of thunder"), "the phenomenal world can be populated with a host of agents and agencies that are presumed to exist behind it."[26]

The question, then—as illustrated in the preceding section on Northup and Adorno—is how to understand the relationship between the textual, micrological scale manipulations and reductive moves that metonymic rhetoric enables at the sentence level and the macrological political assumptions about causality and responsibility that follow from writing history in a metonymic mode. One obvious maneuver is to consider the question from a basic compositional level, where one could argue that the passive voice, indicated by the absence of an active verb, renders any sense of cause and effect unclear. A classic example is Nixon's lament, "Mistakes were made," which clouds the sense of causality and responsibility conveyed in an active, agent-based confession such as "I made mistakes." This compositional interpretation again brings us back to prosopopoeia, which, according to Pierre Fontanier, "consists in staging, as it were, absent, dead, supernatural or even inanimate beings. These are made to act, speak, answer as is our want. At the very least these beings can be made into confidants, witnesses, accusers, avengers, judges, etc."[27]

Moving from the compositional level to a more overarching historical perspective, it is not difficult to see how apprehending history in this metonymic or prosopopoeic passive voice enables specific actions or effects to appear agentless or uncaused. As Fontanier argues, and as Northup and Adorno demonstrate, metonymically attributing causality to abstract forces suggests a world driven by the inexpressible contours of nameless larger powers that are "absent, dead, supernatural, or even inanimate" and that therefore cannot respond to questioning. Hence, when Northup tells us that "it is not the fault of the slaveholder that he is cruel, so much as it is the fault of the system under which he lives" (157), he makes a metonymic argument. Indeed, one may be predisposed to see individual slavers as the causal forces behind the system of slavery; from this perspective, social barbarism (effect) is produced by the specific greed of individual slavers (cause). Northup reverses this perspective, however, so that slavery as a system becomes the agent or cause of the slavers' brutality, which is no more than the effect of something too big to check—slavery is not the slavers' fault but rather the cause of their (and our) predicament.

Much as Adorno's use of metonymy indicates a disempowered radicalism regarding modern capitalism, Northup's metonymy regarding antebellum slavery can be seen as disempowering as well, for if individual slavers are not to blame for slavery, then who is? If the system is not the product of their intentions, then how does one account for its strength and support? Where did it come from? And if one cannot locate the causes, origins, or driving forces of the system, then how can one attack it? How can one find any political or rhetorical leverage against something that simply is, that has no cause, no agents? Despite my questions about causality and responsibility, Northup's contemporaries would have read this argument less as disempowering than as simply familiar or even conventional. Indeed, at least since Jefferson's 1774 "Draft of Instructions to the Virginia Delegates in the Continental Congress" (a document that has since then come to be known as *A Summary View of the Rights of British America*), Americans have thought of slavery as having originated elsewhere. For example, amid a discussion of the slave trade, Jefferson claims:

> The abolition of domestic slavery is the great object of desire in those colonies where it was unhappily introduced in their infant state. But previous to the enfranchisement of the slaves we have, it is necessary to exclude all further importations from Africa. Yet our repeated attempts to effect this by prohibitions, and by imposing duties which might amount to a prohibition, have been hitherto defeated by his majesty's negative: thus preferring the immediate advantages of a few British corsairs to the lasting interests of the American states, and to the rights of human nature deeply wounded by this infamous practice.[28]

Thus Jefferson attributes slavery not to the political, economic, and cultural interests of his fellow plantation gentlemen—some of the wealthiest, most powerful men in the world—but rather to those British corsairs who plunged his fellow good Virginians into their burdensome plight many unfortunate generations ago. This claim illustrates clearly a metonymic reversal of cause and effect, from active, agency-possessing American slave masters (cause) who govern the system of slavery (effect) to an abstract system of British-produced slavery (cause) that has entrapped passive, agency-lacking slave masters (effect). The passage also illustrates a metonymic manipulation of scale, from responsible and historically situated individuals who are corporeal and tangible to a prehistoric legacy that is incorporeal and intangible, literally unalterable. Such metonymic rhetoric served the slaveholding yet democracy-loving Jefferson well, for it enabled him to blame Britain for the catastrophe of slavery while simultaneously using this charge to argue that only a democratic revolution could rescue America from continued British barbarism. Jefferson thus dissents from continued British rule by assenting to the promises of American democracy while ironically refusing to take any responsibility for slavery;

hence the paradox of democracy-loving slaveholders found rhetorical expression via Jefferson's metonymy. In fact, this cultural fiction—*we hate slavery and we love democracy, but we cannot abolish slavery in the name of democracy because the rotten British saddled us with it, and ending it would be too difficult*—worked so well that slaveholding Americans relied on it for the next seventy-five or so years, countering attacks on slavery with the familiar chant: *It's not our fault, but we love democracy; it's not our fault, but we love democracy.*[29]

This Jeffersonian mantra lamenting the muted wish for an impossible abolition was sufficiently ubiquitous to appear among the cultural fictions Lydia Maria Child attacks in her seminal manifesto *An Appeal in Favor of That Class of Americans Called Africans* (1833). Participating in the radical abolitionist momentum begun in 1829 with the publication of David Walker's *Appeal* and then advanced by the 1830 British parliamentary debates on abolition, the 1831 launch of William Lloyd Garrison's *Liberator,* the 1832 founding of the New England Anti-Slavery Society, and the 1833 founding (in Philadelphia) of the AASS, Child's call to action stands among the foundational texts of antebellum abolitionism.[30] In a chapter entitled "Free Labor and Slave Labor—Possibility of Safe Emancipation," Child mockingly observes that "the tolerator of slavery will say 'No doubt the system is an evil; but we are not to blame for it; we received it from our English ancestors. It is a lamentable *necessity;*—we cannot do it away if we would;—insurrections would be the inevitable result of any attempt to remove it'—and having used the word *lamentable,* they think no more upon the subject."[31]

Child displayed awesome courage in publishing her *Appeal,* and her sarcastic tone nicely skewers the insincere hand-wringing of many proslavery proponents—including Jefferson—yet, as do Adorno and Marx in the previously quoted passages, she writes with an unmistakable tone of indignant righteousness. It is difficult to decide, then, whether we should praise such rhetoric for refusing to negotiate with evil—hence the AASS's bold motto, "No Union with Slaveholders"—or question the efficacy of treating one's political opponents as little more than cheats and liars. If we agree with Robert Hariman that "political style is a coherent repertoire of rhetorical conventions depending on aesthetic reactions for political effect," then we must ask what reactions Child's mocking style is likely to elicit.[32] Along with raising these political questions regarding the rhetorical means of persuasion (to which I return later), note that Child attacks the Jeffersonian cultural fiction that slavers want to but cannot abolish slavery specifically because of the fiction's metonymic strategy of reversing cause and effect. Indeed, Child clearly recognizes that the metonymic rhetoric slavers had favored at least since Jefferson's "Draft" amounts to a carefully choreographed displacement of causality and responsibility. Like Marx, then, Child sees proslavery cultural fictions as willful, selfish misconceptions.[33]

Unlike Child's sarcastic critique of the way "tolerators" used causality- and responsibility-clouding metonymy, Northup's *Twelve Years a Slave* attempts to use the explanatory power of metonymy to make sense of history while simultaneously chronicling in relentless detail the specific causes of and agents responsible for the brutality of slavery. Hence, foreshadowing the tension between Adorno's content and form, Northup's occasional metonymic generalizations contrast with the novel's many passages describing the complexities and intricacies—the ungeneralizable details—of the system of slavery. One obvious result of this irony-producing tension is that readers are *not* asked to recognize selfish misconceptions on the parts of others (such as Ford, the good, kind Christian); rather, they are enabled to contemplate the genuine difficulty of human choice. Actors are not so much willfully delusional or blinded by self-interest as simply confused, baffled, or scared. Indeed, although the novel's unflinching condemnation of the system of slavery leaves little doubt regarding the need for abolitionism, its paradoxically metonymic portrayal of slaveholders as this systems' dumbfounded victims enables readers to see them as familiarly human, historically situated, politically compromised fellow citizens. Thus, in what feels like a paradoxical yet productive combination of Jefferson's long-standing excuse for slavery and familiar Christian moralism, readers are encouraged to hate the sin (slavery) while forgiving the sinner (the slaveholder). By recognizing the plight of both slaves and slaveholders, then, Northup provides an enabling rhetorical space from which to contemplate abolitionism not as a threatening and revolutionary attempt to overthrow a culture but rather as a generous, necessarily cross-racial attempt to relieve tragedy.[34] In this sense, then, one may postulate that Northup's metonymy fulfills pedagogical and explanatory roles.

It is instructive to compare how some of Northup's contemporaries also attempted to revise abolitionism from a radical critique of slavery to a prudent call for relief from tragedy. Northup pursued this strategy through humble irony, and Robert Rantoul Jr. pursued this strategy by assenting to the mantra *Washington, the Constitution, freedom, liberty,* but Frederick Douglass relied instead on what he called "scorching irony." I thus now turn to Douglass's "What, to the Slave, is the Fourth of July?" Delivered in Rochester, New York, on 5 July 1852, Douglass's speech is rightly considered one of the masterpieces of radical abolitionist oratory. Although contemporaries may not think of Rochester as a hotbed of either abolitionist activism or modernist progress, it was home to Douglass's abolitionist newspapers (first *The North Star* and then *Frederick Douglass's Paper*); an important stop on the Underground Railroad; and, thanks to the Erie Canal (completed in 1825), "America's first inland boom town," complete with some of the nation's first mass-produced housing and most advanced commercial agriculture. The Douglasses accordingly had ample opportunity to witness the transformations and paradoxes of modernity up close; they partook of this opportunity by attacking slavery in speech and print and by offering runaway slaves their last American shelter before crossing the border into Canada. For Douglass and his comrades in the bustling Rochester of 1852, then, the stakes were high, even deadly.[35]

Indeed, the passage of the Fugitive Slave Act in 1850 and its brutal enforcement in Northern states the following year made anywhere within American borders unsafe for all African Americans, since bounties and a lack of due process meant that even "free" blacks were falsely charged and sent into slavery. In this sense, the act institutionalized precisely the conditions that led to Northup's kidnapping in 1841.[36] Northup's novel and Douglass's speech are thus both in large part rhetorical responses to this act. The two men's situations differed crucially, however: whereas Northup was born free, kidnapped into slavery, and then freed again by the interventions of progressive white lawyers, Douglass was born enslaved, escaped into freedom, and then—even though British friends purchased his freedom for £150—still felt vulnerable to reenslavement at the hands of compromising white politicians and (forgive the ugly pun) black-market kidnappers. Douglass is thus more desperately endangered by the Fugitive Slave Act, which perhaps accounts at least partly for the scathing tone of his speech. Additionally, in 1851 Douglass hid three men who had shot and killed a slaveholder pursuing them. Despite the ensuing manhunt, Douglass made the perilous trip with the (now doubly damned) fugitives to the boat that would take them to Canada.[37] Hence, whereas Northup's novel looks back to reflect on a triumph over slavery, Douglass's speech looks forward to confront the ongoing life-and-death struggle between abolition and slavery as inflected by the newly urban, capitalist, boomtown of Rochester.

Accordingly, Douglass's speech is a fiery, uncompromising polemic against both the institution of slavery and the Northern white racism that enables many Americans to look the other way, pretending that slavery is not their problem. Douglass attacks this cultural fiction with the thesis that slavery is a *national* problem, that it pollutes not only the South but the nation as a whole. In one of his most famous passages Douglass explodes: "The existence of slavery in this country brands your Republicanism a sham, your humanity a base pretense, and your Christianity a lie. . . . it makes your name a hissing and a byword to a mocking earth . . . Oh, be warned! A horrible reptile is coiled up in your nation's bosom."[38] These "thunderbolts of condemnation" are launched from the natural-law position that reads Jefferson's "We hold these truths to be self evident, that all men are created equal" not as a culturally conditioned example of the nuanced ambiguities and realities of political exclusion but rather, as a universal, inclusive statement of principle.[39] As Charles Mills has noted, "The great virtue of natural law and natural rights theory . . . is that it provides one with a preexisting and enduring Archimedean moral vantage-point from which to denounce actually existing human laws and practices." Mills concludes that "the uncompromisingly absolutist character of natural law prohibitions precludes any appeal to contingent circumstances."[40]

One of the central curiosities of Douglass's speech, however, is the relatively little relief his claim for such an Archimedean moral vantage point grants him. In fact, Douglass appears so weary of having to explain the self-evident, so sick and tired of trying to reason with listeners whose prejudices place them firmly beyond the reach of reason, that he finally blurts out, "What, then, remains to be argued? . . . The time for such argument is passed. At a time like this, *scorching irony,* not convincing argument, is needed" (257, emphasis added). Scorching irony is thus the rhetoric of last resort for the activist who has tried more traditional means of persuasion and found them ineffective.[41]

Curiously enough, William Harper proposes a similar thesis in his proslavery manifesto *Memoir on Slavery,* where he claims that slavery "is no longer regarded as a subject of argument and investigation. The opinions referred to are assumed as settled, or the truth of them as self-evident. If any voice is raised among ourselves to extenuate or vindicate, *it is unheard. The judgment is made up. We can have no hearing* before the tribunal of the civilized world."[42] Thus, much as Douglass argues that slavers and their supporters are beyond the reach of rational argument, Harper argues that abolitionists and their supporters refuse to listen to counterarguments. Both speakers believe that their interlocutors have made up their minds and can give no hearing to alternative views. In short, both Douglass and Harper lament the fact that speech and print fail them in the face of stubborn political realities. These are curious claims, for the period witnessed the most explosive growth of publishing in America's history. Indeed, the combination of modernist transformations in rapid production techniques, inexpensive printing materials, ease of transportation, and the availability of gas lamps and reading glasses combined to produce a capitalist print revolution that flooded the nation with papers, magazines, broadsides, pamphlets, and copies of popular speeches. There is thus a paradoxical and perhaps even pathetic slippage between the reality of a nation devouring persuasive materials at a historically unprecedented rate and the perception, shared by both Douglass and Harper, that no one is listening.[43]

Nonetheless, faced with such supposedly impossible communicative situations, Harper resorts to an elaborate series of rhetorical gymnastics regarding the support for slavery found in natural law, the Bible, ancient history, and science. On the abolitionist side, Douglass resorts to his scorching irony, including his famous—and fatally flawed—attempt to read the radical, democratic promises of the Declaration of Independence against the conservative, slavery-enabling compromises of the Constitution (264–67).[44] Ironically, then, both Harper and Douglass try to persuade their audiences even while arguing that persuasion is impossible. Douglass deepens this sense of scorching irony by turning his listeners' expectations on their heads, using what is supposed to be a celebratory moment to engage in a serious critique.[45] Indeed, while Douglass launches what everyone present must no doubt have anticipated—a blistering attack against both slavery in particular and white racism in general—he also lambastes the duplicity of his audience and the hypocrisy of a nation that dares to celebrate independence while supporting slavery. In a claim echoing a similar charge from *Uncle Tom's Cabin,* Douglass seethes: "I am not included within the pale of this glorious anniversary! Your high independence only reveals the immeasurable distance between us. . . . This Fourth of July is *yours,* not mine. *You* may rejoice, *I* must mourn" (255).[46] Hence, "for revolting barbarity and shameless hypocrisy, America reigns without a rival" (258). One can imagine the faces of Douglass's audience that day, with his fellow abolitionists clapping frantically while the finely attired moderate Whig bourgeoisie of Rochester sat next to them squirming, their skin crawling, their minds racing with fear and doubt and anger—*Am I complicit with terror, or is this man crazy? How dare he speak for the founders? But perhaps he's right. Disunion is madness, but so is slavery. What to do? What to do?*

Whereas Jefferson's metonymy displaces the causes and effects of slavery and hence minimizes America's guilt over the peculiar institution, Northup's metonymy creates a humbly ironic space of empathy and hence maximizes the possibility for understanding between radically different cultures. Child's mocking sarcasm and Douglass's scorching irony, however—much like Adorno's angry irony in *Negative Dialectics*—force readers and listeners to rethink their commitments by escalating their anxiety regarding their implication in a system that they had previously thought dirtied the hands of others without compromising their own actions. Each of these three rhetorical strategies—minimizing guilt, maximizing understanding, and escalating anxiety—seems bold compared to the nuanced prudence of Rantoul and yet mild compared to the secessionist calls of the AASS, the incendiary tirades of Garrison (which sometimes included torching copies of the Fugitive Slave Act and the Constitution), and the calls to arms launched by black abolitionists (who sometimes spoke while wearing firearms for protection) such as Henry Highland Garnet, Charles Lenox Remond, William Wells Brown, Samuel Ringgold Ward, and Rev. Jermain Wesley Loguen.[47] Moreover, all these rhetorical strategies differed from the sentimental, almost gothic rhetoric of Ernestine Potowski Rose, a leader of the then rising women's rights movement who, regarding the Fugitive Slave Act, asked listeners to "look at that infamous, detestable law, which was written in human blood, and signed and sealed with life and liberty, that eternal stain on the statute book of this country."[48]

Americans were thus confronted with an overwhelming array of rhetorical appeals, all of which both illustrate the nuances and possibilities of what Hariman calls political style and subtly use irony and metonymy to convey notions of causality and responsibility. The central interpretive tasks are to question how these various rhetorical strategies influenced one another and their audiences, coalescing into cultural fictions, and hence to explore the complicated workings of the dialectics of assent and dissent. I propose that one strategy for approaching these difficult questions is to explore how antebellum abolitionists sought to persuade their fellow Americans regarding slavery by appealing to cultural fictions that articulated and celebrated the promises of modernity, the Enlightenment, and capitalism.

Modernity, Capitalism, and Yankee Ingenuity

Although there are no definitive answers to the previously raised rhetorical and historical questions regarding the dialectics of assent and dissent, it is instructive to consider briefly how the various abolitionist camps positioned themselves against slavery by invoking the promises of modernity, the Enlightenment, and capitalism. The idea is to examine how abolitionists sought to persuade their neighbors not only by dissenting from cultural fictions supporting slavery and racism but also by assenting to cultural fictions celebrating the grand march of historical progress (captured in a vague fealty to modernity), political freedom (the Enlightenment), and economic opportunity (capitalism). This strategy of dissenting by assenting entails a rhetoric of regional and historical pride in which Northerners are encouraged to see themselves as the natural heirs to the glorious promises of modernity, the Enlightenment, and capitalism, with these three forces understood as the whizbang ingredients of what, when taken as a whole, Douglass celebrated as "the tendencies of the age." Indeed, as I will show, Douglass, Northup, and Child derived much of their rhetorical power from their gung-ho valorizations of modernity, the Enlightenment, and especially capitalism, with these three tropes condensed into the cultural fiction I hereafter refer to as Yankee ingenuity.[49]

For example, although Douglass usually portrays antebellum America as a cesspool of ethical decline, a compromised and tottering traitor to its founders' greatness (250–55), in the penultimate paragraph of his speech he claims that "intelligence is penetrating the darkest corners of the globe" (267). Antebellum American slavery thus contradicts both the nation's radically democratic past and the march—although currently stalled—of the Enlightenment's penetrating intelligence. Nonetheless, Douglass is hopeful, for he notes that "there are forces in operation which must inevitably work the downfall of slavery." In a paragraph that would make Kant proud, he groups these "forces" as "the obvious tendencies of the age," including the ascent of "knowledge," transportation, and fair-minded international relations among nations. The crucial moment occurs when Douglass supplements his broad thesis that "a change has come over the affairs of mankind" with the Adam Smith–like claim that "the arm of commerce has borne away the gates of the strong city" (267). Modernity, then, the tendency of the age—the procapitalist, liberal, Enlightenment legacy of Kant and Smith alike—produces a combination of knowledge, transportation, and commerce that must inevitably break down old customs. Furthermore, Douglass argues that this enlightened march of progress is based in no small part on modernist and capitalist technologies of production, distribution, and communication. Whereas America's founders struggled to reach the hearts and minds of the masses via hand-cranked printing presses and horse-drawn carriages, activists of Douglass's generation benefit greatly from the new "means of concert and combination" enabled by the fact that "stream" and "lightning" have "been reduced to order and discipline" in the form of canals and railroads, the two chief means of modern transportation (252). Of course, this paean to the liberatory powers of modernity and capitalism may come too late; perhaps Douglass has so completely lambasted America that he cannot, in the closing moments of the speech, reclaim its possible leading role in the inevitable march of the Enlightenment.[50]

Unlike Douglass, with his end-of-the-speech nod to the promises and possibilities of modernity, both Northup and Child repeatedly portray northern Americans as nothing less than proud little engines of progress and industry. Indeed, regardless of the way they interpret Northup's literary merits or the strength of his abolitionist critique, readers are hard pressed not to see *Twelve Years a Slave* celebrating the liberatory, modernizing, opportunity-enhancing, self-making righteousness of Yankee ingenuity. For example, the novel's opening chapter tells readers that his experiences rafting lumber from Lake Champlain to Troy, New York, with the assistance of "several efficient hands," enabled Northup to master "the art and mysteries of rafting." Hence, on his being kidnapped into slavery, Northup is able "to astonish the simple-witted lumbermen on the banks of the Bayou Boeuf" (8). Northern capitalism is thus portrayed as a system of hardworking and efficient individuals mastering nature's bounty, while Southern slavery produces simple-witted morons.

The full complexity of this cultural fiction is not revealed until sixty-three pages later, when Northup, again referring to his skills as a boatman, tells us, "On all sides I heard Ford's Platt [Northup's slave name] pronounced 'the smartest nigger in the Pine Woods'" (71). The comparison here to other slaves is crucial, for it demonstrates that Northup's Yankee ingenuity distinguishes him from the unskilled, lazy, unimaginative drones produced by slavery. The radical implication of this comparison is that the get-up-and-go hustle-and-bustle of Yankee ingenuity transcends race, thus enabling Northup to sound at least in this passage less like a Northern black speaking of abolition and more like a bourgeois modernist speaking of the comparative advantages of capitalism. Parallel comparisons between Northup's Yankee ingenuity and the dumbing-down effect of slavery appear throughout the novel. In one scene depicting the radical differences between Northup and other slaves, the inventive Northup builds "a fish trap," "a new resource . . . hitherto unthought of by the enslaved children of Africa" (154–55). In fact, Yankee ingenuity is so powerful that it even enables favorable comparisons between Northup and Southern whites, such as when Master Epps tells a white friend that Northup is "a reg'lar genius; he can make a plough beam, wagon tongue—anything, as well as you can" (219). Said by one white master to another, the phrase "as well as you can" demonstrates that Northup's "genius"—with that phrase understood as marking the intelligence, job skills, and hard work produced by capitalism—not only towers over his fellow slaves' indolence but also compares favorably to the abilities of Southern white masters. Indeed, not only does Northup show ingenuity as a rafter and fisherman; in addition, dumbfounded whites call on him to make their looms, design better axes, and improve their poorly built furniture (73, 133, 240). Northup thus portrays slavery as a cross-racial system of mass-produced lethargy rendering both whites and blacks lazy and stupid. Yankee ingenuity, however, the necessary response of invention and enthusiasm to the challenges and opportunities of modern capitalism, enables both whites and blacks to achieve their true genius.

Much like Northup, Child seeks to persuade her readers by positioning abolition within the broad historical advances of the Enlightenment, modernity, and capitalism. But whereas Northup bases his observations concerning Southern indolence versus Northern industry on his personal experiences in both the North and South, Child bases her arguments on the testimonies of a politically famous Southerner, Charles Faulkner, and a British man of letters, Robert Sutcliff. Faulkner was among the most eloquent opponents of slavery in the then unprecedented and potentially world-changing 1832 Virginia legislature debates following Nat Turner's revolt in 1831. His arguments were widely distributed in the North. Child accordingly reproduces extensive passages from Faulkner in the hope that his legitimacy as a Southern gentleman will add authenticity and bite to her *Appeal.* For example, she quotes Faulkner asking his fellow Virginians to compare the "division, discontent, indolence, and poverty of the Southern country" with the glorious, modern North, where one finds "happiness and contentment . . . and busy and cheerful sound of industry—the rapid and swelling growth of their population—their means and institutions of education—their skill and proficiency in the useful arts—their enterprise, and public spirit—the monuments of their commercial and manufacturing industry; above all, their devoted attachment to the government from which they derive their protection" (76).[51] If launched by a Northern abolitionist, such claims might strike readers as little more than polemical, but as stated here by a son of the South, such arguments bear the weight of a damning imminent critique. Child weaves such passages into her narrative so seamlessly, and with so few signposts or markings that readers may wonder exactly whose words they are reading. In this sense Child employs the rhetorical strategy of prosopopoeia, advancing her argument by subtly invoking the voice of a guest narrator or witness.

The utopian North's bountiful modernity is again represented on the next page via long passages from Sutcliff's *Travels in Some Parts of North*

America (1815). Based on his various journeys throughout America in 1804, 1805, and 1806, undertaken ostensibly for what he calls "mercantile concerns," Sutcliff's travelogue exemplifies the flood of banal and panoramic surveys that curious foreigners of the period wrote about the young republic. Whereas the genre was later elevated into literary philosophy and made famous by Tocqueville's *Democracy in America,* Sutcliff's contribution is a generally flat, uninteresting, diarylike string of simple observations. Nonetheless, it is useful for Child's purposes, for it demonstrates again and again that slavery looks bizarre not only to committed abolitionists but also to supposedly "objective" foreigners. For example, Sutcliff notes that in Pennsylvania he saw wagons "drawn by four or more fine fat horses, and carriages firm and well made, and covered with good stout linen, bleached almost white." "The appearance of things in the slave States is quite the reverse of this," for wagons there, "if [they] may be called such," "appear in as wretched a condition" as the "ragged black boy or girl driving a team consisting of a lean cow or a mule, sometimes a lean bull, or an ox and a mule" (77). In short, Child argues through Sutcliff that the slave South suffers from a distinct lack of Yankee ingenuity.[52]

Indeed, Sutcliff's testimony enables Child to cast the argument that slavery produces a deadening drag on the modernizing pull of capitalism as not simply a rhetorical ploy forwarded by abolitionists but an observable fact witnessed by anyone who travels the country with open eyes and minds. The fact that Child quotes Sutcliff for three long paragraphs that, like the text she quotes from Faulkner, bear little indication of authorship other than quotation marks at their beginnings again shows the subtle uses an author may make of prosopopoeia. More important, though, these passages demonstrate that Child's critique of slavery—much like the arguments offered later by Douglass and Northup, as well as Joshua Leavitt and Wendell Phillips—depends on building common ground with readers by invoking their shared assent to the cultural fiction that Yankee ingenuity makes the capitalist North more productive, advanced, bountiful, and moral than the slavery-based South.[53]

If Douglass, Northup, and Child constitute representative examples, then the leading abolitionists felt that even the most scathing dissent from slavery should include equally energetic assent to the North's modernity. Moreover, although abolition was still very much a contested ideal up to and during the Civil War, few Americans would not have been moved by the abolitionists' tributes to their favorite cultural fiction: that America is the land of opportunity, of progress, of pulling one's self up by the bootstraps of righteous good deeds and morally uplifting labor. The awesome persuasive power of this cultural fiction is attested to not only by its repeated inclusion in abolitionist attacks against slavery but also by the fact that it could so easily have been seen as poppycock yet was not. For example, the Yankee ingenuity celebrated by Douglass, Northup, and Child was, at least in the more industrialized Northeast, a necessary cultural fiction justifying the fact that poorly paid workers were suffering through seventy-two-hour workweeks in hellish factories—the "busy and cheerful sound of industry" indeed.[54]

In addition, although Douglass argues that "the arm of commerce has borne away the gates of the strong city" (267), a cursory analysis of the distribution of wealth and property indicates that the capitalist commerce of modernity was not so much breaking down these gates as erecting new versions of social power and privilege. For example, Edward Pessen observes that by 1845 the wealthiest 3 percent of New York City's elite owned over 66 percent of the city's wealth; in 1841 Brooklyn, 66 percent of the city's population owned less than 1 percent of its wealth. Such inequalities were not restricted to major metropolitan areas, for Jonathan Prude has shown that in 1860 the richest 10 percent of the small rural Massachusetts towns of Dudley, Oxford, and Webster controlled 47 percent, 56 percent, and 63 percent, respectively, of their communities' wealth. Conditions were equally bad on the frontier, where in St. Louis the wealthiest 20 percent of the city owned 93 percent of the city's property. Perhaps even more significantly, Bruce Laurie notes that in Newark, "the proportion of self-employed craftsmen declined from 1-in-5 in 1840 to less than 1-in-10 in 1860." Whereas nearly 33 percent of Cincinnati's mechanics were homeowners in 1820, "the proportion plummeted to 6% in 1838 and to under 5% in 1850."[55] The progress of capitalist modernity thus had less to do with the spread of democratic equality and economic opportunity and more to do with the acceleration of gross class divisions—precisely the opposite of the cultural fiction endorsed by Northup, Child, and Douglass.

Moreover, whereas Northup, Child, and Douglass each supported the cultural fiction that modernity entails an inevitable advance toward intelligence, knowledge, and opportunity, Pessen's research suggests the opposite: as capitalism progressed spatially across the nation and technically into new means of production, divisions between workers and elites multiplied. Indeed, whereas the wealthiest 4 percent owned 49 percent of New York City's property in 1828, by 1845 they owned over 66 percent—an increase of almost 35 percent. Likewise, the richest 4 percent owned 59 percent of Boston's wealth in 1833 but over 64 percent in 1848, with similar patterns discernible in Brooklyn, Philadelphia, and a host of other Northern urban centers. There can be little doubt, then, that descriptions portraying Jacksonian America as a modernist paradise of economic opportunity and democratic equality are patently fictional, for research demonstrates that the period was marked by accelerating downward mobility for workers and multiplying riches for elites.[56]

Despite such harsh conclusions, one is obliged to recognize that Douglass, Northup, and Child derived much of their rhetorical power from their assent to the cultural fiction of Yankee ingenuity. That such astute political activists relied on this cultural fiction only demonstrates how completely their rhetorical dissent from slavery was intertwined with their rhetorical assent to the promises—albeit predominantly false—of modernity and capitalism. Indeed, the fact that these intertwined rhetorics of assent and dissent stood in such verifiable contradiction to the economic and political factors to which they supposedly pointed and yet were still persuasive demonstrates how heavily our means of persuasion rely on fiction—cultural fictions.

I have argued that no analysis of the dialectics of assent and dissent in abolitionist rhetoric can proceed without simultaneously examining the abolitionists' relationships to the promises of modernity, the Enlightenment, and capitalism, with these three terms understood as the key ingredients to the overarching cultural fiction of Yankee ingenuity. As noted in the introduction, I am also committed to an interdisciplinary and comparativist position that requires any analysis of the rhetorics of abolitionism, modernity, or capitalism, if it is to be even remotely helpful in a broad historical sense, to address the cultural fictions that supported slavery. In the following chapter I accordingly analyze both the structural, materialist realities of slavery (who owns what? who owns whom? who benefits from the system and how?) and the corresponding rhetorics of proslavery cultural fictions. As I will show, proslavery cultural fictions, much like their abolitionist counterparts, were framed in large part as forays into a larger cultural debate regarding the relationships among democracy, capitalism, and modernity. But whereas abolitionists attacked slavery through appeals to a federally based democracy empowered by capitalist modernity, proslavery cultural fictions marshaled the language of states' rights democracy against the custom-destroying powers of modern capitalism. Before addressing these questions, however, the chapter opens with a discussion of Franklin and Paine's abolitionism, which, paradoxically, established the rhetorical foundations of America's fear of certain race-related "serious evils."

2 *Proslavery Cultural Fictions, White Fear, and the Rhetoric of Serious Evils*

> Since the time of Reformation came . . . Christians have been taught to account all men their neighbors; and to love their neighbors as themselves; and to do to all men as they would be done by; and to do good to all men—*and man-stealing is ranked with enormous crimes.*
>
> —Thomas Paine, "African Slavery in America"

Thus Thomas Paine, writing from Philadelphia in heady, revolutionary March 1775, still ten months before he would electrify the world with his outrageously wonderful *Common Sense,* attacks the "enormous crime" of slavery. Paine escalates the palpable sense of contempt behind such slavery-as-crime imagery when he charges that slave dealers "may as well join with a known band of robbers."[1] Such moral and political outrage led Paine to join the Society for the Relief of Free Negroes Unlawfully Held in Bondage the same year his antislavery article appeared in print. It was not until nine years later, after the all-consuming passions of America's War of Independence had subsided, that this society again became active, now calling itself the Pennsylvania Society for Promoting the Abolition of Slavery, for the Relief of Free Negroes Unlawfully Held in Bondage, and for Improving the Condition of the African Race.[2] Writing as the president of this society five years later, in November 1789, Benjamin Franklin celebrates its work: "In prosecuting the design of our association, our endeavors have proved successful, far beyond our most sanguine expectations."[3] Despite this self-congratulatory opening claim, Franklin quickly slides into the more ominous issue at hand: "Slavery is such an atrocious debasement of human nature, that its very extirpation, if not performed with solicitous care, *may sometimes open a source of serious evils*" (518, emphasis added). The president of one of the young republic's first abolitionist societies thus acknowledges that although slavery constitutes an atrocious debasement, freeing the slaves may be worse.

Outlining the reasoning behind this thesis, Franklin argues that "the unhappy man, who has long been treated as an animal, too frequently sinks beneath the common standard of the human species. . . . Under such circumstances, freedom may often prove a misfortune to himself, and prejudicial to society" (518). Following this realization that slavery amounts to the mass production of barbarity and that abolishing it will therefore unleash a tidal wave of black zombies "accustomed to move like machines," without "the power of choice," "reason," or "conscience," Franklin suggests—in a passage that sounds hauntingly prophetic considering the racial bias of current imprisonment rates—that "attention to emancipated black people, it is therefore hoped, will become a branch of our national police" (518).[4] This attention, as outlined by the society in its "Plan for Improving the Condition of Free Blacks," includes convening four regularly scheduled committees: a "committee of inspection," charged with "superintending the morals, general conduct, and ordinary situation of the free Negroes" (519); a "committee of guardians," who will teach free blacks "some trade or other business . . . during a moderate time of apprenticeship, or servitude " (520); a "committee of education," which will not only teach free blacks "generally acknowledged moral and religious principles" but also, and strangely, "procure and preserve a regular record of the marriages, births, and manumissions of all free blacks" (520); and a "committee of employ," "as the want of this would occasion poverty, idleness, and many vicious habits" (520).[5] Although a pragmatic spirit of enlightened reform clearly pervades this document, it also clearly expresses white fears of a postslavery world.

Franklin's proposals are therefore remarkable for two reasons. First, in arguing for immediate emancipation he places himself at the forefront of the then nascent abolitionist movement. Second, while making this bold, radical call for emancipation, he simultaneously illustrates how powerfully the dread of emancipation haunts even abolitionists. This claim is particularly poignant since in 1789 there was no national police, let alone organized local or state police forces. Hence, even while calling for abolition, Franklin imagines the construction of a historically unprecedented and racially specific disciplinary apparatus, thus linking through fear freedom and bondage, emancipation and surveillance, hope and terror. Even Paine, in his typically uncompromising and consequences-be-damned article of 1775, foreshadows the difficulties of integrating ex-slaves into existing cultural practices, for he observes that "the past treatment of Africans must naturally fill them with abhorrence of Christians" (55). The nation's leading abolitionists of the revolutionary period were therefore terrified at the prospects of abolition.

I have opened this chapter by discussing Franklin and Paine's fears regarding the "serious evils" that could follow abolition because they illustrate the rhetorical foundations underlying what became one of the three fundamental paradoxes of antebellum American democracy. That is, although many antebellum Americans were opposed to the criminal debasement of slavery, they simultaneously lived—as did Franklin and Paine before them—in fear of the presumed catastrophes that might follow from emancipation. Slavery is clearly, as Paine's melodramatic prose describes it, a "savage practice" undertaken by "desperate wretches" (52), yet despite this realization, white thought regarding slavery in both the revolutionary and antebellum periods could not escape the assumption that freeing the slaves, while perhaps redeeming the promise of democracy—and, as noted in chapter 1, the promises of the Enlightenment and modernity in general—would certainly lead to serious evils. It comes as no surprise, then, to learn that proslavery cultural fictions were based in large part on manipulating this white fear. Consider Thomas Roderick Dew's remarkable threat from his canonical proslavery manifesto "Abolition of Negro Slavery": "The history of the world has too conclusively shown, that two races, differing in manners, customs, language, and civilization, can never harmonize upon a footing of equality. One must rule the other, or exterminating wars must be waged."[6] The first paradox to be discussed, then, is that even those Americans who loathed slavery were terrified—like Dew—by the prospect of its abolition.

The second crucial paradox of antebellum American democracy involves the existence of slavery as a set of embodied, material practices within a nation ostensibly founded on the textual claim that "all men are created equal." Indeed, attempting to reconcile the progressive, enlightened, and liberating rhetoric of democracy with the barbarity of slavery left many Americans not only perplexed, outraged, and flabbergasted by the profligate moral compromises built into their government but also confused by the radically indeterminate, textual nature of their new democracy.[7] For example, Peter Dorsey has recently observed that whereas in 1847 Frederick Douglass considered the Constitution to be "radically and essentially slaveholding," by 1851 he claimed that "not one word can be found in the Constitution to authorize slavery" and that the Constitution therefore is "a warrant for the abolition of slavery in every state." This was certainly Douglass's position by the time he gave his Fourth of July speech addressed in chapter 1. Dorsey contends that this dramatic shift in perspective illustrates Douglass's growth from accepting "the received authority of history" to his actively participating in "the openly textual possibilities of reinterpretation."[8] Nevertheless, the threat of abolitionism implied in such potentially radical possibilities of reinterpretation clearly persuaded some citizens of the need for ambiguity- and discussion-ending reinterpretations in which the Constitution could be upheld as a fundamentally and irrevocably proslavery charter. The paradoxical idea here is to engage in an interpretation-ending interpretation of the Constitution, to produce a proslavery reading to end all further readings. For example, Chief Justice Roger B. Taney's majority opinion in *Dred Scott v. John F. A. Sanford* illustrates the desire for a final, nonnegotiable proslavery version of the Constitution: "Negroes were *not intended* to be included under the word citizens in the Constitution, and therefore can claim none of the rights and privileges which that instrument provides for and secures to citizens of the Unites States."[9]

Douglass and Taney illustrate the fact that antebellum debates regarding the paradoxical presence of slavery within a democratic nation were—because of the originary, nation-founding legitimacy of both the Declaration and the Constitution—inescapably hermeneutic, which explains why many of the attendant arguments were based in large part on claims about the founders' intentions. One of the central issues regarding debates over slavery, then, involved determining which group could provide rereadings of the Declaration and Constitution persuasive enough to prompt a wholesale reinterpretation of slavery's legal and political status in America. In short, arguments regarding the status of slavery as an embodied, physical praxis within the new democracy focused in large part on questions about the way to read the nation's founding cultural fictions.

Of those Americans striving to perform a persuasive revision of the nation's founding cultural fictions in the cause of antislavery politics, perhaps none was more successful than John Quincy Adams. Indeed, his success as an antislavery activist illustrates the third paradox of antebellum American democracy. Adams's attacks on slavery were particularly persuasive among white Northerners because he articulated slavery primarily neither as a moral offense to Christians and the promise of the

Enlightenment (as did Paine and Child) nor as an institution leading to undesirable outcomes that might bedevil the future management of the nation (as did Franklin and Dew) but rather (more like Douglass and Rantoul Jr.) as an immediately relevant, insidious institutional apparatus perverting the Constitution's promise of democracy for property-holding white men. For example, in a 21 October 1843 address to his constituents in Dedham, Massachusetts, Adams details the myriad offenses of President Tyler. Regarding Tyler's push to annex Texas, Adams makes the following incendiary claim: "Your country is no longer a democracy, it is no longer even a republic—it is a government of 2 or 300,000 holders of slaves, to the utter exclusion of the remaining part, and all the population of the other States in the Union." Adams refers here to the representative imbalances caused by the three-fifths clause, which he calls "fraudulent, because under the name of a representation of *persons*, it was a representation of *property*."[10] In identifying the curious political alchemy that treats persons (slaves) as property but that simultaneously endows this property as pseudo-persons who count for three-fifths of a vote, Adams—observing the same phenomenon that Marx would later characterize as "reification"—points to a fundamental contradiction within the Constitution:

> Your property, what you have virtuously and honestly acquired, is excluded, while the owner of the slave is not only represented, as you are, in his person, but also in the persons of his slaves. Does the slave give his vote? No. Who gives the vote? The owner of the slave. He has a vote then for himself, and three votes for every five of the slaves of which he is the owner. . . . Now I ask you, Fellow Citizens, to reflect upon this: . . . If there be propriety in admitting a representation of property, upon what ground is it that your house and land, your shop and merchandise, should not be represented as well as slave property? (239–40)[11]

The question here, then, is not about the moral or political status of slavery as an institutional practice that consigns millions of Africans to bondage, drudgery, and brutality but about the impact this institution has on the democratic rights of Adams's compatriots. Prudently seeking to short-circuit possibly inflammatory misreadings of his position, Adams offers the following crucial qualification: "I beg that I may be understood that I am not now speaking as an abolitionist. I do not put it upon the question of the propriety or justice of the abolition of slavery, but upon the ground of your equal rights, in the Constitution of the United States, and in the representation of them in the legislative body" (240). Adams's delimiting tone here—denying his identity as an abolitionist—should remind readers of Rantoul's cautionary caveat from his Grand Massachusetts Convention speech, where he notes that despite his opposition to the Fugitive Slave Act, he has no truck with "new-fangled doctrines" such as "fanaticism or abolitionism."[12]

The third paradox of antebellum American democracy, then, as illustrated by Adams's and Rantoul's meticulously nuanced oratory, is that the period's debates regarding slavery's status in the democracy frequently were not about slavery as an embodied, institutionalized system of exploitation, racism, and violence. Rather, they concerned the ways in which slavery, understood as a *metaphor* for a host of egregious moves by Southern politico-economic elites (the so-called Slave Power), compromised the economic opportunities, democratic rights, and cultural privileges of white Northerners.[13] This rhetorical strategy was so successful that manipulating the ambiguities of this third paradox eventually became the driving strategy of Lincoln's Republican party. For example, consider the following claim, which Lincoln made at the first Ottawa, Ill., debate with Stephen Douglas:

> I have no purpose directly or indirectly, to interfere with the institution of slavery in the states where it exists. I believe I have no lawful right to do so, and I have no inclination to do so. I have no disposition to introduce political and social equality between the white and the black races. There is a physical difference between the two, which in my judgment will probably forever forbid their living together on terms of respect or social and political equality, and inasmuch as it becomes a necessity that there must be a superiority somewhere, I, as well as Judge Douglas, am in favor of the race to which I belong having the superior position.[14]

This passage demonstrates that even a man considered to be among the most important antislavery politicians of the period viewed white supremacy as an accepted and even desirable fact of life. Indeed, in claiming a physical difference between the two races that would prevent their social and political equality, Lincoln mimics the fundamental premises of proslavery cultural fictions: *they are different from us, they are inferior to us, and they will never live as equals among us.*

Antebellum America thus faced three interrelated paradoxes regarding slavery. First, although many Americans believed slavery was a heinous crime, they simultaneously feared that freeing the slaves would be even more damaging to the republic. Second, although the young nation was in large part founded on empowering notions regarding the transparency and veracity of the popular will, and hence on a radically new, immediatist concept of the body politic, debates regarding the status of slavery frequently revolved around mediated and nonverifiable rhetorical issues of textual interpretation. Third, although slavery was an incredibly popular subject of discussion, much of this discourse addressed not slaves and slavery per se but rather slavery as a metaphor for a host of historical issues, including the supposed encroachment of Southern politico-economic power over free white Northerners, the increasing tension between political liberty (democracy) and economic inequality (capitalism), the fate of democracy amid unprecedented geographic expansion, and the crumbling of traditional social hierarchies as America marched into modernity. Each of these three paradoxes was saturated with white fear regarding the potential catastrophes of emancipation, and furthermore, each of them—even when approached via the statements of leading antislavery activists—illustrated profound, unsettling levels of commitment to white supremacy.

Given the remarkable intelligence, humanitarian passion, and rhetorical genius of the previously mentioned antislavery figures—almost literally a pantheon of great Americans: Paine, Franklin, Adams, Douglass, Lincoln, Rantoul—it is more than a little disconcerting to notice that their antislavery pronouncements (excluding those made by Douglass) contained explicit appeals to fear-based, racist sentiments. Indeed, the fact that even the leading anti–Slave Power activists of the period pursued political agendas that were directed neither at the abolition of slavery itself nor at the pursuit of equality for blacks, and that these leaders assented to many of the main premises underlying many proslavery cultural fictions, should be cause both for reconsidering the history of arguments about race and slavery in the United States and for recognizing just how radical the abolitionists addressed in chapter 1 were compared to their fellow Americans. This is a question not of assigning blame or moral rebuke to some of our ancestors but rather of reconsidering the central role that slavery, racism, and white supremacy played in antebellum American culture. To put this in less dramatic terms, it is evident that antebellum America was saturated with images, stories, scientific theses, biblical parables, economic analyses, and any number of other cultural fictions—offered by anti–Slave Power and proslavery figures alike—explaining supposedly irreconcilable differences between whites and blacks.

Indeed, it is clear that the discourse of antebellum America, even when ostensibly addressing congressional minutiae, tariffs, westward expansion, or banking politics, was in large part driven by white fear regarding the "serious evils" both slavery and the possibility of emancipation foisted on the land. The leading proslavery individuals of the period addressed this point explicitly. For example, in "Abolition of Negro Slavery," Thomas Roderick Dew argues that the debate about slavery "involves the whole framework of society" (24). Later in this same text Dew observes that "all the sources of wealth and departments of industry, all the great interests of society, are really interwoven with one another—they form an indissoluble chain; a blow at any part quickly vibrates through the whole length—the destruction of one involves another" (41). "The whole framework of society," "all the sources of wealth," "all the great interests of society," "an indissoluble chain," "the whole length"—these phrases indicate that proslavery advocates understood discourse about slavery synecdochically as discourse about the nation: talk about slavery (as a part) and you inevitably talk about America (as a whole). Thus, whereas Northup's metonymy encourages empathic understanding across political boundaries, and whereas Jefferson's metonymy minimizes white guilt over slavery, Dew's synecdoche strives *to implicate everyone* in slavery.

Furthermore, whereas much antislavery literature was framed in morally blistering yet logistically vague language, pro-slavery advocates pursued precision, for their vested interests in expanding slavery forced them to detail in clear expository language slavery's economic, cultural, and political benefits, the damage that would result from abolition, and even the long-term historical advantages of slavery over what George Fitzhugh lambasted as the "tumults, uproar, mendacity and crime of free society."[15] Proslavery cultural fictions, then, because they aspired to be about everything else important to antebellum America, continually examined the promises and possibilities of democracy, capitalism, and modernity. The synecdochic nature of proslavery cultural fictions means that they offer remarkable opportunities not only for reconsidering the central role of slavery, racism, and white supremacy in antebellum American culture but also for observing how Americans responded to the wrenching economic, cultural, and political changes that marked the rise of modernity. I proceed, then, with the proposition that proslavery cultural fictions articulate a coherent and considered worldview and that understanding this worldview in turn teaches us important lessons about the way antebellum Americans argued not only about race and slavery but also about democracy, capitalism, and modernity.[16]

The first crucial step for approaching proslavery cultural fictions in this humbly ironic manner is to recognize that the proponents of slavery were not crazed fanatics. For example, in a recent review of William Miller's glorious study *Arguing about Slavery,* Eric McKitrick describes how, by 1860, Northerners "had run out of tolerance for the Southerners' mad efforts not only to push their system into the unsettled territories but to cut off the least discussion of it." McKitrick's rhetoric echoes Louis Hartz's charge, from his classic text *The Liberal Tradition in Amer-*

ica, that "fraud, alas, was the inevitable fate of Southern social thought."[17] Both McKitrick and Hartz overstate and simplify the case, for the elite slaveholding Southerners' politics were no more mad than those of their Northern counterparts, and the cultural fictions they constructed to explicate their agenda were not based on fraud. Indeed, although it may be reassuring to think of slavery as the fraudulent product of premodern lunatics who hatched bizarre plots and repugnant conspiracies, this perspective does nothing to advance our knowledge regarding how and why slavery lasted as long as it did precisely because it fails to explain slavery in the economic, cultural, political, and rhetorical terms of the period.

Justin Smith, in *The Annexation of Texas,* offers a more intellectually nuanced and historically productive method of approaching the thought of proslavery advocates. In a passage describing the expansionist, proslavery positions held by President Tyler and Abel Upshur, he suggests that "it must always be borne in mind that Upshur and Tyler considered slaves a form of property quite as legitimate as a mackerel fleet. To protect it seemed to such men a right and a duty; and it should certainly occasion no surprise that Southerners, finding themselves in possession of the government, used the power frankly in defense of their interests, just as Webster would no doubt have employed it in support of the tariff, which multitudes of good citizens regarded as merely highway robbery legalized."[18] Thus, in contrast to Dew's synecdochic thesis that discourse about slavery amounts to discourse about America as a whole, Smith's approach reminds us that although slavery may now appear to be a thoroughly repudiated form of social organization (note that Smith wrote in 1911), before the Civil War it was mostly considered but one element among a wide series of contested political issues, many of which struck Americans as more immediately pressing than slavery. Explaining slavery as the work of Southern lunatics erases this fact from our national history, thus enabling an unfortunate simplification of the issue that elides questions about Northern white complicity with slavery.

My subsequent concerns in this chapter, then, are twofold. First, I consider proslavery cultural fictions seriously, examining them as a systematic form of rhetoric, a series of economic, political, cultural, and historical arguments that articulate an antibourgeois, anticapitalist, antimodern worldview. Second, I attempt to demonstrate that these proslavery cultural fictions relied heavily on Northern white fears regarding the serious evils assumed to follow abolition. To pursue these dual concerns, I offer two interrelated areas of analysis. With respect to the first, I address the question from a primarily economic perspective, demonstrating that much of white Northerners' complicity with slavery followed from the fact that Northerners benefited from slavery as much as Southerners did. Put simply, it was widely understood that acting against slavery would hurt the economic interests of the North and that slavery, although possibly a moral problem, would therefore have to be tolerated in the name of continued healthy profits. The next section accordingly examines the structure of the political economies of both the slave South and the "free labor" North, arguing that comparative differences between the levels of economic development in the two regions sprang from their different forms of capitalism. With respect to the second area of analysis, I present an extended series of case studies in the rhetorical analysis of cultural fictions addressing three of the major premises and recurring rhetorical tropes of proslavery cultural fictions, particularly as they involve the three paradoxes discussed previously. For purposes of organizational clarity I have divided this work into subsections that address what I call "paralyzing rhetoric," "indecipherable rhetoric," and "nostalgic rhetoric." The analyses in these sections are based on readings of works by Thomas Prentice Kettell, Edmund Ruffin, and David Christy; other lesser-known writers from *The Southern Literary Messenger* and *De Bow's Review*; and especially Thomas Roderick Dew, William Harper, and George Fitzhugh. Continuing my commitment to comparativist scholarship, I supplement my analysis of these proslavery cultural fictions with frequent comparisons to the ostensibly antislavery comments of Lincoln, Hinton Rowan Helper, Catharine Beecher, and Alexis de Tocqueville and the abolitionist arguments of Solomon Northup, John Greenleaf Whittier, Lydia Maria Child, and David Walker.

The Political Economy of Complicity

In 1860 an anonymous author in the *Vicksburg Daily Whig* offered the following description of the relationship between New York City and the South: "New York City, like a mighty queen of commerce, sits proudly upon her island throne sparkling in jewels, and waving an undisputed commercial scepter over the South. By means of her railways and navigable streams, she sends out her long arms to the extreme South; and with avidity rarely equaled, grasps our gains and transfers them to herself—taxing us at every step and depleting us as extensively as possible without actually destroying us." Bracketing this passage's curious gender politics, it appears that, for our anonymous author, the political economy of slavery is the province not exclusively of premodern Southern lunatics but rather of a national system of mutual dependency and exploitation in which the rapidly modernizing capitalists of the "free"

North profit just as handsomely as their slaveholding Southern counterparts. Indeed, in *Business and Slavery: The New York Merchants and the Irrepressible Conflict,* Philip Foner estimates that by controlling shipping fees, insurance costs, brokering charges, and the other business transactions required for engaging in multinational commerce, New York City interests pocketed up to forty cents out of every dollar spent on cotton.[19] There is thus more than a little truth to the following claim William Harper makes in his influential *Memoir on Slavery:* "The prosperity of those States [the North], and the civilization of their cities, have been for the most part created by the existence of slavery."[20] As was frequently the case with such claims, this thesis received its most economical expression at the hands of J. D. B. De Bow, who referred with more than a little disdain to Northerners as those "*slave-made* capitalists."[21]

My first point regarding the political economy of complicity, then, as illustrated by the damning rhetoric of the anonymous author from the *Daily Whig,* Foner's meticulous research, Harper's *Memoir,* and De Bow's essay, is that the economic developments fueling the North's transformation into a modernist and capitalist juggernaut were financed in great part with capital made through lucrative dealings with the slaveholding cotton growers of the South. Indeed, although the ostensibly free North was not saddled with the obvious ethical baggage of engaging openly in slavery, many Northern merchants were nevertheless deeply implicated in the economic benefits of cotton and were therefore complicit with the political economy of slavery. Thus, although many abolitionists attacked slavery by assenting to the cultural fiction that capitalism was modernizing and enlightening the world, the recognition that Northern capitalism was dependent on Southern slavery forced some abolitionists to attack Northern capitalism as but a permutation of Southern slavery. This relationship underlay Lydia Maria Child's following cautionary reminder: "While we bestow our earnest disapprobation on the system of slavery, let us not flatter ourselves that we are in reality any better than our brethren of the South. . . . they tell us that Northern ships and Northern capital have been engaged in this wicked business; and the reproach is true. Several fortunes in this city have been made by the sale of Negro blood."[22]

Thus abolitionists and proslavery writers often agreed that Northern capitalism was growing fat on the blood of slavery. Historians trained to see the long view will find this argument obvious, for of course the historical purpose of slavery was to provide metropolitan capitals and centers of production with the resources necessary to advance market domination. Indeed, in the relationship between America's modernizing capitalist North and its agrarian slave-based South, no less than in the relationship between industrial Britain and its slave colonies, one sees the interaction of two dramatically different yet mutually dependent stages of capitalism. Child's claim that many Northern fortunes had been based on the slave trade, then, no less than De Bow's cutting reference to "*slave-made* capitalists," indicates not so much a radical rhetorical ploy to align fellow citizens against slavery (or for it, in De Bow's case) as a historically accurate description of the way modern capitalism's remarkable successes were based largely on comparative market advantages secured through the monopolies of labor and material that slavery made possible.[23]

As detailed in the closing pages of chapter 1, a vast body of economic research demonstrates that antebellum capitalism dramatically accelerated the divisions among rich, middling, and poor Americans. This is true regarding the relationships between North and South as well. Whereas the Northeast was rapidly modernizing via new means of production, distribution, and marketing, the South's reliance on slavery and cotton led to both a diminished consumer-goods economy (because slaves could not participate as consumers in the same way as Northern workers could) and to an apparent lack of investment in what we now call "research and development." Gavin Wright provides an example of this lack of investment in new technologies with respect to mechanical devices for harvesting, threshing, and cutting corn and various grains (predominantly Northern crops) versus those for harvesting, picking, and chopping cotton (exclusively a Southern crop): the years between 1837 and 1849 averaged ten patents for the former but fewer than one for the latter. Between 1850 and 1860 the disparity increased slightly, to twenty-nine patents per year for the former versus two-and-a-half patents per year for the latter. Wright's point is that the North's productive capabilities, enhanced by the technological innovations formally recognized in new patents—and fueled with capital made from slavery—were advancing at a rate far greater than the South's.[24] Entrepreneurial Northerners were obviously willing to take advantage of this situation; given the laws of capitalism, they would have been foolish to do otherwise. Thus, following a period of heavy antislavery organizing in Cincinnati, the city's proslavery *Enquirer* editorialized on 11 September 1841 that "a miserable clique of fanatics" was jeopardizing the "friendly relations with" and lucrative "trade and travel of the South."[25] Profits are profits, this article suggests, regardless of their source.

Nonetheless, certain Southerners perceived these relations as having gradually reduced the South to little more than an abused colonial exporter of raw materials. Hence North Carolina's most famous antislavery advocate, Hinton Rowan Helper, argued dramatically in his manifesto *The Impending Crisis of the South* (1857): "It is a fact well known to every intelligent Southerner that we are compelled to go to the North for almost every article of utility and adornment, from matches, shoepegs and paintings up to cotton mills, steamships and statuary. . . . All the world sees, or ought to see, that in commercial, mechanical, manufactural, financial, and literary points of view, we are as helpless as babes in comparison with the Free States."[26] In protesting the gross imbalance of trade between North and South, Helper points to two popular arguments. First, many claimed that the South's lack of investment in research and development hindered its ability to advance new technologies of production, distribution, and marketing and thus left its citizens helpless before the modernizing North. Second, this claim implies as a corollary that the predominantly monolithic economic system created by a slavery-based plantation economy offers few opportunities for the diversification of job skills necessary to launch an economy into full modernization.

Sweeping generalizations about the state of regional economies are obviously difficult to make without oversimplification, but Helper's arguments seem not far off the mark. For example, in their controversial *Time on the Cross: The Economics of American Negro Slavery,* William Fogel and Stanley Engerman report that 73 percent of all slave labor was directed into cotton production, with 14 percent invested in the production of tobacco, 6 percent in sugar, 5 percent in rice, and 2 percent in hemp.[27] In his more recent *Without Consent or Contract: The Rise and Fall of American Slavery,* Fogel modifies these figures to suggest that cotton production required 38 percent of slave-labor time, with 31 percent of slave-labor time spent on the "growing of corn and the care of livestock," and 31 percent spent on "land improvements, the construction of fences and buildings, the raising of other crops, domestic duties, and home manufacturing (especially the production of clothes)."[28] This second set of figures suggests that the South's economy was more diversified than Helper thought, yet it nonetheless reveals the remarkably lopsided nature of a slavery-based plantation economy that thrived overwhelmingly on the single cash crop of cotton.

Fred Bateman and Thomas Weiss observe similarly telling disparities for 1860: whereas the average capital investment per establishment for northeastern manufacturers was $12,456, the figure for Southern manufacturers was but $4,827; whereas output per establishment averaged $22,669 in the Northeast, the figure for Southern manufacturers was but $8,034; and whereas average capital per worker was $82 in the North, it was but $11 in the South.[29] These numbers indicate not value judgments regarding the two systems' ethical or political natures but rather differing levels of capitalization and modernization. Despite these obvious disparities in patterns of capital investment, manufacturing output, and capital per worker, however, Bateman and Weiss also observe that although each manufacturing employee in the Northeast produced $1,196 worth of goods per year, those in the South produced $1,466 worth of goods per year (184, table 1). Hence, although the technological capabilities, job skills, and capital investment patterns of the South appear to indicate that it faced less favorable long-range economic prospects than did the North (and more specifically the Northeast), Southern capitalists were nevertheless operating a remarkably profitable economic system. That is, the South was not modernizing as quickly or in the same manner as the North, yet Helper's claim about the South's relative helplessness notwithstanding, its profits indicate a healthy, thriving capitalist economy.

One of the paradoxes of antebellum Southern wealth, then, is that while slavery enabled the plantation elite to approach a grand lifestyle comparable to that of the world's most wealthy aristocratic families, the infrastructural limitations in the political economy of Southern cotton production meant that the Southern slaveholders, despite their monopolistic control of the world's largest cash crop, had to import from the North both goods (including a majority of their shoes and farming tools) and the skilled workers needed to repair their carriages, roads, and ships.[30] The South's need to import goods and skilled labor from the North helps to explain the common cultural fiction in which slavery is portrayed as producing a slothful workforce and a lazy, decadent master class that suffers from a crippling shortage of Yankee ingenuity. Indeed, recall that in *Twelve Years a Slave* Solomon Northup continually portrays both his slaveholders and his fellow slaves as muddle-headed boors incapable of performing creative labor. For example, toward the end of the tale, as Northup has finally secured his freedom and is bidding farewell to his contacts on the plantation, the plantation mistress sidles up to him to lament pathetically, "Now there is no one left who can mend a chair or a piece of furniture—no one who is any use about the house."[31]

This portrayal of an incompetent South, while obviously hyperbolic in the service of creating dramatic narrative contrast, has some truth in it, for numerous observers have noted that the rising bourgeoisie of the Northeast provided a majority of the ships necessary for the national and international distribution of Southern cotton, the insurance on crops and ship cargoes, the advance funds necessary for planting new crops in the spring, and a majority of both the domestic merchandise—basic daily items as well as luxuries—and supplemental labor purchased by Southern consumers.[32] Indeed, Northup's narrative is more than simply a celebration of Yankee ingenuity enmeshed within antislavery propaganda, for his portrayal of the South's long-term economic prospect, indicated by the plantation mistress's lament, is consistent with the views expressed by forward-looking Southerners. For example, in *The Five Cotton States and New York* Stephen Colwell estimates that, much to his chagrin, the South spent $131,000,000 on goods and services made or produced in New York City during 1859 alone.[33] Thomas Prentice Kettell laments this trade imbalance in his popular *Southern Wealth and Northern Profits,* where he observes that "all the profitable branches of freighting, brokering, selling, banking, insurance, etc., that grow out of the Southern product, are enjoyed in New York."[34] Along these same lines, a Natchez newspaper editorial laments the fact that "the large planters—the one-thousand bale planters—do not contribute most to the prosperity of Natchez. They, for the most part, sell their cotton in Liverpool, buy their wines in London or Le Havre; their Negro clothing in Boston, and their plantation implements in Cincinnati."[35] What angered Colwell, Kettell, and this anonymous Natchez editorialist—and what left Northup, Helper, and many promodernity and procapitalism Northerners scoffing at the long-term viability of the plantation system—was the Southern economic elite's failure to reinvest their considerable profits back into the South's domestic economy. In short, the South's cotton elite were spending their surplus capital in manners that did not benefit the region's long-range economic modernization.[36]

To summarize: although the South's economic elite invested less heavily than did their Northern counterparts in the technological innovations and market transformations associated with modernization, the *superexploitation* of labor made possible by slavery enabled them to reap incredible profits.[37] Indeed, while the South's need to import basic goods and services looked like a sign of economic weakness from the Northeast's modernizing and gung-ho capitalist perspective, from the South's would-be aristocratic, even feudal perspective, this arrangement constituted a logical, cost-efficient way to meet needs while not redirecting labor from the true engine of growth and prosperity—cotton. This apparent paradox, of the South's remarkable "revenue efficiency" in the face of the North's overwhelming "technical efficiency," has frequently left historians confused regarding the structure of the South's political economy; hence, historians have frequently portrayed the South as backward and premodern.[38] More recently, however, scholars have come to realize that the South was one of the early to mid-nineteenth century's leading worldwide economic engines enabling the international transition into modernity. For example, Fogel and Engerman argue that the antebellum South was the Western world's third richest nation in terms of per-capita income, ranking behind only England and northeastern America (including Massachusetts, New Hampshire, Vermont, Pennsylvania, New York, Connecticut, and New Jersey) but substantially ahead of France, Germany, Switzerland, the Netherlands, Belgium, Denmark, what is now Italy, and Austria.[39] Furthermore, with respect to capital accumulation, Fogel observes that "nearly two out of three males with estates of $100,000 or more lived in the South."[40] This second figure tells us more about the wealth of the South's economic elite versus that of the North's than it does about the overall structure of the two regions' economies, yet Fogel's point is clear: the South was not a backward and pauper-ridden region but rather a prosperous economic zone managed by some of the world's most wealthy capitalists.

In attempting to comprehend the complex issues of economic growth and the distribution of wealth, it is instructive to address the basic numbers in terms of slave ownership, circa 1860; table 1 shows some of the relevant data. According to these figures, slaves constituted roughly 41.5 percent of the South's total population. Since on average only 34 percent of white families in these states owned slaves, fully 66 percent did not. These calculations indicate that the two largest population groups living in the South were slaves, who constituted 41.5 percent of the total population, and nonslaveholding white families, who constituted approximately 39 percent. The numbers on slave ownership require another level of specification, however, for Stampp argues in *The Peculiar Institution* that 88 percent of all slaveholders owned fewer than twenty slaves,

Table 1.

State	Total Slaves	Total Whites	Percentage of Slaves in Population	Total Slaveholders	Percentage of Slaveholding White Families
Virginia	490,865	1,047,299	32	52,128	27.3
North Carolina	331,059	629,942	34	34,658	29.1
South Carolina	402,406	291,300	58	26,701	47.1
Georgia	462,198	591,550	44	41,084	37.6
Florida	61,745	78,680	44	5,152	34.5
Alabama	435,080	529,121	45	33,730	35.1
Arkansas	111,115	324,335	26	11,481	20.1
Mississippi	436,631	354,674	55	30,943	49.2
Louisiana	331,726	376,276	47	22,033	31.0
Texas	182,566	420,891	30	21,878	28.5

Sources: Compiled from *The United States Eighth Census* (1860) and matched against figures in Michael Holt, *The Political Crisis of the 1850s* (New York: W. W. Norton, 1978), 229; and Douglass North, *The Economic Growth of the United States, 1790–1860* (New York: W. W. Norton, 1966 [1961]), 129.

meaning that they were not part of the dominant "planter class." Furthermore, using the ownership of fifty or more slaves as the mark of membership in the ruling "planter aristocracy," Stampp found only 10,000 families in the class (30). Multiplying Stampp's 10,000 families by the generally accepted average of 3.1 white males per family suggests that the real powerbrokers—those elite white plantation "aristocrats" who owned fifty or more slaves—made up considerably less than 1 percent of the South's overall population.[41] These numbers thus indicate in dramatic fashion that proslavery cultural fictions needed to persuade a vast amount of citizens to support a politico-economic system from which they derived little power or wealth.

Nevertheless, although the planter aristocracy may have made up less than 1 percent of the total population, 34 percent of white families did own some slaves, meaning that a remarkably large percentage of citizens were directly invested in the politico-economic system. Otto Olsen puts this number in perspective by comparing slave ownership in the South to stock ownership in post–World War II United States. Taking a $5,000 stock investment to be a 1949 equivalent to owning one slave in 1860, Olsen found that only 2 percent of U.S. families were directly invested in the nation's political economy at this level. Olsen concludes from these figures (34 percent vs. 2 percent) that the political economy of slavery was not "exceedingly oligarchical" but rather "created one of the largest percentage groups of investors in the direct exploitation of labor that the world has ever seen."[42]

Wright contests Olsen's view, arguing that the percentage of slave owners was declining over time, from 36 percent of white families in 1830, to 31 percent in 1850, and to 25 percent in 1860. These figures suggest that the antebellum South, much like the North, was experiencing an expanding division of wealth between an increasingly elite class of the superrich—the plantation aristocracy involved in cotton and sugar production—and those nonslaveholding farmers and merchants struggling to stay one step ahead of insolvency.[43] Wright summarizes this trend as producing "an increasingly staggering differential" between slaveholders and nonslaveholders.[44] Hence, despite Olsen's provocative comparative claims, I am inclined to agree with Wright that the South was a community divided deeply not only by the obvious racial differences between whites and slaves but also by the severe class distinctions between a remarkably wealthy handful of elite plantation aristocrats and the majority of economically disempowered self-sufficient rural farmers and small-time urban manufacturers and merchants.

The crucial point that many historians overlook, then, is that while

Northerners were trumpeting the lack of modernity in the South, the Southern elite were only too happy to have the bustling midlevel merchants and grubby workers of the North fill those labor gaps not covered by slavery or local poor working whites. Indeed, as Anderson and Gallman argue, "What needs to be emphasized is that [the planter's] decisions were altogether rational. . . . where mechanization could serve his interests—as in sugar refining—he was no laggard in accepting new methods and making the necessary, heavy investment in machinery. . . . the fact that the South lagged behind the North in mechanizing harvest procedures is not clear evidence of a general Southern technological weakness in agriculture."[45] In short, Northern capitalists' deep involvement in the political economy of cotton does not necessarily indicate a comparative economic weakness on the part of the South; rather, it shows only the differences between the means of production in the modernizing, increasingly industrial, capitalist North and the patriarchal, agrarian, slavery-based South. This thesis suggests that Yankee ingenuity is less a better system of living, as many Northerners believed, than simply a different system of living.

This subtle slippage from exposition to moralizing encouraged Northern complicity with slavery, for entrepreneurial Northern merchants, bankers, shippers, workers, and so on could rely on the remarkable engine of the slave-based cotton plantations to promote continued economic prosperity in the North while simultaneously deriding the South's slavery as immoral and premodern. Thus, with the empowering belief that their own hands were clean and their own politico-economic system—the culture of Yankee ingenuity—was more modern, more moral, and more productive, many Northerners marched proudly and righteously into the future fully complicit with slavery. Of course, as my discussion of Lydia Maria Child suggests, not all Northerners were pleased by the fact that the economies of the South and North were so inextricably interwoven. For example, the *Annual Report of the American Anti-Slavery Society* of 1855, amid its scathing critique of the New York City business community's much-publicized support for the Compromise of 1850, claims that the New Yorkers supported the legislation not out of a sense of duty to the nation but rather for the personal goal of maintaining "the clipper ships, Government contracts, warehouses bursting with merchandise, large profits, and great dividends" that resulted from their lucrative dealings with the South. The Northern merchants indicted in this report responded quickly in brave capitalist fashion, arguing that their involvement with Southern slavery—although repugnant to them morally—was nonetheless crucial for the economic security of the nation.

Hence an anonymous New Yorker responded as follows: "We are not such fools as not to know that slavery is a great evil, a great wrong; but there are millions upon millions of dollars due from Southerners. We cannot afford the overthrow of slavery; It is not a matter of principle with us—It is a matter of business necessity."[46] Thus, just as many of the South's cotton-growing elite viewed their dealings with the North to be the unfortunate yet necessary requirements of doing business in an international capitalist market, so the Northern businessman quoted here held dealings with the slave-holding elite to involve not moral but only commercial issues. In short, however the different factions may have viewed their uncomfortable interactions with one another, there was a considerable interlinking of Southern and Northern business interests. That is, *slavery was not only a Southern problem but also the economic engine propelling the North's drive toward modernity.*

As I discussed in chapter 1, one of the most unsettling conclusions of examining Southern slavery, Northern capitalism, and the onset of modernity in antebellum America is that conditions of property ownership and wealth were no more egalitarian in the North than they were in the South. The figures cited previously suggest this conclusion, as does the popular New York City essayist George Foster, who lambasted the period as one drunk with the "spirit of mercantile exploitation and multiplied profitmaking."[47] Proslavery advocates such as George Fitzhugh argued along similar lines. Indeed, although Fitzhugh's work tends toward hyperbole, these figures demonstrate that legitimate economic reasoning may lie behind his categorical charge, from *Sociology for the South,* that "the laboring millions are in worse condition (in free society) than they ever were before" (52). One cannot draw too firm a conclusion from the caustic pens of Foster and Fitzhugh alone, yet I hope to have persuaded readers that both the North and the South were marked by profoundly inequitable economies in which the majority of the population had little or no direct stake in the production of goods, the accumulation of capital, or the ownership of property.

It is clear, then, that the politico-economic elite of both the North and the South desperately needed cultural fictions that could justify and explain their profound economic, political, and cultural power as enmeshed in larger issues of nationality, freedom, race, and even historical destiny. Indeed, considering the dramatic economic inequalities just detailed, it is a wonder that poor working people in both the North and the South were not up in arms. The politico-economic elite's success in keeping the "riff-raff" in line no doubt depended in large part on their ability to create cultural fictions that provided clear meanings and obligations to citizens who—at least based on economic factors—might otherwise have been in revolt against their "betters." The rest of this chapter explains how these proslavery cultural fictions were based on *the rhetoric of paralysis, the rhetoric of indecipherability,* and *the rhetoric of nostalgia.*

Proslavery Cultural Fictions and the Rhetorics of Paralysis, Indecipherability, and Nostalgia

At the close of his influential *Memoir on Slavery* (1838), following page after page of detailed economic, cultural, political, and historical reasoning regarding the benefits of slavery and the anticipated catastrophes of abolition, William Harper arrives at a dramatic and sweeping religious claim that I suspect indicates his position on slavery more truthfully, honestly, and immediately than do the preceding, more nuanced arguments. Indeed, in a moment of stark rhetorical candor that betrays his frustration at having to explain something so obvious, Harper blurts out: "Does not the finger of heaven itself point to a race of men . . . on whose whole features, mind and character, nature has indelibly written slave?" (120–21). Unfortunately for Harper and his fellow proslavery advocates, heaven's intentions are not so easily verified; hence, while clearly believing that slavery is ordained by no less an authority than God, the proslavery faction was nonetheless obliged to resort to more common, pedantic, earthly forms of persuasion. I will thus eschew discussions of proslavery cultural fictions based on religious arguments, for while claiming direct access to the finger of heaven may have proven reassuring (and was in fact a popular form of discourse), proslavery thinkers appear to have realized that metaphysical arguments were not nearly as likely to persuade readers as were arguments regarding economic security, racial purity, and the fate of both democracy and national unity.[48] I accordingly address three significant tropes within proslavery cultural fictions specifically as they correspond to the three paradoxes outlined in the introduction to this chapter.

PARALYZING RHETORIC

I described the first of the three paradoxes regarding slavery in antebellum America as follows: although many Americans believed slavery to be a heinous crime damaging the democracy, they simultaneously feared that freeing the slaves would be even more damaging to the republic. Proslavery advocates, fully aware of the rich contradictions embedded in this paradox, clearly sought to drive popular thought regarding slavery and the possibilities of abolition toward paralysis. More specifically, if they could refute the first aspect of the paradox (by proving that slavery is not a heinous crime but rather a positive good) while simultaneously exaggerating the second aspect of the paradox (by demonstrating that abolition would wreck the Union), then they could immobilize possible antislavery sentiments in a wash of paralyzing contradictions. The first major trope of proslavery cultural fictions, then, entails combining what historians call the "positive good" thesis with what I call the "impending doom" thesis.[49] Furthermore, the attempt to combine these theses into an argument that predicts the future of a postabolition America (understood here as exemplifying the rhetorical trope of prolepsis) and that, based on these proleptic acts, accordingly calls for a politics of moderation, caution, and fealty to tradition (understood here as exemplifying the rhetorical trope of prudence) amounts to an attempt to construct a rhetoric of paralysis.

Among proslavery advocates arguing that slavery is a positive good, perhaps none was as influential as Thomas Roderick Dew, the well-known political activist; lecturer; professor of history, metaphysics, and political law; and president of Virginia's William and Mary College from 1836 until his death in 1846. Dew's positive good thesis, as he presents it in "Abolition of Negro Slavery," is that "the menial and low offices being all performed by blacks, there is at once taken away the greatest cause of distinction and separation of the ranks of [white] society. The man to the North will not shake hands familiarly with his servants. . . . But go to the South, and you will find that no white man feels such inferiority of rank as to be unworthy of association with those around him. . . . it is this spirit of equality which is both the generator and the preserver of the genuine spirit of liberty" (66–67). Slavery is a positive good, then, because it enforces an inviolable color line that serves as a marker dividing menial and low labor (anything done by a slave) from respectable labor (anything done by a white). Additionally, this color/labor line enables unprecedented levels of equality and liberty among citizens who, despite the obvious disparities of wealth and political power among them, recognize one another as neighbors in the congenial fraternity of free whites.

This positive good thesis is important historically, for Dew wrote "Abolition of Negro Slavery" explicitly as a response to debates within the Virginia legislature following Nat Turner's August 1831 rebellion. According to Laurence Shore, these debates took an overwhelmingly antislavery tone, stemming from both fear of further rebellions and "the State's predominantly (Western) non-slaveholding population's anger over politico-economic servitude to the Eastern slaveholding population."[50] Dew's positive good thesis was also a response to a marked rise in abolitionist activism in the South and a prolonged economic slump in both land values and export profits.[51] Dew thus offered his article as a revisionary rhetorical response to what the Southern elite perceived as major challenges to the system of slavery, traditional class relations, and the South's long-term economic and political viability. That is, Dew's positive good thesis was not so much a celebration of slavery per se as a rhetorical defense of status-quo politics prompted by a series of historical crises.

Despite its origins as a defensive response to crisis, the positive good argument quickly became popular, for it appeared to capture a common sentiment, expressed here by George Fitzhugh in one of his 1854 *Richmond Examiner* editorials: "We have stood on the defensive long enough. We can throw fire-brands as well as the abolitionists."[52] David Christy argued along these lines in his 1855 manifesto *Cotton Is King* (not to be confused with Elliott's 1860 anthology of the same title), stating that slavery had yielded several benefits: "Our exports are increased; our foreign commerce advanced; the home markets of the mechanic and the farmer extended, and the wealth of the nation promoted."[53] Edmund Ruffin, a prominent Virginia planter and proslavery spokesperson, also defended slavery on positive grounds, claiming in *The Political Economy of Slavery* that it was only by imposing slavery that "leisure could be afforded to the master class to cultivate mental improvement and refinement of manners."[54] The appendix to this small pamphlet, entitled "The Influence of Slavery, or of Its Absence, on Manners, Morals, and Intellect" (the text of Ruffin's 16 December 1852 presidential address to the State Agricultural Society of Virginia), repeats the thesis: "By confining the drudgery and brutalizing effects of continued toil or menial service to the inferior race . . . [slavery] gives to the superior race leisure and other means to improve mind, taste, and manners" (26). Perhaps the most categorical versions of the positive good thesis are found in Harper's *Memoir on Slavery*, where he claims that "the institution of slavery is an essential process in emerging from savage life" and that "every society which has attained civilization, has advanced through this process" (91, 81).[55] Dew, Fitzhugh, Christy, Ruffin, and Harper thus all claim slavery to be a positive good that provides the foundation for unprecedented levels of cultural refinement, limitless politico-economic expansion, genuine democratic equality among white men, and, ultimately, civilization itself.

Given the dramatic economic inequalities in both the South and North, such promises of cultural refinement, economic prosperity, guaranteed democratic equality, and the continued progress of civilization appealed strongly to poor whites who felt themselves economically and politically disempowered. For example, while describing the "pass" system that allowed slaves to move from one plantation to another while conducting officially sanctioned business, Northup observes, "Those having the air and appearance of gentlemen, whose dress indicated the possession of wealth, frequently took no notice of me whatever; but a shabby fellow, an unmistakable loafer, never failed to hail me, and to scrutinize and examine me in the most thorough manner" (118). The point is that the latter individual, a representative of that economically disempowered class Northup later refers to as "mean whites," derives a sense of cultural privilege and political authority from reinforcing slavery, for this enables him to enact his aspirations to wield the authority of the plantation aristocrats. Indeed, in his study of the political bonds among plantation aristocrats and poor whites, Eugene Genovese notes that the plantation elite's overwhelming economic, political, and cultural clout made it "natural, as a matter of inclination and social conscience, [for lower-class whites] to be ready to ride patrol, to help discipline the slaves, and to take part in the political and police aspects of the slave regime—in short, to think and act like slaveholders even before becoming one." Poor whites were thus encouraged to think of themselves "as aspiring slaveholders or as non-slaveholding beneficiaries of a slaveholding world."[56] Thus, in the face of the glaring economic inequalities between the so-called slave aristocracy and the 66 percent of whites who did not own slaves, the color line served as a sweeping cultural fiction that buried the contradictions attendant on the aristocracy of wealth within the putative neighborly democracy of white supremacy.

Viewing slavery in this manner obviously appealed markedly to Southerners, for the positive good thesis enabled elites to see themselves, via their captaining of the plantations, as the fathers of civilization while simultaneously enabling poor whites—who otherwise had considerable economic reasons to challenge the plantation elite—to see themselves, via their membership in the great white family, as respected and important citizens in the democracy.[57] For many Northerners, however, assenting to this cultural fiction could easily be taken as a sign of support for the Southern aristocracy, an act that was tantamount to renouncing the modernist and capitalist values embodied in the cultural fiction of Yankee ingenuity. The rhetorical dilemma for proslavery proponents concerned with appealing to Northerners was thus to present a cultural fiction that supported the maintenance of slavery without necessarily endorsing the values and interests of the Southern cotton elite.

Hence the positive good thesis is supplemented with a variety of hyperbolic scenarios portraying slavery as the primary protective measure holding back the imminent disasters imagined as following abolition. The corollary to the positive good thesis, then, is the impending doom thesis, which represents society as an intricate web of politico-economic institutions and finely balanced cultural norms that, if altered through the drastic measure of abolition, will collapse into economic ruin and devastating racial warfare. For example, the anonymous "J" addresses the question of abolition in *The Southern Quarterly Review* of 1850: "Two billions of property extinguished at a blow. To what condition would this reduce us? To hopeless universal ruin. Our fields waste—our cities in ruin—industry paralyzed—commerce fled; we would be compelled to abandon the homes we now repose [in,] in peace, our genial soil and delicious climate to utter desolation and barbarism."[58] The obvious shortfall of this cultural fiction is that by identifying the focus of this imagined universal ruin as exclusively Southern ("our fields," "our cities," "our homes," etc.), the author unwittingly suggests that Northerners are distanced from the threat of disaster, that their world is somehow removed from the devastation to follow abolition.

This shortcoming explains why the most astute proslavery advocates, clearly following the rhetorical lead of their counterparts in the earlier debates in Britain, attempted to articulate the impending doom as broadly historical (that is, as entailing the fate of civilization itself) and to cast their arguments as national rather than regional appeals.[59] For example, Kettell writes in *Southern Wealth and Northern Profits* that curtailing the growth of slavery will "jeopardize the national prosperity, the domestic peace, the safety of life and liberty, and the very existence of the Nation" (5). Kettell is a master of such incendiary proleptic rhetoric; he claims, for example, that abolition will cause "servile insurrection, bloodshed and annihilation of person and property," not only resulting in the destruction of the South but also "involving ultimately the ruin of the North" (5).[60]

Numerous impending doom theses went so far as to predict civil war. For example, the Democratic party mouthpiece, *The Madisonian,* again in response to a speech by John Quincy Adams, declared in an article ominously entitled "White Slavery" that the "hypocritical zeal" of Adams and his "pretended philanthropists" was "eager to precipitate the country into the horrors of a civil and servile war."[61] This charge echoes Dew's proleptic vision of abolition: "We shall wake at last to all the sad realities of savage warfare and increasing barbarism" (48). In *Memoir on Slavery* Harper nicely summarizes such impending doom theses when, after discussing the forthcoming "utter poverty," "misery," "desolation," "discord," "horror," and "atrocity" of a postabolition America, he concludes that freeing the slaves "would overturn the fundamental institutions of society" (128, 130, 135). Such doomsday prophesies epitomize proslavery advocates' proleptic efforts to portray abolition as a surefire means of plunging the Union into economic decline and race-based warfare and, ultimately, of instigating the dissolution of the Union and even civilization itself.

Such proleptic rhetoric was not considered extreme or outlandish. Indeed, most Americans were familiar with any number of bloody events that lent credibility to these charges. The most obvious and frightening example of impending doom was the carnage of the 1791 Haitian revolution. In terms of domestic politics, the "Christiana Tragedy" is a good example. This incident took place 11 September 1851 in Christiana, Pennsylvania, where Edward Gorsuch attempted to retrieve four slaves who had recently escaped from his Maryland farm. The runaway slaves' attempts to rebuff Gorsuch received support from over one hundred local residents, mostly black but some white; the ensuing melee left Gorsuch dead, his son wounded badly, and scores of whites and blacks either clubbed, shot, or beaten. Gorsuch was technically within his legal rights, since he was enforcing his property claims under the provisions of the Fugitive Slave Act. In fact, Northern whites were frightened less by political battles over enforcement of this act than by the violence it provoked. That is, they perceived such situations—where blacks did not hesitate to defend themselves against whites, where Northern whites would take up arms against their Southern compatriots, and where tensions over slavery could erupt in terrifying interracial battles—as troubling signs of terrible things to come. The impending doom thesis gathered credibility from such events. In fact, in his remarkable analysis of the Christiana Tragedy, Thomas Slaughter concludes that "no single event before John Brown's Raid contributed more to the decline of confidence in the nation's ability to resolve the controversy over slavery without wholesale resort to arms."[62]

One of the fascinating aspects of antebellum debates regarding slavery—as noted earlier in my discussions of Franklin, Paine, Adams, and Lincoln and as demonstrated by observing the chilling implications of events such as the Haitian Revolution and the Christiana Tragedy—is that many antislavery figures adopted language that echoed some of the key rhetorical strategies of proslavery cultural fictions, particularly the impending doom thesis. For example, John Greenleaf Whittier, one of the most ardent antislavery poets of the period, employs the trope of impending doom in his poem "Our Countrymen in Chains!"

O, rouse ye—ere the storm comes forth,—
The gathered wrath of God and man,—
Like that which wasted Egypt's earth,
When hail and fire above it ran,
Hear ye no warnings in the air?
Feel ye no earthquake underneath?
Up—up—why will ye slumber where
The sleeper only wakes in death?[63]

Whereas I have cited Lincoln, Franklin, and Rantoul counseling various plans for moderating the serious evils of abolition, Whittier here argues that only immediate abolition may spare the nation from the imminent cataclysm fostered by slavery. Whittier's poem thus illustrates the rhetorical dialectics of dissent, for although he pursues an antislavery agenda, the poem's ominous biblical imagery of forthcoming disasters, which clearly relies on the rhetoric of serious evils, cannot help but reinforce the rhetoric of impending doom forwarded by proslavery advocates.

Perhaps the most dramatic example of an antislavery figure employing the rhetoric of impending doom is David Walker's *Appeal to the Coloured Citizens of the World,* where Walker writes: "I tell you Americans, that unless you speedily alter your course, *you and your country are gone!!!!!!* For God Almighty will tear up the very face of the Earth!!!"[64] Later in this same manifesto Walker barks, "you are ruined!!!" (47), and "Wo, wo will be to you if we have to obtain our freedom by fighting" (70). Then, in a passage whose threat of doom contemporary readers certainly understood, he writes: "My colour will yet root some of you out of the very face of the earth!!!!!!" (72). Even Alexis de Tocqueville, in a passionate chapter of *Democracy in America* that excoriates slavery as a "total perversion" of "the laws of humanity," cautions readers that "a conflict between the white and the black is inevitable" and that this conflict will likely escalate into "the most horrible of civil wars and perhaps the extirpation of one or the other of the two races."[65] Whittier, Walker, and Tocqueville were courageous advocates of abolition, yet by employing the hyperbolic and proleptic rhetoric of serious evils, in which America's future is imagined as a catastrophe of racial warfare and perhaps even biblical destruction, they each enliven the rhetoric of impending doom.

It thus appears that much of the period's political discourse, antislavery and proslavery alike, was littered with the rhetorical tropes of *cataplexis* (traditionally understood as the rhetoric of threats), prolepsis (traditionally understood as the rhetoric of forestalling objections by predicting the future), and categorical propositions (traditionally understood as the rhetoric of sweeping, all-inclusive generalizations), all of which were used in dramatic, hyperbolic, emotionally charged arguments. Confronted with all these impending doom appeals and a barrage of arguments regarding slavery's benefits, even the most conscientious citizen's thinking regarding slavery might tend toward caution, if not paralysis.

Somewhat ironically, given their predilections for these forms of rhetorical manipulation and outright bombast, proslavery advocates were simultaneously adamant proponents of a sly variation of the trope of prudence. Whereas this trope is ideally enacted as a performative yet pragmatic, democracy-enhancing example of *phronesis,* or provisional eloquence, Robert Hariman observes that it "too often seems to be invoked in defense of the status quo" and that prudence therefore "relies heavily on common sense, unspoken agreements, and traditional values." Understood in this fundamentally conservative light, prudence amounts to "a means of maintaining the community's traditional alignment of its social practices."[66] For example, in a letter to the *Baltimore Republican and Argus,* Thomas Walker Gilmer suggests that "it should be the first wish of every American to allay an excitement which is fast ripening into crime."[67] In this same year *The Madisonian* cautioned, "We think it becomes the people among whom such things can occur, to be a little more moderate in their invectives against slave-holders."[68] Dew echoes this call for moderation, submitting that "it behoove[s] even the wisest statesman to approach this august subject with the utmost circumspection and diffidence" (24). Thus Gilmer, *The Madisonian,* and Dew, each having employed any number of aggressive impending doom theses, here invoke prudence as the best course of action in the face of abolitionist fanaticism.

Indeed, one of the more consistent (and certainly ironic) proslavery charges against abolitionists was that their rhetoric was imprudent. For example, Dew characterizes the public excitement following Turner's rebellion as based on "rumor, with her thousand tongues . . . , [where] reason is almost banished from the mind," and chastises the official debate in the Virginia legislature as a "zealous" discussion that "boldly set aside all prudential considerations" (25, 28). Likewise, Ruffin refers to abolitionists as "enthusiasts and fanatics" who, mimicking the "revolutionary madness" of France, engage in "violent attacks and denunciations . . . without the least regard for the evils that will follow" (13). An anonymous essayist in *De Bow's Review* even claims that the imprudent rhetoric of abolitionists, whom he labels "ranting atheists, law-breakers, and crazy utilitarians," is so extreme that it amounts to nothing less than "a virtual encouragement to crime."[69] Even Catharine Beecher, one of the more widely respected women in American politics of the era and a strong opponent of slavery, invoked this trope in a letter responding to Angelina Grimké's call for women to join abolitionist societies: "The second reason I would urge against joining the Abolitionist Society is that its character and measures are not either peaceful or Christian in tendency, but they rather are those which tend to generate party spirit, denunciation, recrimination, and angry passions."[70] Thus, whereas the abolitionists articulated what was widely perceived as a consequences-be-damned "firebrand" rhetoric, the previously cited examples demonstrate proslavery advocates (and even one antislavery but not immediately abolitionist woman) appealing to prudence—"be a little more moderate"; "allay an excitement"; "try some circumspection and diffidence"—as the best means of avoiding the impending doom awaiting those who would pursue the dangerous course of abolition. The endlessly deferring, perpetual wait-and-see policy of what Freehling calls "Do Nothingism on slavery" may thus be understood as the rhetorical product of arguing for both positive good and impending doom theses, the combination of which produces a rhetoric of paralysis.[71]

INDECIPHERABLE RHETORIC AND THE POLITICS OF AMALGAMATION

I described the second paradox regarding slavery in antebellum America as follows: while the new democracy was in large part founded on empowering notions of the transparency and veracity of the popular will, and hence on a radically new, immediatist conception of the body politic, debates regarding slavery frequently revolved around fundamentally mediated and nonverifiable rhetorical questions of textual politics. In short, antebellum Americans were confronted with the challenge of squaring their rhetorical and textual sense of the revolutionary promises of democracy with their embodied and experiential sense—perhaps best illustrated via slavery—of democracy's compromised status. Understandably, antebellum Americans were perplexed by this gap between rhetoric and experience, promise and practice, the mediated and the immediate, the body politic and the body. One response involved attempting to show that slavery abased the nation's founding cultural fictions. This led to a vast amount of interpretive work regarding both the legal, textual status of slavery within the Constitution and the political and cultural status of slavery in the light of the Declaration of Independence's thundering claims.[72] A second response to this paradox, the response that I examine here, comprised proslavery attempts to contrast the unknowable, potentially dangerous effects of revisionist hermeneutics—that is, the work of antislavery forces providing reinterpretations of the place of slavery within the Constitution—against the tried-and-true experiences of custom and tradition. Proslavery proponents accordingly argued that the only way to understand the relationships among race, slavery, and democracy was not to engage in revisionary textual hermeneutics, which were portrayed as leading inevitably to a series of indecipherable rhetorical dead ends, but rather to return to customary, traditional means of framing the world. As William Harper argues in *Memoir on Slavery,* such questions must "be settled by convention" (84). These customary, conventional, antirhetorical values were, of course, white supremacist.

One of the most consistent manifestations of this appeal to custom and convention in the face of indecipherable rhetoric was a constant harping on proslavery cultural fictions invoking the threat of amalgamation. Indeed, proslavery cultural fictions rely in great part on expanding the immediate, bodily threat of amalgamation (the popular term that preceded *miscegenation*) into a metaphor representing the threat of rendering the entire body politic indecipherable, confused, muddied beyond repair.[73] Just as a couple's sexual relations could mix races and thus cloud questions of ownership and ethics, the argument goes, so amalgamation could cloud the economic and racial boundaries framing the nation. The remarkable number of speeches and texts dedicated to this argument suggests that fear of amalgamation became one of the period's most ubiquitous cultural fictions. And whereas proslavery advocates came to see revisionary hermeneutics as dallying amid the indecipherable, they portrayed amalgamation as a physically embodied and easily visible example of the damage that followed from race mixing. Thus, whereas textual and rhetorical arguments regarding the nation's founding promises and premises were indecipherable, the body politics of amalgamation were obvious and clear and could be understood by anyone armed with the commonsense wisdom of which custom and convention are made.

One of the many contradictions of this argument, of course, is that amalgamation itself was largely indecipherable. For example, consider these passages from Gustave de Beaumont's novel *Marie; or, Slavery in the United States* (1835):

> "That woman," he replied, "is colored."
> "What? Colored? She is whiter than a lily!"
> "She is colored," he repeated coldly; "local tradition has established her ancestry, and everyone knows that she had a mulatto among her forebears."
>
> "That lady who has attracted your attention is white."
> "What? White! She is the same color as the mulattoes."
> "She is white," he replied; "local tradition affirms that the blood which flows in her veins is Spanish."[74]

Whiteness and blackness are thus not always visible signs but rather culturally crafted positions within hierarchies of power, wealth, and privilege as determined by the obscure folklore and mythology that underpin local tradition.

This negotiated and therefore potentially destabilizing racial and thus political ambiguity—*Is she white or black? How can one tell?*—appears in proslavery cultural fictions as one of the most potent threats to the stability of custom. For example, Harper claims in *Memoir on Slavery* that amalgamation can produce "nothing but pure, unmixed, dephlegmated, defecated evil" (134). As I will show, this argument surfaced in almost all the most important proslavery cultural fictions. Indeed, proslavery advocates used the threat of amalgamation as a means of rendering moot the endlessly open, textual nature of democracy, for no textual or constitutional debate could override the absolute evil of interbreeding. Hence, faced with the new republic's complicated textual indeterminacies, proslavery advocates attempted to justify traditional cultural politics by invoking the literally pretextual, immediately physical customs of body politics. In so doing, they hoped to interject into debates about race and slavery a semblance of certainty, of common sense.

Before examining examples of this argument, it is important to note again that cultural fictions addressing amalgamation derived their persuasive power largely from the overwhelming nationwide presence of white supremacist attitudes. For example, on 7 November 1837, while an Alton, Illinois, mob was attacking (for the third time that year) the press responsible for printing Elijah Lovejoy's abolitionist *Observer,* Solomon Morgan, when stopped by the mayor and asked why he was engaging in such antidemocratic violence, responded, "How would you like a damned nigger going home with your daughter?"[75] Three years earlier, following the bloody race riots that rocked New York City for five days (7–11 July 1834), the American Anti-Slavery Society was so concerned about its cause's having been linked to amalgamation that it released a postriot handbill, announcing: "We entirely disclaim any desire to promote or encourage intermarriages between white and colored persons."[76] Abolitionists released a similar disclaimer, reading, "We are not amalgamationists," following race riots in Cincinnati in September 1841.[77] Seventeen years later, at a Democratic rally in Indianapolis, a banner read, "FATHERS, SAVE US FROM NIGGER HUSBANDS!"[78] These brief examples demonstrate that some Northerners were quick not only to associate antislavery activism with proamalgamation stances but also to employ amalgamation as a sweeping metaphor for voicing social unease.

Leonard Richards summarizes this point when he argues in *"Gen-*

tlemen of Property and Standing" that "for most white Americans amalgamation meant miscegenation, the debasement of their posterity, and the downfall of white America. For [Northern] 'gentlemen of property and standing,' however, it also symbolized the breakdown of distinctions among white men, the blurring of social divisions, and the general leveling process they saw enveloping ante-bellum America" (166). Richards's summary points to the fact that proslavery cultural fictions regarding amalgamation were based mostly on the rhetorical trope of metonymy. Specifically, they portrayed amalgamation not as the effect of slavery, as the inevitable result of a brutalizing system in which white men acted with impunity toward black women, but rather as the cause of social breakdown. Furthermore, in keeping with Burke's notion that metonymy strives "to convey some incorporeal or intangible state in terms of the corporeal or tangible," proslavery cultural fictions portrayed amalgamation as the corporeal and tangible source of the nation's difficulties.[79]

Indeed, proslavery cultural fictions employed metonymy to rearticulate amalgamation not in its literal sense as the bodily mixing of races but rather as a complicated metaphor linking "improper" sexual conduct with the broad degeneration of morals and standards that accompanied the confusing social transformation of late-Jacksonian America. For example, in *Two Lectures on the Natural History of the Caucasian and Negro Races* (1844), Dr. Josiah C. Nott of Mobile, Alabama, argues that amalgamation produces "hybrids" and that human hybrids are a "distinct species"; he draws this conclusion from the example of breeding a horse with an ass, which produces an impotent, lesser creature, the mule. According to Nott, the proliferation of such "distinct species" amounts to nothing less than the undermining of Western civilization: "This adulteration of blood is the reason why Egypt and the Barbary States never can rise again, until the present races are exterminated, and the Caucasian substituted. Wherever in the history of the world the inferior races have conquered and mixed in with the Caucasians, the latter have sunk into barbarism."[80] Nott's claim that amalgamation results in a desperate sinking into barbarism—unless, of course, this slide into oblivion is prevented by the extermination of the polluting races—was repeated by Dew in "Abolition of Negro Slavery," where he too argued that in those cases where the "commingling of races ensued, it has been found that the civilized man has sunk down to the level of barbarism, and there has ended the mighty work of civilization" (47). Hence, much as Jefferson metonymically displaced cause and effect to appease American guilt by blaming the British for slavery, these examples portray catastrophe as the result not of slavery but rather of sinful and civilization-wrecking amalgamationists. As does Jefferson's argument, the amalgamation argument shifts blame, in this case from slave masters to slaves, from the system of slavery to individual immorality.

Perhaps the most immediate example of the havoc caused by amalgamation—short of wrecking civilization in toto—was the slew of complaints disgruntled Southern white women filed against philandering husbands. For example, in an 1849 trial before the North Carolina Supreme Court, Ruthey Ann Hansley charged that her estranged husband, Samuel G. Hansley, in addition to rumbling through frequent bouts of drink-induced violence, had fallen into the "intolerable" habit of "bedding and cohabitating with a negro woman named Lucy." Amalgamation's crisis-causing nature is most obvious, however, in the charge that Samuel, in his drunken infatuation with a slave, "deprived the petitioner of the control of all those domestic duties and privileges connected with the house, which belong to a wife, and placed the said Lucy in the full possession and enjoyment of those privileges and duties."[81] Thus, Samuel Hansley disrespects his wife, "hybridizes" the gene pool, and, perhaps most important, destroys the proper hierarchy of plantation control, all concrete signs showing how amalgamation can wreck civilization. (Interestingly, such fears assume that traditional hierarchies of gender, regardless of race, will remain firmly in place.) The examples from Nott, Dew, and Hansley demonstrate that discourse regarding amalgamation relies on a sophisticated and two-tiered metonymic strategy. First, it reverses relations of cause and effect, arguing not that slavery causes amalgamation but that amalgamation causes social degeneracy. Second, via the use of what Burke calls "scale manipulation," it escalates the impact of amalgamation into a civilization-ending threat.[82]

Astute antislavery figures accordingly attacked this metonymic portrayal of amalgamation. For example, in his famous debates with Stephen Douglas, Lincoln repeatedly attacks the proslavery tactic of describing even the mildest anti–Democratic party rhetoric as if it were a clarion call for amalgamation. In their first debate, at Ottawa on 21 August 1858, while replying to Douglas's opening comments, Lincoln notes with more than a touch of sarcasm that Douglas has hyperbolically portrayed him as having a "tendency . . . to set the states at war, and to set the niggers and white people to marrying with one another" (67). Lincoln again attacks Douglas's metonymic version of amalgamation when, in the sixth debate, at Quincy on 12 October, he caustically jokes: "Mr. Douglas will insist that I want a Nigger wife" (318). The pro-Republican *Chicago Tribune* reports that both lines triggered "great laughter." The interesting point here is that Lincoln's responses succeeded only because the audience found these assertions to be absolutely absurd. Both lines thus worked as comic relief while simultaneously deflecting Douglas's exaggerated claims regarding Lincoln's status as a "Black Republican." Lincoln's responses, then, while denying Douglas's charge through a dismissive, joking version of reductio ad absurdum (*Of course I do not want a nigger wife, and isn't Douglas a dolt for saying that I do when he knows damn well that I don't?*), depend on the all-important assumption that no one in the audience will consider, even for a moment, the plausibility of Douglas's charge. Thus, while Lincoln and Douglas are battling over the way to manipulate most productively the slur of amalgamation—understood in this case as a sweeping trope for casting doubts on the moral standing of their interlocutor—both men share the same fundamentally white supremacist assumptions about the body politics of amalgamation: *it is historically dangerous, it is practically evil, and it is so morally unforgivable that it works nicely as a vicious, crowd-pleasing joke.*

The numbing complexity of popular thought regarding amalgamation was expressed even more succinctly when Lincoln, in the fourth debate, at Charleston on 18 September, attempted to smear Douglas with the shame of amalgamation. Referring to Douglas's repeated descriptions of Lincoln as a "Black Republican" favoring amalgamation, Lincoln responds: "I recollect of but one distinguished instance [of amalgamation] that I have heard of a great deal so as to be entirely confident of it, and that is the case of my friend Douglas' old friend, Col. Richard M. Johnson" (190). Lincoln refers here to the much-publicized case of Johnson's "amalgamating" with Julia Chinn, one of his many slave mistresses. What makes the Johnson case so interesting, however, aside from that fact that it was one of the leading topics of trashy gossip and race-baiting banter in the 1836 presidential election (in which Johnson, a Southern Democrat, ran successfully as Van Buren's vice president), is that Johnson's error was not in taking a slave as his lover—for this was common, accepted practice—but in treating the daughters of this relationship as if they were white. Indeed, the popular press rebuked Johnson not because he had produced children with a slave but because he secured white husbands for Imogene and Adaline, his two daughters with Julia Chinn. Southern custom (in its fully American, post–French colonial variation) holds a single great-grandparent with "black blood" sufficient to confer "blackness"; hence, in marrying his daughters to prominent white Southern gentlemen, and thus in attempting to "pass" the illegitimate offspring of what should have remained a private, purely sexual affair as the legitimate heirs of public, property-holding status, Johnson violated the color line.[83]

Lincoln was therefore astute to attack Douglas by associating him with Johnson's well-known faux pas, for when considered in tandem with his pointed jokes referring to amalgamation (not to mention his repeated charge that Douglas was involved in a conspiracy to extend slavery into the western territories),[84] such rhetoric sends two clear messages. First, it reconfirms unequivocally that Lincoln was as repulsed by amalgamation generally, and by Johnson's actions specifically, as the next man. The implied tone here is white supremacist, thus enabling Lincoln to appeal to the racism of the audience. To put this another way, Lincoln's barbed reference to Johnson demonstrates that one may oppose the Slave Power yet not be "soft" on race issues; this is clearly an appeal to the latent racism of wavering Democrats. Second, it demonstrates that amalgamation is caused by slavery, practiced by slaveholders, and likely to continue if Douglas and his fellow expansionists have their way in opening the territories to slavery. The implied tone here is cautionary, thus enabling Lincoln to appeal to the trope of impending doom. To put this another way, Lincoln here suggests the following: *Just imagine Kansas and Nebraska spoiled with swarming herds of Johnson's mulatto bastards! That's the nagging little truth of what expanding slavery will give us.* This is clearly an appeal to the latent racism of waffling former Free Soilers. Lincoln's pointed reference to Johnson therefore serves a doubly productive rhetorical function, for it demonstrates the foolish, hyperbolic nature of Douglas's attack on Lincoln while simultaneously appealing to the racist sentiments shared by both of the crucial swing vote populations: wavering Democrats and waffling former Free Soilers.[85]

By raising the Johnson case to exemplify the specter of amalgamation, Lincoln acknowledges the difference between amalgamation as an accepted physical practice of sexual, body politics and as a controversial semiotic practice of legal, textual politics. Harper addresses this rift between practice and rhetoric, sex and semiotics, in *Memoir on Slavery,* where he grants that "the licentious passions of men overcome moral repugnance, and find transient gratification in intercourse with females of the other race. But this is a very different thing from making her the associate of life, the companion of the bosom and the hearth" (131). Bracketing the unspeakable horrors of "moral repugnance" (Harper cannot even name that "other race") and the illicit pleasures of purely physical sex, what clearly offends Harper is the thought that a black woman might ascend to a legally, textually sanctioned position of power and privilege. Indeed, both the Lincoln and Harper quotations demonstrate that amalgamation as sex (in which a woman is a disempowered object) is morally unfortunate yet culturally accepted, whereas amalgamation as marriage (in which a slave woman is recognized as an empowered subject) is something else entirely, for—as witnessed in the Johnson case—it amounts to a blurring of the color line. Whereas having your way with a slave is but one of the various brutal privileges of white supremacy, striving to include the offspring of such indiscretions in the carefully sanctioned world of white property owners violates every principle of Southern culture. The distinction then, is between acceptable private sexual encounters with someone who lacks legal and political agency and unacceptable public or legal acknowledgment of someone with legitimate claims to social standing.[86]

One of the more elaborate discussions of this dual standard (oscillating between amalgamation's private, body politics and its public, textual politics) appears in Eva Saks's "Representing Miscegenation Law," which argues that "because the deviance of social form from legal form makes social form an unreliable sign of legal form (and vice versa), this deviance causes a crisis of representation." The crucial source of this crisis, according to Saks, and as illustrated in the Johnson case, is that "interracial sex and marriage had the potential to threaten the distribution of property, and their legal prohibition was an important step in consolidating social and economic boundaries." As the earlier quotations from Beaumont indicate, attempts to consolidate such boundaries along strictly racial lines present problems because there are no objectively verifiable means for deciphering race. As Saks observes, "To substantiate blood, to substantiate what is neither a mimetic description nor a tangible entity but instead a semiotic figure, is impossible."[87] This perhaps explains why the legal records of planters who tried to bequeath property to their mulatto children and slave mothers consistently contain petitions filed by furious white relatives claiming that in the face of nonverifiable claims of lineage, custom suggests that they (the acknowledged and historically accepted white relatives) should retain legitimate ownership over both the property and even the mulattos in question.[88]

Indeed, given the lack of any objective measure for blood or race (the key terms underpinning the metaphor of amalgamation), all one can do, following proslavery thinking, is fall back on the timeworn impressionism of accepted custom.[89] And accepted custom for most white antebellum Americans was white supremacist, which meant that any crisis of representation, any confrontation with a legal or textual question of inheritance and ownership that appeared to be written in the indecipherable rhetoric of race, was resolved in favor of a hard-line defense of tradition. This point underlies Harper's argument that "the opinion which connects form and features with character and intellectual power, is one so deeply impressed on the human mind, that perhaps there is scarcely any man who does not almost daily act upon it, and in some measure verify its truth (114). This customary privilege of controlling the meaning of black bodies as both sexual or physical and textual or legal objects is expressed explicitly in "Abolition of Negro Slavery," where, addressing the possibility of a new law to emancipate slaves, Dew argues: "The law would make them freemen, but custom or prejudice, we care not which you call it, would degrade them to the condition of slaves" (55). The democratic law of the land therefore can do nothing in terms of altering custom or prejudice. Amalgamation thus stands as a trope for everything about which the South refuses to compromise: the laws may change, but custom still rules the body politic.

One obvious manifestation of this threat that textual discourse will never alter tradition and custom—basically, the charge that some things will never change—is the use of amalgamation as a trope that metonymically condenses vague white fears of imagined black retribution into scenes of sexual terror. Put simply, this cultural fiction argues that since textual politics can never modify the deeply embedded, experiential base of body politics, the lust for black vengeance (in the form of sexual assault on white women) will continue regardless of any potential legal emancipation. For example, a mysterious series of fires swept across Texas in July 1860, prompting one local settler, Benjamin Bowman, to charge, "Abolition Emissarys ar going through this country instigating Negros to Burne the towns and kill there Masters. . . . allso they was to kill all the Wimmin and Children that they could—all the likly young ladies they Was to save for Wives for themselves." Randolph Campbell observes that the fires most probably resulted from a recently introduced type of phosphorous match, yet Texans, bereft of this cool-headed analysis, apparently preferred to believe that the fires were started as a diversionary tactic to pave the way for the amalgamationist intentions of vengeance-driven blacks.[90]

Harper's *Memoir on Slavery* offers a similar scenario. After predicting that, following abolition, "the blacks will be tempted to avenge themselves by oppression and prescription of the white race," Harper proceeds immediately to discuss the "unspeakably loathsome" act of amalgamation (130). Thus the threat of forced, revenge-based amalgamation serves the larger rhetorical purpose—which can be grasped here as a variation on the impending doom thesis—of outlining the imminent catastrophes that await abolition. Fires erupt inexplicably, crops die, stray looks become accusations, strange and bizarre things happen without rhyme or reason; in this vacuum of understanding, in this whirlwind of indecipherable acts, amalgamation serves as a catchall threat of lurking black sexual mischief. Thus amalgamation, when understood through the previously detailed metonymic processes, ultimately serves the rhetorical function of cataplexis; that is, it stands as a threat of the terrible misfortune that awaits those who ignore the accepted racial boundaries of custom and tradition.

NOSTALGIC RHETORIC I: FITZHUGH AND THE CRIMES OF MODERNITY

I described the third paradox regarding slavery in antebellum America as follows: while slavery was an incredibly popular subject of discussion, much of this discourse did not concern slaves and slavery per se; rather, it used slavery as a metaphor for a host of historical issues, including the supposed encroachment of Southern politico-economic power over free white Northerners, the increasing tension between political liberty (democracy) and economic inequality (capitalism), the fate of democracy amid unprecedented geographic expansion, and the crumbling of traditional social hierarchies in the face of America's transition into modernity. Such substitutions generally figured in antislavery discourse, but slavery served as a sweeping metaphor as well for proslavery advocates, for whom it indicated not only the proper racial and hierarchical order of the world but also the differences between the genteel stability and deferential order of the South's would-be aristocratic world and the North's rough-and-tumble class competition, political "leveling," godless modernizing, and dog-eat-dog capitalism. George Fitzhugh summarizes this point when he observes that "the true cause of quarrel lies deeper. It is not mere Negro slavery, but the slavery principle."[91] For both anti–Slave Power and proslavery advocates, then, debates regarding slavery frequently amounted to a form of rhetorical sublimation: that is, in the face of life's jarring complexities, attacking or supporting slavery enabled Americans to voice political ideas in readily recognized political language that, like most acts of sublimation, amounted to a redirection or refocusing of energies that could not find more articulate expression.[92] More specifically, proslavery cultural fictions rely in large part on a simplifying rhetoric of nostalgia, in which timeworn cultural tradition and racial purity are offered as solutions for what Tocqueville referred to in *Democracy in America* as the nation's "strange confusions" (11).

One of the central debates of antebellum America concerned whether the idealistic democracy enshrined in the Declaration of Independence could withstand the pressures of maintaining a nation as geographically diverse, as culturally fractured, as economically disparate, and as politically contentious as America. One ghost haunting this debate, of course, is the nostalgic cultural fiction that European-style aristocracy is somehow more orderly, more coherent, and more manageable than American-style democracy. For example, Tocqueville observes that as democracy marches forward, "the barriers which imprisoned society and behind which it was born are lowered; old opinions, which for centuries had been controlling the world, vanish; a course almost without limits, a field without horizon, is revealed" (43). There is a utopian sense of possibility here, of a world of endless options, yet Tocqueville, like many of his contemporaries, is concerned that such a world may spin out of control. Indeed, he later notes that without the "natural associations [of the old aristocratic order] which check the abuses of power," America might decline into "the most galling tyranny" (195). After all, antebellum America amounted to a renunciation of all previous life-ordering norms; Tocqueville thus describes it as "a nation where the old customs of people are changed, public morality is destroyed, religious beliefs shaken, and the spell of tradition broken" (242).

This context makes it clear that much of the antebellum debate regarding slavery attempts to reconfigure this spell of tradition in a new, particularly American vernacular. For example, at the second Lincoln-Douglas debate, at Freeport on 27 August 1858, Harold Holzer notes that (in addition to Douglas's getting pelted with a rotting melon rind) one of the many banners in the audience read "NO NIGGER EQUALITY" (88). This banner is curious for two reasons. First, Freeport is a small town just south of the Wisconsin border, a long way from slave country, in a state with almost no free black population to speak of, which means that the slogan is probably less a political endorsement of any practical, local political issue or platform—*since no sane person would espouse such a philosophy*—than a hackneyed call supporting the traditional, customary, metapolitical values of white supremacy. Second, the Lincoln-Douglas debates were ostensibly not about the question of racial equality, for both Lincoln and Douglas had repeatedly made their white supremacist positions clear. Decrying racial equality, then, amounts to both a gigantic simplification of the debate's real issues and a redundant statement of the all too obvious. The banner therefore condenses a series of complicated political issues into a catchall assertion that denies the specificity of the moment to reassert the already understood: *whatever happens here, in these debates, or in the coming elections, or in the unfolding of democracy across the new lands of the West, let us agree that niggers are inferior, have always been inferior, and always will be inferior.* Politicians come and go, parties align and disintegrate, but the one great spell of tradition remains: "no nigger equality."

Granting, then, that the ultimate spell of tradition in antebellum America was the lingering fealty to white supremacy, it is not surprising that the proslavery rhetoric of nostalgia primarily left the race question sleeping—*Everyone agrees on this issue anyway, so why bother?*—and proceeded instead to engage the troubling question of the ways modern capitalism was changing America. But whereas much public debate in the new democracy focused on methods of closing the gap between the rhetoric of equality and the economic reality of oligarchy, certain patriarchal Southerners portrayed modern capitalism as nothing less than a destructive, godless, world-changing onslaught against traditional values. For example, in a letter of 27 April 1843, written in the midst of the Texas annexation controversy, President John Tyler reports: "Duff Green returns to England with a view to negotiate with the Capitalists."[93] This remark presents another example of metonymy, for it conflates the multiple and conflicting interests of Britain regarding the fate of Texas, the abolition of slavery, and the global balance of power into the all-inclusive sign of "the Capitalists." Indeed, Tyler here uses metonymy to condense the complicated historical, political, and economic debates at hand into a stark choice between the genteel grandeur of Southern patriarchy and the selfish, money-grubbing, imperialist ambitions of British capitalism.[94]

Although not frequently stated with as much rhetorical efficiency as in the Tyler example, the attempt to link capitalism with the destruction of traditional values constitutes a central trope of proslavery cultural fictions.[95] For example, Dew clearly contrasts Southern elegance and patriarchal order with the unruly "selfish principle" that drives capitalism in England and northern America: "Look to the slave-holding population of our country, and you everywhere find them characterized by noble and elevated sentiment, by humane and virtuous feelings. We do not find among them that cold, contracted, calculating selfishness which withers and repels everything around it" (58, 64). According to such proslavery rhetoric, the cold and calculating selfishness of Northern capitalism amounts to a cruel deception, for even though workers there are ostensibly free, most of them are shackled by an economic system that allows little possibility of improving their circumstances. Slavery, however, holds out no such cruel illusion of betterment yet cares for its laborers in a manner not possible under capitalism. Harper thus argues that slavery is a morally superior form of social organization because slaves, confident of their places in the world, are "secured against the temptation to greater crimes" and the "more avaricious vices and miseries" that follow from the chimerical freedoms of capitalism (108). In fact, while slaves repose contentedly in the unchanging certainty of the slaveholder's patriarchal order, Northern workers suffer a constant barrage of hardships and indignities: "There is continual apprehension for the future—for themselves—for their children—of sickness and want, if not of actual starvation. They expect to improve their circumstances! Would any person of ordinary candor, say that there is one in a hundred of them, who does not well know, that with all the exertion he can make, it is out of his power materially to improve his circumstances?" (109).

In short, this cultural fiction argues that capitalism destroys the souls of workers who, according to Harper, are "worn out in the struggle with fortune" (109), while slavery guarantees a stable, unchanging social order. The *Madisonian*'s provocatively entitled editorial of 30 October 1843, "White Slavery," repeats this thesis: "It is well known that the condition of the poorer classes of the population, in any part of Europe, even the freest, is worse in every respect that that of our negro slaves" (245). Even Walter Whitman, the brash young reporter who eventually became Walt the poet, argued in 1842 that "the British have within the borders of their own country miseries comparable to which those of the southern slaves are as a ward to Ossa."[96] Edmund Ruffin echoes Whitman's charge when he claims in *The Political Economy of Slavery* that modern capitalism has created "another kind of slavery—*pauper slavery*" (7). George Holmes succinctly summarizes the proslavery attack on the moral degradation caused by modern capitalism in "The Failure of Free Societies," where he charges: "That religion has been undermined, morals contaminated, crime increased, misery extended, deepened and multiplied, want and starvation augmented, society agitated, and orderly government endangered by the progress of the so called prosperity of the free labour system, is evident without further proof to any one who reads contemporary literature, (or) who pays attention to the statements of newspapers."[97] Thus Tyler, Dew, Harper, the anonymous author of "White Slavery," Ruffin, Holmes, and even the young Whitman position capitalism as the real slavery, whereas Southern slavery is but a kind, moral, paternalistic managing of naturally preselected hierarchies.

The proslavery attack on capitalism therefore relies on the rhetoric of nostalgia, for in the face of modern capitalism's messy, amoral, voracious destruction of custom, proslavery cultural fictions appeal to the traditional values of white supremacy, elitism, and antimodernism. The most ardent proponent of this argument is George Fitzhugh, whose two major works, *Sociology for the South; or, The Failure of Free Society* (1854; hereinafter *SS*) and *Cannibals All!; or, Slaves without Masters* (1857; hereinafter *CA*),[98] amount to a scathing attack on liberalism, capitalism, democracy, and modernity itself. To pursue my thesis regarding the rhetoric of nostalgia, I discuss first Fitzhugh's characterization of the differences between slavery and capitalism and then the three major tenets of his attack on modernity.

Fitzhugh assaults modern capitalism's free-labor system with consistently incendiary rhetoric. For example, he claims that "the South, quiet, contented, satisfied, looks upon all socialists and radical reformers as madmen or knaves. . . . We turn away from them with disgust, as from something unclean and vicious. . . . From their own mouths we can show free society to be a monstrous abortion" (*SS*, 81). In comparison to such vitriolic, even implicitly violent rhetoric, Fitzhugh portrays slavery as a gentle, caring system of naturally ordered cohabitation. In fact, in an argument that has confounded historians for a long time, Fitzhugh argues that "slavery is the very best form of socialism" (*SS*, 27–28) and that "a Southern farm is a sort of joint stock concern, or social philanstery, in which the master furnishes the capital and skill, and the slaves the labor, and divide the profits not according to each one's in-put, but according to each one's wants and necessities" (*SS*, 48).[99]

Comparing Fitzhugh's contemptuous, vicious rhetoric describing capitalism with his gentle, dreamy, even strangely utopian portrayal of slavery, it is not difficult to understand how historians have generally characterized Fitzhugh as "that most cranky and extreme" of proslavery writers, as an example of a "mutant strain," as a rhetor who was "in many ways atypical and even antithetical to the moral-philosophical mainstream of pro-slavery thought."[100] My interest in Fitzhugh, however, stems from the fact that while his rhetoric may initially appear ill-tempered and extreme, his critique of modernity nicely captures one of the central concerns of antebellum America. Indeed, while making hyperbolic claims about both slavery and capitalism, Fitzhugh nonetheless offers a provocative and three-tiered critique of modernity, defending regionalism over internationalism, promoting traditional authority over modern liberty, and valorizing the stability of "old ways" over the passing fashion of the moment.

The first major theme within Fitzhugh's rhetoric of nostalgia involves his defense of regionalism against internationalism. If one recalls that the unequal trade balance between the North and the South caused Southerners much distress and constituted a primary motive for Northern merchants' support for moderate, antiabolition sentiments, then it comes as no surprise that Fitzhugh, like many of his contemporaries, addresses modern capitalism's impact on regional economies. Fitzhugh's position on the increasingly interregional and international nature of capitalism differs significantly from that of his contemporaries, however, for instead of calling for reformist modifications in the capitalist system, Fitzhugh offers the thoroughly nostalgic and antimodern proposal that economic production should remain exclusively regional. For example, Fitzhugh argues that "providence has wonderfully adapted the productions of each section to the wants of man and other animals inhabiting those sections. It is probable, if the subject were scientifically investigated, it would be found that the productions of one clime when used in another are injurious and deleterious" (*SS*, 19). Three years later Fitzhugh condenses this argument into the simple claim that in the face of the capitalist and abolitionist assault launched from London and Paris, Americans "must become national, nay, provincial, and cease to be imitative cosmopolitans" (*CA*, 59).

It is hard to imagine that Fitzhugh failed to realize that shipping Southern cotton to the North and then on toward London and Paris was a foundational economic reality of Southern culture. Thus Fitzhugh's argument here appears to be purely performative. More specifically, the reference to Providence clearly strives to invoke a familiar, comforting sense of God's transcendent authority against capitalism's world-changing secular humanism. The off-handed proposal about investigating the subject scientifically clearly indicates that Fitzhugh's argument is not empirical but rather rhetorical. The claim regarding the undesirable effects of interregional trading seeks to reinforce the us-versus-them regionalism prevalent in the South. Finally, the call for a renewed provincialism completes the rhetorical barrage by appealing to the popular perception that both capitalism and abolitionism were flowing directly from swarming urban centers bent on the destruction of the South's cherished rural states' rights. These four moments of persuasion, in which Fitzhugh appeals to God over humanism, common sense over science, regionalism over nationalism, and provincialism over worldliness—each of which clearly contradicts the one undeniable fact of Southern economic prowess, namely, the global demand for cotton—amount to a tour de force of nostalgic rhetoric.

I have already noted that numerous historians have dismissed Fitzhugh's arguments as out of step with those of his fellow proslavery advocates, yet his nostalgic emphasis on provincialism was consistent with the popular call to defend states' rights against the assumed centralizing forces of urban modernity. Thus Genovese observes that "the provincial rejection of an outside world which threatened to impinge on the culture as well as the material interests of the local community" constituted a central tenet of the South's attempt "to defend local rights against the pressures of centralization."[101] Indeed, in his 1857 essay "The Conservative Principle" (hereinafter "CP") Fitzhugh clearly links states' rights to antimodernism. Following two pages of attacks against liberalism, democracy, and the Republican party, he barks: "Hands Off! is what we ask and demand. . . . Each state has the right, and best understands how to manage its own social and domestic affairs" ("CP," 426). Fitzhugh's call for provincialism may therefore be read not only as a critique of the centralizing forces of modern, urban capitalism but also as a representative example of the defense of states' rights. In this sense Fitzhugh appears less an outlandish extremist than an exemplary figure in the defense of a nostalgic and specifically Southern anticapitalist Republicanism.[102]

The second major trope within Fitzhugh's rhetoric of nostalgia involves his call for traditional authority against modern liberty. This argument is encapsulated in the simple, almost childish charge that "good men obey superior authority, the laws of God, or morality, and of their country; bad men love liberty and violate them" (*SS,* 30). The philosophical premise underlying this claim involves a more sophisticated attack on the fundamentally modern notion that society is an artificial, intentionally constituted compact of equals. Indeed, modern liberty poses a threat to divinely constituted laws and morality precisely because it encourages people to believe that they have some active, empowered role in building their social order. Fitzhugh accordingly abhors the "monstrous vision" of both Locke and Smith, on whom he places considerable blame for the unfortunate "social contract that presupposes the sovereignty of each individual" ("CP," 428). Providing an alternative to such idealistic liberal nonsense, Fitzhugh observes that "man is born a member of society, and does not form society. Nature, as in the case of bees and ants, has it ready formed for him. . . . Society is the being—he one of the members of that being. He has no rights whatever, as opposed to the interests of society; . . . Whatever rights he has are subordinate to the good of the whole; and he has never ceded rights to it, for he was born its slave, and had no rights to cede" (*SS,* 25–26).

The rhetoric here, like much proslavery writing, is relentlessly antimodern, antiliberal, and ultimately antidemocratic.[103] Indeed, whereas the Declaration of Independence and the Constitution both emphasize the liberal belief that government consists of a social contract based on the intentional negotiation of rights and privileges among empowered citizens, Fitzhugh argues through a long chain of association that society is a preformed fact of nature; that this ontologically given order amounts to an organic, literally prehistoric being; and that—contrary to the tenets of liberalism, capitalism, and modernity—the individual is born into this organic being not with rights but as a slave. Fitzhugh thus portrays society as an organic being furnished with a prechosen elite of superior beings and a laboring class of inferiors, those drones who constitute what Governor Hammond labeled the "mud-sill" class.[104] Indeed, whereas "the little experiment of universal liberty" is but a "predatory and nomadic" facade that places "the rich and the poor, the weak and the powerful" in "positions of antagonism and war," Southern society has wisely chosen to pursue the orderly, deferential world of slavery, in which lesser men naturally recognize "a common despotic head or ruler" (*SS,* 70, 43, 34, 61).

Fitzhugh's argument may strike postmodern readers as absurd, yet recall the brief discussion earlier in this section, via Tocqueville's *Democracy in America,* of the widespread antebellum fear of democracy. In that context Fitzhugh's antimodern, antiliberal, anticapitalist arguments read less like the ravings of a fringe fanatic and more like a fully articulated example of one of the period's most prevalent concerns.[105] Thus, when Fitzhugh argues that modern liberty has created a chaotic world in which "revolution follows revolution with electric speed" (*SS,* 41), he simply voices the deep fears left lingering in Tocqueville's observation that modern liberty has created a nation where old beliefs and social systems are shattered. Indeed, the central thesis of Marvin Meyers's classic study of Jacksonian America, *The Jacksonian Persuasion* (1960), is that Jackson successfully appealed to Americans' fears of modernity by invoking the nostalgic theme of "restoration." Like Fitzhugh's, Jackson's thundering morality and antimodern rhetoric sought "to restore the solid virtues of the Old Republic."[106] By acknowledging the similar arguments offered by Dew, Harper, Christy, Ruffin, J. D. B. De Bow, L.C.B., and the anonymous author of "Modern Philanthropy and Negro Slavery"; granting the accuracy of Meyers's characterization of the period; and recalling the grim tone of Tocqueville's *Democracy in America*—by doing all this, we can see Fitzhugh's rhetoric of nostalgia not as betraying the outmoded extremism of a fanatic but as echoing the nostalgic theme of restoration pervading Jacksonian America.[107]

The third major trope in Fitzhugh's rhetoric of nostalgia involves his tribute to the stability of "old ways" as superior to the passing fashions of the moment. For example, he bluntly claims: "We have already stated that we should not attempt to introduce any new theories of government and of society, but merely try to justify old ones" (*SS,* 82). This position follows from the impending doom thesis, for the new theories of government all amount to a recipe for disaster. Thus Fitzhugh argues that "immediate interest is all the mass look to; and they would be sure to revolutionize government, as often as the situation of the majority was worse than that of the minority" (*CA*, 245). Fitzhugh's rhetoric here may strike readers as harsh, yet the charge that the masses are driven solely by immediate interests is again consistent with one of the central fears of the young republic. For example, even that classic homage to liberal modernity *The Federalist Papers* amounts to a lengthy treatise on (among other things) the best way to harness the impetuous energy of the masses so that they will not continue to pursue what Madison refers to as "improper or wicked projects."[108] Indeed, nervous antebellum elites in both the North and the South—like Madison before them—were plagued by the fear that if left to govern themselves, the unruly masses, driven blindly by their selfish, short-sighted goals of immediate advancement, would do no more than flounder in the destructive will to revolutionize.

In Fitzhugh's nostalgic worldview, however, the fad of revolutionizing means that life's organic foundations of truth and beauty are abandoned for the shallow seductions of modernity. Hence, in a classic example of the rhetoric of nostalgia, Fitzhugh laments that "now the world seems to regard nothing as desirable except what will make money and what costs money. There is not a poet, an orator, a sculptor, or painter in the world. The tedious elaboration necessary to all the productions of high art would be ridiculed in this money-making, utilitarian, charlatan age. Nothing now but what is gaudy and costly excites admiration. The public taste is debased" (*SS*, 93). According to this cultural fiction, the unholy triumvirate of liberalism, capitalism, and modernity produce a thoroughly shabby, absolutely fake, utterly debased world run solely for the "sybaritic pleasure and practical epicureanism" of that cheap, visionless, horde of money-grubbing Northerners lambasted by L.C.B. as "an aristocracy of the Money Bag."[109]

In the face of the precipitous decline fostered by this capitalist aristocracy, it is no wonder that, according to Fitzhugh, "riots, mobs, strikes, and revolutions are daily occurring" (*CA*, 248). Hence Fitzhugh closes his argument in *Cannibals All!* with the charge that "the mass of mankind cannot be governed by Law. More of despotic discretion, and less of Law, is what the world wants. We take our leave by saying, THERE IS TOO MUCH OF LAW AND TOO LITTLE OF GOVERNMENT IN THIS WORLD" (248). Fitzhugh states the chilling implications of this nostalgic vision even more bluntly in "The Conservative Principle," where he calls for nothing less than an aristocratic purge of all modern "isms": "We want no theorizing do-nothings, no bland, cunning, non-committal courtiers, no transcendental abstractionists. The times need stern, active, rigid, severe men. Armed with the Constitution, the common law, and the bible, such men will cleanse the augean stable of the isms" (427–28).

Fitzhugh's rhetoric in these passages is obviously extreme: he tends to generalize hastily; his vocabulary swerves toward polemical tirades; he frequently relies on categorical propositions rather than more measured, nuanced phrases; and he has a penchant for slipping into a dramatic, declarative tone likely to strike readers as overblown or even somewhat hysterical.[110] I have argued throughout my reading of Fitzhugh, however, that his arguments, even while rhetorically outrageous in certain places, nevertheless exemplify some of the period's dominant philosophical and political tenets. Before closing this chapter, then, I again shift my attention from a Southern proslavery advocate to compare Northern actions and statements regarding similar issues—in this case, the relationship of modern capitalism and antebellum democracy—hence demonstrating the national scope of the rhetoric of nostalgia.

NOSTALGIC RHETORIC 2: NATIVISM, PRINT CAPITALISM, AND NORTHERN ANXIETIES

Recall that the fundamental logic of capitalism (*attack slavery and you attack our business partners*) and the overwhelming presence of white supremacist attitudes (*"I, as well as Judge Douglas, am in favor of the race to which I belong having the superior position"*) led many Northerners to accept perpetuating and even extending slavery. In closing this chapter on white fear and the rhetoric of serious evils, I will demonstrate that the rhetoric of nostalgia played as significant a role in Whitman's North as it did in Fitzhugh's South. Indeed, by comparing the proslavery writings of Fitzhugh and his colleagues with the words and actions of his compatriots in the North, particularly the words and events surrounding the nativist movement, antiabolitionist mobs, and their joint attack on modern print capitalism, I hope to show that Northern acquiescence to slavery, much like Fitzhugh's defense of it, was based at least in part on deep-seated fears regarding the onslaught of modernity.

These fears are perhaps most evident in the popularity of "defense organizations" that were aggressively racist, antidemocratic, and prone toward mob violence. Indeed, Northerners' anxieties regarding modernity, which were articulated in a lively mix of protective unionism, racism, white nationalism, and anti-Catholicism, were crucial to, among others, the Know-Nothing party, the Order of the Star Spangled Banner, the Mechanics Mutual Protection Association, the American Protestant Association, and the Order of United American Mechanics. These groups directed much of their violence against Irish laborers, as in the 1844 riots in Philadelphia, in which, according to Bruce Laurie, "Nativist invaders and besieged Irish" battled for three bloody days, leaving "dozens of buildings in rubble and the streets strewn with sixteen dead men and boys, most of them Irish." The Irish had their own scapegoats, of course, and were quick to attack free blacks, as in the 1842 Philadelphia riots, in which Irish workers attacked a parade celebrating both temperance and Jamaican Emancipation Day and set fire to more than twenty black-owned houses and churches.[111]

The Irish were more often the victims than the aggressors, however, for the Know-Nothing party—the political embodiment of the nativist movement's cultural anxieties and a significant transitional step toward the Republican party—waged a sustained terrorist campaign against the very presence of Irish immigrants in the United States.[112] For example, in Louisville in 1855 nativists blockaded voting booths against Irish immigrants, resulting in over twenty deaths, while that same year in Massachusetts Governor Gardner proposed a "twenty-one year waiting period after naturalization before foreign born citizens could vote."[113] The vehemence of the Know-Nothings' anti-Catholicism was so strong, and their showing in the 1854 elections so successful, that one Whig observer stated, "This election has demonstrated that, by a majority, Roman Catholicism is feared more than slavery."[114] Such fears had been trumpeted a decade earlier in a nativist broadside from Kingston, New York (figure 2), that warned Americans to fear "the most dangerous influence of Popery," which attempts "to control every thought, feeling, and motion" of those who fall under the spell of its "Anti-Christian Power."[115] In retrospect, it appears that both Roman Catholicism and slavery were feared only slightly more than the moderating tendencies of the democratic process itself, for Holt observes that although the nativists were remarkably successful in electoral politics during the 1854 and 1855 seasons, they nonetheless "resorted to mayhem and murder to stop immigrants from voting" and relied on a widespread policy of "seizing the ballot boxes in immigrant districts."[116] These brief examples represent a much wider policy of nativist violence against both Irish immigrants and free blacks and demonstrate that the antebellum combination of racism and antimodernism was strong enough to compromise the very premises of democracy.

It is interesting to observe, then, that directing violence against Irish workers and preventing them from voting appear to have served the same nostalgic function for Northern workers as arguing against modern capitalism served for Southerners such as Fitzhugh. That is, when confronted with a rapidly changing economic and cultural landscape—one clearly complicated by the devastating economic crash of 1837 and the recession plus drought of 1854–55—both Northerners and Southerners sought

AMERICAN REPUBLICAN

TOWN NOMINATIONS.

"BEWARE OF FOREIGN INFLUENCE." [WASHINGTON.

ADDRESS.

Fellow-Citizens:—We most earnestly solicit all who can have the proud boast of saying that they are of American birth, or have American hearts in their bosoms, now to come to the rescue, and support the *American Republican Ticket*. Let us now take the solemn admonition of the Father of our Country to "*Beware of Foreign Influence.*" Can it be that we have amongst us yet political demagogues and partizan office-seekers who dare presume to have the hardihood to throw obstacles in the way to prevent the success of our ticket?—We can hardly believe there is any foul enough to do it! We now ask every honest voter in the town, and particularly solicit an answer at the ballot box, is not the cause we have espoused a most noble one? Are not those principles worthy of support which avow the protection of the American born against the most dangerous influence of Popery? That influence is now most fearfully making against us from all the Roman Catholic countries on earth, which are sending their millions of offcasts and vagabonds here annually, to take from us the liberties we now enjoy. These immigrants can never be *Americanized*, and their children will be separated from ours by their mode of education. Thus they will form a distinct and hostile race; and they will, like the Romanists of all other countries, ever regard the native born and Protestants of this republic as heretics, accursed of God, conceiving it their duty to annihilate and destroy such as soon as they attain the power. Can any one in his senses doubt that such a population must be dangerous to our liberties? We know full well the character of the *Anti-Christian Power* which will control every thought, feeling and motion of these enslaved masses. Revelation has admonished us of its rise and reign. History tells us of the millions it has slain—of its imposters and blasphemies—of its Inquisitions and *Autos de Fe*. We can now see with our own eyes the pitiful wrecks of the nations it has emasculated, brutified and devoured. All its present movements show that its principles are unchanged, that its lust for dominion is now as insatiable as ever, that its thirst for blood is restrained only, not extinct.

Fellow-Citizens of all parties, it is with pain we look forward to that which will inevitably follow these movements, if not checked in time. When the hour shall arrive for Popish Priests, backed by European arms and sustained by foreign subsidies, to put in motion the millions of offcasts from all the Romish countries then congregated here, then will be the time of weeping, wailing and lamentation with us, as has already been the case with all the nations which have underwent a like fate. Then, fellow-citizens, the time will come when the acts, principles and doctrines of the *American Republican Party* will be most justly and properly appreciated. Then will come the time that those political demagogues and partizan office-seekers, who are now endeavoring to put every obstacle in our way, to prevent our cause from progressing, will receive the scorn and condemnation of the American people, so justly merited.

But, fellow-citizens, we tell you that the American ball is in motion, and no human power can stop its progress. God grant that every man whose blood courses thro' American veins, who stands in its way, may give it a touch—keep it moving, until it shall have rolled through every nook and corner of this country, and brought out the doctrines of American Republicanism everywhere. For that a salutary alteration in our Naturalization Laws, according to the doctrines of our party, will continue to be the great rallying cry of the American people, independent of demagogues and partizan office-seekers, there can be no sort of doubt. The great deep of public opinion is now aroused, and no human power can stay its onward progress. The frauds, the perjuries, the violence and villanies which now disgrace our elections and pollute our ballot boxes are having the happiest effect, for they are opening the eyes of the American people to the danger which surrounds them, to the volcano which slumbers beneath their feet. They see and appreciate their peril, and they are DETERMINED to act promptly, fearlessly and energetically. The cause is one that appeals to the strongest feelings and warmest sympathies of the American people, and they cannot, WILL NOT, DARE NOT, hesitate. He who falters or hangs back in this great movement, may be considered as a TRAITOR to the land that gave him birth!

JOHN YOUNG, Chairman.

E. W. WATSON and JOHN VANDERLYN, Jr. } SECRETARIES.

AMERICAN REPUBLICAN MEETING.

At a meeting of the American Republicans of the town of Kingston, in favor of the elevation of none but the American born to public office, held at the house of Solomon Brown, on the 23d January, Dr. JOHN YOUNG was called to the Chair, and E. W. WATSON and JOHN VANDERLYN, Jr., were appointed Secretaries. A Committee of five persons from each of the districts of the town, was, together with the Chairman, appointed to select Town Officers, who reported the ticket printed below, which was unanimously adopted by the meeting. The Committee on Resolutions reported the following:

1. RESOLVED, That we will most cordially unite in the support of all the candidates on the American Republican Ticket for Town Officers, that they are all men who, if elected, are pledged to carry out the principles of our Party.

2. RESOLVED, That it is the duty of every individual who has enlisted under the banner of American Republicanism, as well as all others who feel friendly to the cause, to be active and vigilant in warding off the foul corruptions that are made to bear against us by the corrupt Leaders of both the old parties.

3. RESOLVED, That we hold in utter detestation any individual who is a candidate for office, who will in any way attempt to secure the votes of foreigners to elevate himself to power; that if office is conferred on him it ought to be done by the voice of the American-born, or not at all.

4. RESOLVED, That we, as American Republicans, avowedly set forth our principles and doctrines to shield and protect the American born against Foreign influence, which is now most fearfully making against us

5. RESOLVED, That in doing this we do no more than our patriotic fathers did, who defended our rights and liberties, and enjoined upon us; that if we had taken Washington's advice, we would have no cause for complaint against foreign influence at the present time.

6. RESOLVED, That as both the old parties have for years professed to be in favor of Retrenchment in the County Expenditures, whilst refusing and neglecting to do anything to accomplish that object, and whilst some of their candidates for re-election continue to run their hands deeply into the County Treasury, we have no confidence in them; they have been tried and prove faithless, we therefore look to our own efforts for any reform of public abuses.

7. RESOLVED, That we do profess, and pledge ourselves to carry out our professions when opportunity shall occur, in favor of reducing the emoluments of office to a standard equal with the rewards of other occupations of life.

8. RESOLVED, That we admonish the friends of American Republican principles to be aware of the acts and devices of the leaders and electioneerers of both of the old parties, and to turn a deaf ear to the Locofoco demagogue who denounces the American Republican movement as a "Whig trick," and also to the no less unprincipled Whig demagogue who denounces it as a "Locofoco trick." This cry, it is hoped, has now become too stale to deceive any intelligent and sensible man, and is only kept up by the demagogues on both sides with a view of retaining the simple and shallow portions of their followers in their old ranks.

9. RESOLVED, That we view the increase of Foreigners over American born as most alarming in our voting population; that fifteen years ago they had every twentieth vote—seven years ago they had every tenth vote, and last fall, at our Presidential Election, they had every fifth vote. At the same ratio of gain, in seven years more they will have the majority of votes that are cast for our rulers. Can any honest-hearted American, who takes these things rightly into consideration, refuse to vote the American ticket? We say no.

JOHN YOUNG, Chairman.

E. W. WATSON and JOHN VANDERLYN, Jr. } SECRETARIES.

The Alms House Committee of the New York City Council have made the following astonishing report, concerning the importation of paupers and criminals from abroad.

The report states that the bonds of nine firms in the city exhibit the enormous liabilities of $16,000,000—that of the 652 children in the Farms-school, 457 are children of Foreigners and 195 American. The whole number of inmates in the penitentiary is 1419, showing an increase of 400 since July last—of these 333 are Americans and 1198 Foreigners. The number of prisoners and paupers to support is 4344—showing an increase since July last of nearly 1,000; and we know, as they become a burthen on our large cities, that they in the same ratio become a burden on the country at large. Now does it become us as American citizens, when we know that they are such a moth upon us, to encourage their importation as is now going on, merely to gratify those political demagogues who are engaged in it to elevate themselves to power by securing their votes?

[*From the N. Y. Express of Jan.* 26.]

EMIGRANTS.—The Emigrant Society petitioned the Board of Aldermen last night, for the use of a dock at the foot of Rector street. They state that they are possessed of the fact that, over one hundred thousand Irish and German emigrants will be landed in this city for each year, for the next five years. Their petition was referred to the Alms House Committee. If this number is to be landed here from these two countries, we would enquire what will be the number from these and all other [illegible]

AMERICAN REPUBLICAN TICKET
FOR TOWN OFFICERS.

For Supervisor,
Peter J. Dubois.
For Town Clerk,
Caleb S. Clay.
For Justice of the Peace,
Jonathan D. Wilson.
For Collector,
John D. Osterhoudt.
For Town Superintendent,
William H. Dederick.
For Assessors,
Morgan Everson,
John C. Jansen,
Philip Hendricks.
For Commissioners of Highways,
Abel Winchester,
Thomas Scott,
Job C. Champlin.
For Overseers of the Poor,
John D. Middagh,
Charles Stone.
For Constables,
William Vredenburgh,
George W. Dunn,
Richard Colvill,
George Gibbs,
Benjamin Lockien.
For Town Sealer,
William T. Hall.
For Bridge Commissioner,
Benjamin Joy.
For Pound Master,
James B. Wilson.
For Inspectors of Election,
District No. 1.
Peter Delamater,
John Young.
District No. 2.
Thomas G. Van Steenbergh,
Tjerck Wynkoop.
District No. 3.
James A. Taylor,
Charles S. Traver.
For Path Master,
District No. [illegible]
[illegible]

Figure 2. "American Republican Town Nominations. Beware of Foreign Influence," an 1844 nativist broadside from Kingston, New York. (Reproduced courtesy of the Gilder Lehrman Collection, Pierpont Morgan Library, New York City, GLC 7450.)

refuge in cultural fictions that both celebrated traditional, premodern, racially homogeneous means of social order (artisanal organizations in the North; aristocratic privilege in the South) and attacked easily scapegoated others (Irish and free black "invaders" in the North; abolitionists and modernizing capitalists in the South).[117] Thus Sean Wilentz describes Northern nativists as practicing "a true politics of nostalgia," for "while they offered no criticism of the ethics of liberal economic expansion . . . , their cultural approach to political disorder revealed a genuine longing for a supposed golden age, before poverty, before immigration, before social conflict."[118]

Paradoxically this violence-prone nostalgia was frequently orchestrated by the same local elites whom an economic analysis might recognize as the immediate sources of the disgruntled workers' anxieties. The crucial study here is Leonard Richards's *"Gentlemen of Property and Standing": Anti-Abolition Mobs in Jacksonian America,* where of the over 150 antiabolition mobs reported prior to the crash of 1837, Richards studies those he argues were "congregated intentionally and planned and organized" by "high-ranking commercial and professional men of old American stock" (82, 144). Richards concludes that "anti-abolition mobs saw themselves defending the established order against encroachments of internal subversives and foreign agents" (69). Accordingly, "the typical anti-abolition mob should be regarded as an attempt by an aggrieved class to protect its social dominance and to reinforce its traditional values" (150). In chapter 1 I offered this as the central thesis of William Thomas's *Enemies of the Constitution.* It is difficult to read Richards's historical description of these mobs, Wilentz's historical description of the nativists, or Thomas's firsthand account of antiabolitionist violence without recognizing the parallels to Fitzhugh's rhetoric of nostalgia.

As I noted in chapter 1 (see figure 1), the antimodern underpinnings of this nostalgia are particularly evident in the energy with which antiabolitionist mobs and nativists attacked the new means of mass communication made possible by modern print capitalism. Indeed, the rise of modern print capitalism, entailing the convergence of new means of production, new modes of transportation, and new methods of networking and organizing, enabled activists of all varieties to make significant inroads into communities that just a decade earlier had been dominated almost exclusively by the authority of local elites. For example, Richards notes that the American Anti-Slavery Society, based in New York City, distributed over one million pieces of antislavery literature in 1835 alone, which indicates a dramatic "shift in the centers of opinion-making from county seats and capital cities such as Albany, Richmond, and Washington to metropolitan centers" (52, 72). As an example of the activist possibilities of early-modern print capitalism, consider the back flap of Lydia Maria Child's *Evils of Slavery,* which includes an offer for "abolition libraries furnished on the most favorable terms" from the Charles Whipple publishing house, including assorted "Anti-Slavery Hymns, Cards, and Handbills" and works by such antislavery leaders as Child, Phillis Wheatley, and John Quincy Adams. Or consider the back page of Child's 1839 *Anti-Slavery Catechism* (figure 3), which offers cheap copies of Child's *Appeal,* Stroud's *Compendium of the Slave Laws,* John Rankin's *Letters to a Slaveholding Brother,* and other popular abolitionist materials.[119] Similar catalogs of abolitionist materials may be found in virtually any issue of the period's radical journals and papers, including *The Liberator, The Emancipator,* and *The Prisoner's Friend,* hence demonstrating that antebellum activists were mastering the persuasive possibilities of modern print capitalism.

It comes as no surprise, then, to learn that John Tyler, in a 22 August 1835 speech in Gloucester, Virginia, attacked the merging of abolitionism and modern print capitalism. Tyler bemoaned the fact that the printing revolution had enabled a barrage of incendiary materials to shower down on the South at cut-rate prices: "*Human Rights,* twenty-five cents per annum; *Anti-Slavery Record,* one-dollar-and-a-half per hundred; *Emancipator,* a paper larger than the *Whig* or *Enquirer* [Fitzhugh's paper], fifty cents per annum; *Slave's Friend,* a single number, one cent."[120] I turn in more detail to the political implications of modern print capitalism in chapters 3 and 4; my immediate concern here is to establish that the new communicative possibilities of the print revolution amounted to—as Tyler clearly fears it would—a "disruption of established forms of social control and social organization."[121] Indeed, with the rise of New York City as America's first modern publishing center, and considering the abolitionists' success in blanketing the nation with manifestos, chapbooks, hymn books, and any number of other antislavery documents, it is not surprising that Northern traditionalists—much like Fitzhugh and Tyler in the South—came to regard increasingly centralized urban publishing as a moral onslaught against their traditional, provincial world of local privileges and authority.

As did their Southern counterparts, the more traditional elements of Northern society also sought to protect a racially homogeneous republic. The most direct example of this possibility is the American Society for the Colonization of the Free People of Color in the United States (also known as the American Colonization Society), an organization founded in 1816 or 1817 with the purpose of shipping Africans back to Liberia.

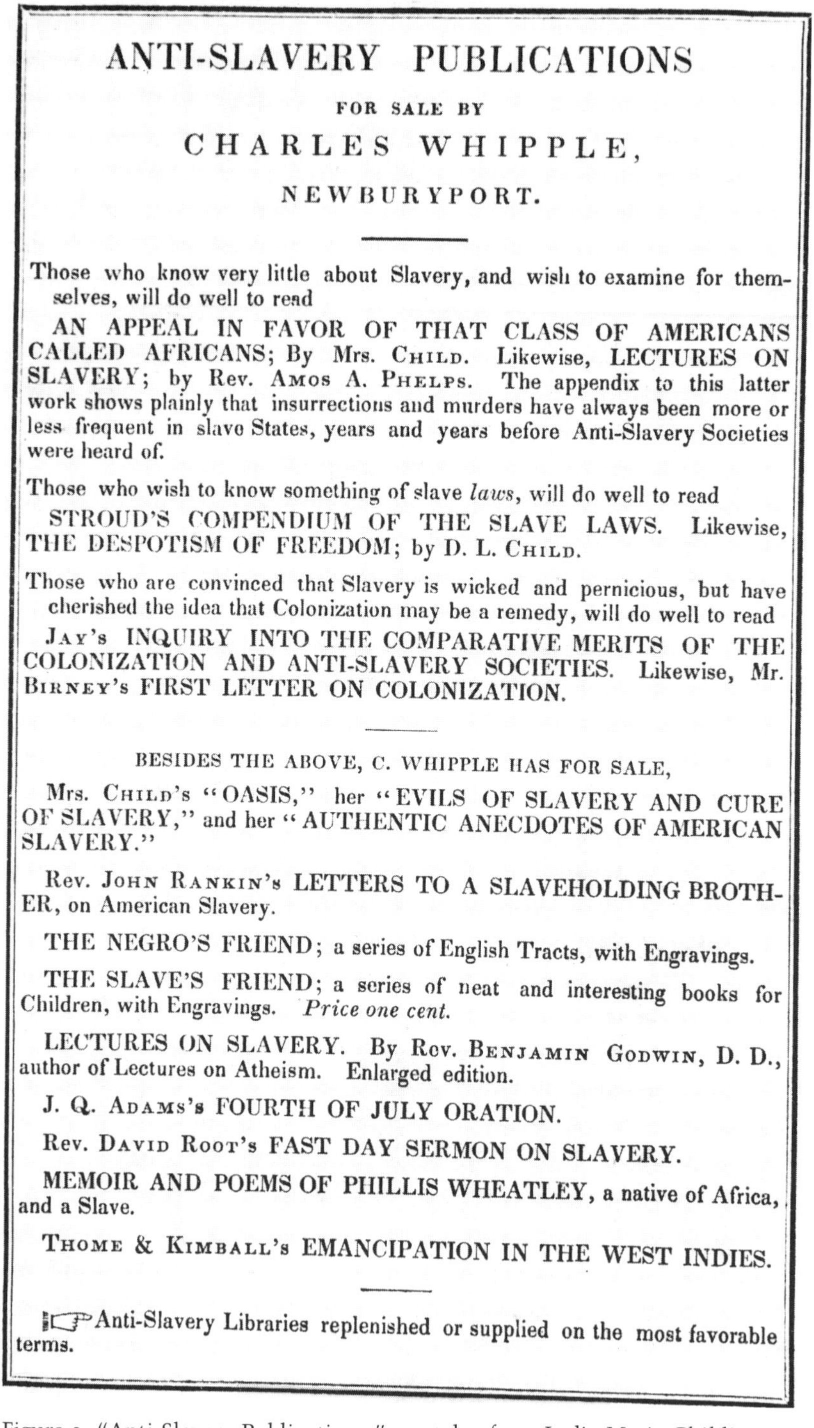

ANTI-SLAVERY PUBLICATIONS

FOR SALE BY

CHARLES WHIPPLE,

NEWBURYPORT.

Those who know very little about Slavery, and wish to examine for themselves, will do well to read

AN APPEAL IN FAVOR OF THAT CLASS OF AMERICANS CALLED AFRICANS; By Mrs. Child. Likewise, LECTURES ON SLAVERY; by Rev. Amos A. Phelps. The appendix to this latter work shows plainly that insurrections and murders have always been more or less frequent in slave States, years and years before Anti-Slavery Societies were heard of.

Those who wish to know something of slave *laws*, will do well to read

STROUD'S COMPENDIUM OF THE SLAVE LAWS. Likewise, THE DESPOTISM OF FREEDOM; by D. L. Child.

Those who are convinced that Slavery is wicked and pernicious, but have cherished the idea that Colonization may be a remedy, will do well to read

Jay's INQUIRY INTO THE COMPARATIVE MERITS OF THE COLONIZATION AND ANTI-SLAVERY SOCIETIES. Likewise, Mr. Birney's FIRST LETTER ON COLONIZATION.

BESIDES THE ABOVE, C. WHIPPLE HAS FOR SALE,

Mrs. Child's "OASIS," her "EVILS OF SLAVERY AND CURE OF SLAVERY," and her "AUTHENTIC ANECDOTES OF AMERICAN SLAVERY."

Rev. John Rankin's LETTERS TO A SLAVEHOLDING BROTHER, on American Slavery.

THE NEGRO'S FRIEND; a series of English Tracts, with Engravings.

THE SLAVE'S FRIEND; a series of neat and interesting books for Children, with Engravings. *Price one cent.*

LECTURES ON SLAVERY. By Rev. Benjamin Godwin, D. D., author of Lectures on Atheism. Enlarged edition.

J. Q. Adams's FOURTH OF JULY ORATION.

Rev. David Root's FAST DAY SERMON ON SLAVERY.

MEMOIR AND POEMS OF PHILLIS WHEATLEY, a native of Africa, and a Slave.

Thome & Kimball's EMANCIPATION IN THE WEST INDIES.

☞Anti-Slavery Libraries replenished or supplied on the most favorable terms.

Figure 3. "Anti-Slavery Publications," a catalog from Lydia Maria Child's 1839 *Anti-Slavery Catechism.* (Reproduced courtesy of the University of Illinois Rare Book and Special Collections Library.)

The American Colonization Society eventually acquired strongholds in Ohio, Pennsylvania, and Connecticut and served, according to Dumond, as "the cohesive force for all the reactionary elements in the slavery controversy."[122] For example, in 1838, some three years before he would succeed Harrison to the presidency but already watching astutely for an opportunity to endear himself with undecided Northern racists, John Tyler became president of the Virginia Colonization Society, thus demonstrating his allegiance with those Northerners who sought a racially pure America.[123] The nostalgia for a racially pure America was so deeply seated, so powerful, that even the ostensibly anti–Slave Power Republicans staunchly supported colonization. Indeed, in a classic study of Republican ideology Eric Foner demonstrates that colonization was one of the key components of Republican thinking. "By early 1860," Foner observes, "Governors Kirkwood of Iowa, Randall of Wisconsin, Bissell of Illinois, and Dennison of Ohio had come out for colonization." Hence, "many political observers expected colonization to be adopted as part of the National Republican platform." It is thus no coincidence that in describing the need for colonization, one anonymous author argued, "We consider this class of people [all blacks, whether free or slave] as a serious evil among us. . . . The only remedy afforded is to colonize them."[124] Northern anxieties regarding race were thus so universal, so unquestioned, that Democrats, Republicans, Free Soilers, and Know-Nothings alike found themselves turning to the cultural fiction that colonization would provide a way of getting rid of the serious evils of slavery and abolition alike.

I have argued throughout this chapter that proslavery cultural fictions, much like the economic benefits of slavery, were not simply a Southern phenomena but part of a much larger, national culture of white supremacy. In this sense, the proslavery writings of Dew, Harper, Ruffin, Christy, and Fitzhugh, much like the ostensibly anti–Slave Power writings of Lincoln, Adams, Whittier, Franklin, Rantoul, and Paine, provide important opportunities for rethinking the historical foundations of modern racism. Indeed, the fact that most of the writers addressed here relied on variations of paralyzing rhetoric, indecipherable rhetoric, and nostalgic rhetoric suggests a new means of understanding how antebellum Americans struggled to make sense of their slave-driven democracy.

Fitzhugh's version of nostalgic rhetoric nonetheless stands out from his contemporaries' arguments as anachronistic—not because of his positions on race, capitalism, modernity, or democracy, however, but because of the incompatibility of his premodern and anticapitalist provincialism with the imperatives of empire. For example, Christy's popular proslavery manifesto *Cotton Is King* ends with the call to "let Africa be once redeemed, let civilization and Christianity spread over a few millions of its population" (200). Such statements make it perfectly clear that ridding the United States of its unwanted Africans presents a golden opportunity not only to protect white wages and women at home but also to finish the righteous evangelical task of "redeeming" Africa to the great white way. The goal of colonization was expressed in an even more belligerent manner by the Knights of the Golden Circle, a group that sought not only to redeem Africa for Christianity by removing Africans from the United States but, better yet, "to rear a powerful slave empire with its center at Havana and a radius long enough to include the slave states, Mexico, and Central America."[125]

Such grand visions of the United States as a hemispheric power, complete with an expanded realm of slave-based operations, may have appealed to Northern racial anxieties, but more important, they expressed a national longing for greatness, for empire. Thus the following chapter examines how Americans struggled to reconcile their fear of blacks, their sense of the impending doom waiting to be foisted on them by the "serious evils" of abolition, and their confusion over the complexities of modern capitalism with their increasing impulse for empire.

3 *Senator Robert Walker's* Letter on Texas Annexation, The South in Danger, *and the Rhetoric of Manifest Destiny*

> Providence has given to the American people a great and glorious mission to perform, of extending the blessings of Christianity and of civil and religious liberty over the whole North American continent. . . . This will be a glorious spectacle to behold. . . . This spirit cannot be repressed, . . . We must fulfill our destiny.
>
> —James Buchanan, speaking in the Senate, 12 March 1844

Buchanan's blustery boast regarding the imminent continental dominion of a glorious nation hurled across the land in a spectacular explosion of Providence's divine will may strike contemporary readers as haughty, ambitious, and perhaps even deluded, yet the period's more thoughtful voices seemed to agree that America's march toward empire was preordained by the hand of God.[1] For example, Alexis de Tocqueville's *Democracy in America,* published in January 1835 in the midst of "King" Andrew Jackson's heroic tenure as president, chief Indian killer, and one of the nation's wealthiest slave owners and real-estate barons, has rightly been hailed as prophetic for a number of reasons, not the least of which is its brilliant analysis of the relationships among American democracy, racism, and empire. Indeed, the book's closing (and by far longest) chapter is entitled "The Present and Probable Future Condition of the Three Races That Inhabit the Territory of the United States." Tocqueville considers here the long-term political prospects of the apparently "insurmountable barriers" raised against both Native Americans and Africans by "the white, or European, the MAN pre-eminently called," and observes that "it has been calculated that the whites advance every year a mean distance of seventeen miles along the whole of this vast boundary.... This gradual and continuous progress of the European race towards the Rocky Mountains has the solemnity of a providential event; it is like a deluge of men rising unabatedly, and daily driven onward by the hand of God."[2] God's hand is so widely assumed to be the force driving America's providential march toward a continental, whites-only empire that Tocqueville submits, "The Americans of the United States must inevitably become one of the greatest nations in the world; their offspring will cover almost the whole of North America; the continent that they inhabit is their dominion, and it cannot escape them" (403).

The categorical claim that Americans—whom Tocqueville designates as whites or Europeans—must inevitably assume dominion of the entire continent would have been comfortably familiar to antebellum Americans, for the dream of empire was synonymous with white supremacy, modernity, and the widespread belief that the rapidly expanding nation had been granted providential blessing. Indeed, well before Tocqueville, Buchanan, and Jackson, no less a source of foundational American cultural fictions than George Washington argued for America's inevitable rise to the status of an empire. For example, Carroll Smith Rosenberg has noted that President Washington's 18 June 1783 letter of retirement as commander in chief of the Armies of the United States "situates Americans as imperialists first and as independent republicans second."[3] Four years later *The Federalist Papers* argued that citizens should support the new Constitution precisely because it would enable the united colonies to proceed more vigorously toward international supremacy than would their continued dallying as a loose association under the Articles of Confederation. Although much of the text engages in painstakingly detailed explanations of the bureaucratic minutiae involved in the labyrinthine distribution of powers within the new Constitution, Madison, Jay, and Hamilton also pepper their text with sweeping, boastful appeals to the then-ridiculous prospect of a forthcoming American empire. Indeed, in 1787, surrounded by hostile, mighty empires and a treacherous wilderness, bankrupt from the War of Independence, and politically fractured, the colonies were in no shape to dream of empire. Given this context, the federalists' (and Washington's) grandiose, imperial vision may be understood as a desperate attempt to persuade the less-than-enthusiastic masses of the need for a constitution by offering the cultural fiction that the battered and tottering confederacy was on the verge of empire.

One version of this argument was negative or disabling, for it argued that not ratifying the Constitution would prevent America from achieving national greatness. For example, Jay argues in *Federalist* number 10 that rejecting the Constitution will merely split the nation "into an infinity of little, jealous, clashing, tumultuous commonwealths, the wretched nurseries of unceasing discord and the miserable objects of universal pity or contempt." The positive, enabling alternative to this gloom appears in *Federalist* number 11, where Hamilton announces the virtues of uniting under the Constitution: "We might soar to dangerous greatness"—dangerous indeed, for Hamilton proceeds to argue that the united colonies will possess "a navy, which, if it could not vie with those of the great maritime powers, would at least be of respectable weight if thrown into the scale of either of two contending parties": "Our position in this respect is a very commanding one . . . We may hope, erelong, to become an arbiter of Europe in America, and to be able to incline the balance of European competitions in this part of the world as our interest may dictate." Hamilton concludes this essay with the enthusiastic charge that if the colonies unite "in erecting one great American system superior to the control of all transatlantic force or influence," then America will "dictate the terms of the connection between the old and the new world!" The telos of such thinking is made even more explicit in *Federalist* number 13, where Hamilton—repeating a projection first launched in *Federalist* number 1—refers to America as an "empire."[4] The essays in *The Federalist Papers* thus imagine the new nation explicitly as an empire; in so doing they bequeath to the nation one of its most enduring cultural fictions. Indeed, the imperialist ambitions of the federalists were not lost on those antebellum Americans arguing in favor of empire. For example, on 7 May 1844, while debating Texas annexation in the House of Representatives, John W. Tibbatts, a Democrat from Kentucky, observed that "the 14th number of the Federalist" supports the national push for expansion. Tibbatts then proceeded to quote Madison at length.[5]

As Buchanan, Tocqueville, Washington, *The Federalist Papers*, and Tibbatts show, then, Americans of the revolutionary, federal, and antebellum periods were enthralled by the prospect of ruling a divinely ordained empire of continental and perhaps even global dimensions. Indeed, many Americans of the late eighteenth and early nineteenth centuries considered what antebellum expansionists later called "Manifest Destiny" to be inherent in the concept of America itself.

The term *Manifest Destiny* was first approached in November 1839 in an editorial by John L. O'Sullivan in his *United States Magazine and Democratic Review.* Echoing Tocqueville's biblical rhetoric of divine guidance, O'Sullivan argues, "The expansive future is our arena, and for our history. We are entering on its untrodden space, with the truths of God in our minds, beneficent objects in our hearts, and with a clear conscience unsullied by the past. We are the nation of human progress, and who will, what can, set limits to our onward march? Providence is with us." The trope of the West as an open horizon of untrodden space provides one of the central rhetorical maneuvers for erasing the multiple histories of indigenous peoples who cultivated the West for untold centuries. The linking of the colonizers' history to the will of God is a crucial component of what historians have referred to as "American exceptionalism." What is perhaps even more interesting in this passage, however, is the revealing confession that America conducts its territorial conquests with a clear conscience, for this conspicuous self-acquittal of the nation's conscience indicates the nagging possibility that perhaps imperial ambition *should* entail questions of conscience. Despite this revelatory moment of rhetorical awkwardness, illustrating what later generations would come to call a "Freudian slip," O'Sullivan appears confident that such bothersome soul-searching is made irrelevant by the fact that Providence ordains America's unstoppable, literally limitless expansion—"*Who will, what can, set limits to our onward march?*"[6] Hence, having dismissed all indigenous cultures, having enlisted the always handy will of God, having disposed of all limits, and having whitewashed the nation's perhaps confused conscience, O'Sullivan announces in the following paragraph that "in its magnificent domain of space and time, the nation of many nations is destined to manifest to mankind the excellence of divine principles." Lest the inattentive reader miss the imperialist vision embedded within this invocation of divinely driven national excellence, O'Sullivan notes that the "noble temple" erected to honor this magnificent domain "shall have for its floor a hemisphere."[7]

The first significant step in constructing this hemisphere-wide temple in antebellum America was the 1845 annexation of Texas. As the prize jewel of the Southwest, whose acquisition entailed the first step toward what many Americans expected to be eventual war with Mexico, and hence the initial move toward the inevitable conquest of the Pacific, Texas was portrayed by proexpansionists of the period as the sine qua non of all imperial ambitions. It is no small coincidence, then, that the first fully articulated use of the term *Manifest Destiny* occurred in another of O'Sullivan's editorials, this one a July 1845 essay written in defense of the recent annexation of Texas. Entitled simply "Annexation," the essay attacks Britain for attempting to "intrude" on America's "manifest destiny to overspread the continent allotted by Providence for the free development of [its] yearly multiplying millions." Furthermore, in a passage linking Texas annexation to American intentions for annexing Oregon (which O'Sullivan and others were convinced would lead to a welcomed war with Britain), O'Sullivan prophesies confidently: "There is a great deal of Annexation yet to take place . . . in the inevitable fulfillment of the general law which is rolling our population westward," hence fulfilling "the manifest design of Providence in regard to the occupation of the continent."[8]

Destined to manifest, manifest destiny, manifest design—O'Sullivan apparently preferred the second phrase, for he used it again in "The True Title," another editorial favoring the annexation of Oregon, this one appearing five month later in the 27 December 1845 *New York Morning News*. Its use here caught the attention of Congressmen Robert Winthrop, a Whig from Massachusetts who, in Congress on 3 January 1846, attacked O'Sullivan's Manifest Destiny argument as an outrageous affront to "the spirit of conciliation, compromise, and peace." Winthrop's eloquent review of the Oregon issue both thoroughly refutes O'Sullivan's swaggering militarism and demonstrates many of the key aspects of Whig opposition to imperialism. "I spurn the notion that patriotism can only be manifested by plunging the nation into war," Winthrop argues, "or that the love of one's country can only be measured by one's hatred to any other country." This noble appeal is followed, however, by a clear statement of the Whigs' lingering sense of their rightful class privilege, as Winthrop predicts that "an appeal to the nonsense of the American people may succeed for an hour, but the stern sense of the country will soon reassert itself." Jacksonian Democrats appeal to the peoples' baser instincts, then, Winthrop argues, while his Whigs speak with the historical clarity and stern sense of right inherited from their federalist and Calvinist forebears. In a more humble tone, Winthrop then asks, "Is there not enough in this historical fact to lead us to distrust our own judgments and our own conclusions, and to warn us of the danger of fixing our views so exclusively on our own real or imagined wants as to overlook the rights of others?" Finally, in an apparently last-ditch attempt to persuade his audience, Winthrop seeks to shame them using what Douglass would later call "scorching irony": "I have no doubt that, if due search be made, a copy of this primeval instrument, with a clause giving us the whole of Oregon, can be somewhere hunted up."[9]

Despite Winthrop's alternately passionate, condescending, and ironic attack on O'Sullivan's Manifest Destiny argument, proexpansionist legislators quickly latched on to the term with both favor and fervor, launching it as one of the period's most powerful cultural fictions.[10] Born of overblown militaristic rhetoric and popularized after having been brought to the attention of Democratic politicians via a moving Whig critique of its basic premises, the term illustrates how history works in strange ways. More important historically, however, and notwithstanding its use in discussions of Oregon and its evocation of divinely preordained destiny, the term was first coined in reference to Texas annexation. *Manifest Destiny,* the brilliant rhetorical phrase originally popularized by the son of a pirate and first used widely in Congress following a passionate plea for moderation in the face of war-mongering expansionists, therefore begins in earnest with Texas annexation.[11]

In appraising the historical and rhetorical relationships between Manifest Destiny and nationalism, Benedict Anderson argues that "the magic of nationalism" "turns chance into destiny" and "contingency into meaning." Furthermore, Anderson suggests that the production of this magic rests on the ability to "imagine a community or nation as deep, horizontal comradeship, regardless of actual inequality and exploitation."[12] Senator Robert J. Walker's *Letter on Texas Annexation* (originally published 3 February 1844) epitomizes both aspects of this process of imagining a community for two reasons. First, it reconfigures the complex politico-economic and cultural contradictions shaping the crisis of Texas annexation as a manageable, functional, political opportunity to realize the United States' manifest destiny. Walker's *Letter* thus responds to a complicated historical and political crisis by offering an explanatory cultural fiction. Second, it vigorously ignores the fact that Texas's slave-based cotton-economy was responsible for profound inequalities, instead representing Texas not as a land of slavery and exploitation but rather as a *fictional* space of unrivaled economic opportunity and political equality. Around 30 percent of Texas's white population owned all its slaves, 72 percent of its real property, and 89 percent of its lucrative cotton market, but, regardless of what Walker's portrayal may imply, only 2.3 percent of the region's white population owned twenty or more slaves (widely considered the dividing line between small-scale farmers and the "planter class"). Hence, even within the ranks of Texas's slaveholding whites, property and wealth were distributed in a strikingly skewed manner.[13] Walker's *Letter* nonetheless portrays Texas annexation not as an expedient imperialist maneuver to support the politico-economic ambitions of the region's slaveholding elite but rather as a burning opportunity to extend the inevitable promise of the United States' heralded democracy and economic equality. It thus attempts to create both a conceptual vocabulary and a revisionist historical narrative capable of organizing complex subject matter into a digestible cultural fiction that appears laden with the ready-made historical legitimacy of Manifest Destiny.

The rest of the chapter unfolds in three sections. The first offers a historical framework situating the debate surrounding Texas annexation within the larger antebellum political battles regarding national expansion and slavery. The second begins by contextualizing Senator Robert Walker within the political milieu of Jacksonian democracy and the presidencies of Tyler and Polk and then proceeds to a detailed rhetorical analysis of the five primary theses of his *Letter.* The third part then concludes by offering observations on the relationships among Walker's *Letter;* the sweeping cultural, technological, and political changes attendant on the early development of print capitalism; and the construction of a rhetoric rationalizing the United States' manifest destiny of eventual continental mastery. Within this third section I address *The South in Danger,* a ferociously polemical pro–Texas annexation pamphlet Walker intended for an exclusively Southern audience (whereas his more nuanced *Letter* circulated primarily in the North). In its first publication, on 25 September 1844, *The South in Danger* was falsely attributed to the pen of James Towles, chairman of the Democratic Association of Washington, D.C. The distribution of such dramatically different documents within the period of seven months, each with its own geographically specific target audience and carefully choreographed rhetorical appeals, and one with faked authorship concealing Walker's hand in its production, justifies considering the rhetoric of these two documents closely. I accordingly limit my comments on U.S. diplomatic intrigue and focus instead on Walker's pamphlets as remarkable case studies of a rapidly modernizing nation struggling to comprehend and rationalize its ascendancy as one of the world's dominant imperialist powers.[14]

Historical Background: Why Annex Texas?

Between 1790 and 1865, 835,000 slaves were relocated westward, with 85 percent of these "exports" initiating from the once dominant tobacco-, sugar-, and rice-based plantations of Maryland, Virginia, South Carolina, and North Carolina. Approximately 75 percent of these relocated slaves ended up on the cotton-based plantations of Alabama, Mississippi, Louisiana, and Texas.[15] This massive transfer of slaves enabled a remarkable increase of cotton production in these states; indeed, the 1860 census found that Alabama, Mississippi, Louisiana, and Texas accounted for over 63 percent of all U.S. cotton production.[16] There is little question, then, that the political economy of cotton was pulling slavery southwestward. This dramatic shift was consistent with the gradual transformation occurring in the economies of Kentucky, Missouri, Maryland, and Virginia, border states that were evolving in directions similar to those of the North, with labor forces comprising increasing numbers of European immigrants and laborers migrating from the North.[17] Laurence Shore thus argues that the increasing presence of wage laborers indicates the border states were undergoing "a pattern of economic development that began to pull them closer to Pennsylvania and Illinois, and further from Mississippi and South Carolina."[18] At the time certain critics even suggested that, together with the devastating collapse in cotton prices following the 1837 crash, this pattern pointed toward the eventual demise of slavery as a viable politico-economic system.[19] Texas was therefore crucial to the way in which the United States understood the cultural and politico-economic consequences of this pattern, for Texas was being touted as the promised land for the perpetuation of slavery. Indeed, Campbell and Lowe report that between 1840 and 1850 the Texas slave population grew from 12,507 to 48,145; by 1861 it surpassed 169,460, an increase from 1840 of 1,300 percent. In 1844 the slave population of Texas was still small compared to those of Alabama and Georgia, yet the planter elite were certain that Texas was, as Campbell describes it, "slavery's frontier."[20]

Texas was also a frontier of another sort: a constant hot spot for military confrontations among westward white settlers, indigenous peoples, Mexican landlords, and pirate slave dealers.[21] As early as 1819 a hodgepodge of squatters, mercenaries, and miscellaneous troops—under the leadership of James Long, a one-time student of Andrew Jackson—marched from Natchez to Nacogdoches to battle Mexican troops in the hope of establishing the Republic of Texas. Long's troops got stomped, but the Texans later won their independence in the infamous eighteen-minute battle of San Jacinto on 21 April 1836. In 1837, however, Mexico (again) abolished slavery, which meant that the continent's newest nation—ripe with the potential to become the most profitable slave-based cotton economy in the world—was bordered not only by an enemy nation but by one whose unpoliced hinterlands offered nearby refuge for runaway slaves.[22] It is no surprise, then, that Native Americans, Mexicans, and runaway slaves, all with legitimate grudges against the Texas cotton elite, formed temporary alliances to battle Texan slaveholders. Indeed, the works of Herbert Aptheker, Wendell Addington, Paul Lack, and Richard Maxwell Brown suggest that such battles were a constant part of life on the Texas frontier, for the expanding geopolitical agenda of the cotton elite and the settlers' attacks on Mexican and native land claims produced a perpetual war economy of roving militias, squads of vigilantes, and gangs of drunken thugs.[23] In fact, Ward Churchill reports Texan-Indian violence to have been so prevalent that "the government of first the Republic, and then of the State of Texas, maintained a bounty on all Indian scalps until well into the 1870s."[24] Texas was thus the new frontier not only for the political economy of slave-based cotton production but also for the many forms of military conflict and Indian removal central to the cultural fictions explaining Manifest Destiny.

Texas was simultaneously a frontier of yet another sort, for it was a constant site of confrontation between the United States and its European competitors, particularly Britain. For example, to offset the United States' international monopoly, the British had tried desperately to grow cotton in India; when that venture failed, they turned toward Texas as a potential colony or politico-economic ally. Britain was not alone in this thinking. P. H. Laurent notes that after a particularly friendly 1841 trade agreement between Texas and Belgium, "Belgian documents" began "to mention a Belgian colony in Texas."[25] Thus, taking full advantage of international interest in its supposedly unmatched promise as the next great cotton-growing region, Texas had by 1842 established formal diplomatic relations with Britain, France, Holland, and Belgium. In fact, Texas-European commerce was so profitable, and the promise of continued European demand for cotton so definite, that Texas president Sam Houston, echoing the fundamental assumption of Manifest Destiny, boasted in December 1844: "If we remain an independent nation, our territories will be extensive—unlimited. . . . the Pacific alone will bound the mighty march of our race and our empire."[26]

The intense emotions surrounding the debates over slavery's future, the perceived threat of imminent British adventurism, recurring Indian violence, and Houston's big talk regarding the imperial future of an independent republic clearly indicate that the push for Texas annexation was in great part a response to what were perceived as impending political crises. Indeed, no less a public hero than the former president Andrew Jackson claimed that annexing Texas was a defensive measure necessary to protect the Union from the triple threat of British economic and military invasion, raids by savage Indians, and slave insurgency. Jackson feared that, if left unchecked, this unholy alliance could "raise a servile war, take New Orleans, arouse the Indians on our West to war, and throw the whole West into flames that would cost oceans of blood and hundreds of millions of money to quench and reclaim."[27] It is not difficult to imagine how such apocalyptic rhetoric aroused the anxieties of the South; given the strength of Northern Whig opposition to annexation, however, it is more difficult to fathom how such predictions of regional catastrophe addressed Northern interests.

The Southern cotton elite responded by portraying Texas annexation not as a desperate situation of crisis management but as a golden opportunity for economic advancement. For example, Senator Ambrose Sevier, a Democrat from Arkansas, argued in an executive session of the Senate on 7 June 1844 that annexing Texas would enable America "to monopolize, through the instrumentality of slave labor, the production of cotton and sugar, and other Southern productions, not only for the supply of our own markets, but the markets of the world."[28] Such grand talk of global monopolies no doubt appealed both to Southern capitalists and to their business partners in the North, yet by including slavery as a prerequisite to this economic mastery, Sevier corroborated Northern fears that Texas annexation was but another maneuver to bolster the fortunes of the "peculiar institution." Indeed, as early as 1836 Benjamin Lundy argued that U.S. interest in Texas was merely the result of "a long premeditated crusade against the government set on foot by slaveholders, land speculators, etc., with the view of re-establishing, extending, and perpetuating the system of slavery."[29] Both Jackson and Sevier thus argued for Texas annexation with rhetoric that clearly represented the exclusive concerns of the South's slaveholding cotton-producing elite, hence confirming the worst suspicions of anti-expansionists such as Lundy. Constructing an argument that could enable a nationwide consensus on the issue required a more inclusive rhetoric. In other words, a persuasive proannexation front could not be built by using such obviously and exclusively pro–Slave Power rhetoric but instead required proannexation cultural fictions that would appeal to small-scale Southern farming and Northern concerns as well.

This is where race becomes a key issue: by linking the annexation of Texas as a defensive measure necessary to protect the Union to ever-present Northern racial fears, proannexation propagandists were able to produce a cultural fiction of apparently *national* perspective. Indeed, one of the crucial factors in articulating this cultural fiction as a national concern was the claim that Texas would act as a "safety valve" that would slowly release surplus and westward-moving slaves down into Latin America. For example, John Calhoun's close colleague Senator George

McDuffie, a democrat from South Carolina, borrowed rhetoric from Senator Walker's *Letter* for a proannexation argument he voiced on 23 May 1844: "If we annex Texas, it will operate as a safety-valve to let off the superabundant slave population from among us," hence offering "some natural and safe process of getting rid of this description of people."[30] Thus the promised removal of Africans—clearly an appeal to racist sentiments in both the North and the South—transformed what was essentially a defensive reaction to a regional politico-economic crisis into a proactive cultural fiction of national proportions.

My thesis is twofold. First, the arguments previously discussed as rationales for annexing Texas, including Jackson's "necessary defense" argument, Sevier's vision of a slavery-based global monopoly on sugar and cotton production, and McDuffie's "safety valve" theory, were preliminary and largely unsuccessful attempts to articulate a cultural fiction broad enough to coalesce the various regional and class-based elements of the debate into a unified national movement. Second, the spectacular success of the *Letter on Texas Annexation* followed from Walker's ability to incorporate these limited regional elements within an even more grandiose, unifying, nationalist rhetoric portraying annexation as the epic work of America's preordained manifest destiny.

Senator Walker's Letter on Texas Annexation

Robert Walker graduated from the University of Pennsylvania in 1819 at the top of his class. By 1822 he was an established lawyer in Pittsburgh, apparently well on his way to fulfilling the legacy of his father, a distinguished Pennsylvania Supreme Court judge and veteran of the Revolutionary War. In the spring of 1825 Walker married Mary Blechynden Bache, the great-granddaughter of Benjamin Franklin and granddaughter of A. J. Dallas, James Madison's secretary of the treasury. Mary Bache was also the niece of George Mifflin Dallas, a pro-Jackson Democrat prominent in Pennsylvania politics. Walker was thus privy to the inner sanctum of the rising Jackson movement, with which he had been active since 1822. In 1826 he moved to Natchez, Mississippi, where he began a lucrative law practice and soon embarked on massive dealings in western land speculation.[31] A brief digression into Walker's history as a land baron establishes some of the political precedents necessary to comprehend more fully his *Letter on Texas Annexation.*

As is well known, Andrew Jackson decimated Indian cultures across the continent. His military victories in the West were "legally" recognized in the 27 September 1830 treaty of Dancing Rabbit Creek and the 20 October 1832 treaty with the Chickasaws, the combination of which opened over 100,000 square miles of new land for realtor speculation. Taking full advantage of his long-standing familial, political, and legal ties to the Jackson movement, and wisely using the newly formed Chocchuma Land Company as his purchasing agent, Walker bought 42,318 acres for himself, another 25,952 acres in league with other investors, and 4,502 acres with yet another set of investors. In fact, Walker and his associates in the Chocchuma Land Company snatched up over 75 percent of the fertile cotton-growing lands of central Mississippi made available by Jackson's militarism. Furthermore, whereas the 1820 Land Act set western land prices at $1.25 per acre for bundles of 80 or more acres, by 1834 Walker and his associates had sold over 25,000 acres of land for the usurious price of $8 per acre. These freewheeling land deals eventually caught the attention of outraged Mississippians who brought charges against Walker and his associates for land fraud. In a remarkable tribute to the power of party and insider politics in the Democrat-controlled state, Walker escaped with a not-guilty verdict. He then used the notoriety he had achieved in the case, along with his legal and financial successes, his strong family ties, and a much-publicized (although apparently forged) letter of support from King Andrew, to win a senate race. Walker thus arrived in Washington in 1836 as a flamboyant, incomprehensibly rich, legally savvy Democratic senator from Mississippi. In 1841 he was reelected and returned to Washington as one of its most respected land barons and power brokers, having become known as the "wizard of Mississippi."[32]

Perhaps because of his success as a land baron in Mississippi, and no doubt drawing on insider information gleaned in Washington, Walker soon became one of the largest holders of land in Texas. This is not entirely exceptional for men of his status and wealth, for speculation in Texas land was a popular means of both sheltering capital and making fast profits. In fact, Elgin Williams argues that "the Texas government was in effect one huge real estate corporation" and that "one of the chief industries in Texas was gulling New York capitalists and other newcomers with moonshine titles."[33] Like many other proannexation Democrats, then, Walker took political interest in Texas because he owned property that, given the flood of immigration predicted to follow annexation, would immediately rise in price, hence making a nifty profit. The records here are confusing, yet it appears that Walker owned Texas property valued at roughly $12,500. Considering that the Galveston Bay and Texas Land Company was selling land in Texas for as little as 10 cents per acre (with Sam Houston as the company lawyer), Walker may have owned as many as 125,000 acres.[34]

By the time of the presidential campaign season of 1844, then, Walker had become deeply implicated in the economics of annexation; not surprisingly, he had also cemented his role as a leading proannexation spokesperson. The latter role put him at odds with Martin Van Buren, who, despite his unpopular opposition to annexation, his inept handling of Jackson's populist legacy, and rumblings of discontent within the Democratic party, appeared a sure bet to win the Democratic nomination.[35] The presidency of John Tyler, who was universally condemned as "His Accidency" after he ascended first to the vice presidency as a reconciliation candidate chosen to placate Southern Whig swing votes and then to the presidency after the death of William Harrison, was a crippled embarrassment, leaving little doubt that the highly respected Henry Clay would receive the Whig nomination for president. Extreme proannexation Southern Democrats thus needed to find someone other than Van Buren who could defeat the Whig's Clay. Unfortunately for them, annexation was still primarily a back-burner issue: Van Buren was fastidiously ignoring the question in the hope that he could return to the White House without having again to combat the imperial legacy of his legendary predecessor, and Clay wisely avoided the issue for fear of its potentially divisive appeal to sectional rather than party allegiances.

Van Buren and Clay thus seemed assured of their nominations and mutually pledged to silence on the potentially explosive issue of annexation, yet a coterie of proannexation Democrats somehow persuaded the lame-duck Tyler to postpone the Democratic convention from November 1843 to May 1844.[36] This postponement gave Walker and proannexation Democrats the crucial window of opportunity needed to launch Texas into the national consciousness. The strategy was to torpedo the nomination of Van Buren (a much-loathed backroom banker from New York) as a first step toward securing the nomination for a properly imperialist Southern aristocrat, who, after defeating Clay in the presidential election, could then grease the political wheels for the annexation of Texas.[37]

Walker's most important contribution to this agenda was his *Letter of Mr. Walker, of Mississippi, Relative to the Annexation of Texas* (figure 4).[38] First published in the *Washington Globe* on 3 February 1844, the *Letter* was an unparalleled media sensation, for it was reprinted millions of times, appearing not only in the *Washington Globe, Philadelphia Pennsylvanian,* and *New York Herald* but also as privately funded chapbooks and pamphlets that, according to Frederick Merk, were "subsidized by a secret 'Texas Fund' established in Washington by wealthy Southerners and speculators in Texas lands."[39] Walker's *Letter* was thus a privately funded piece of propaganda charged with a dual task: throttling Van Buren

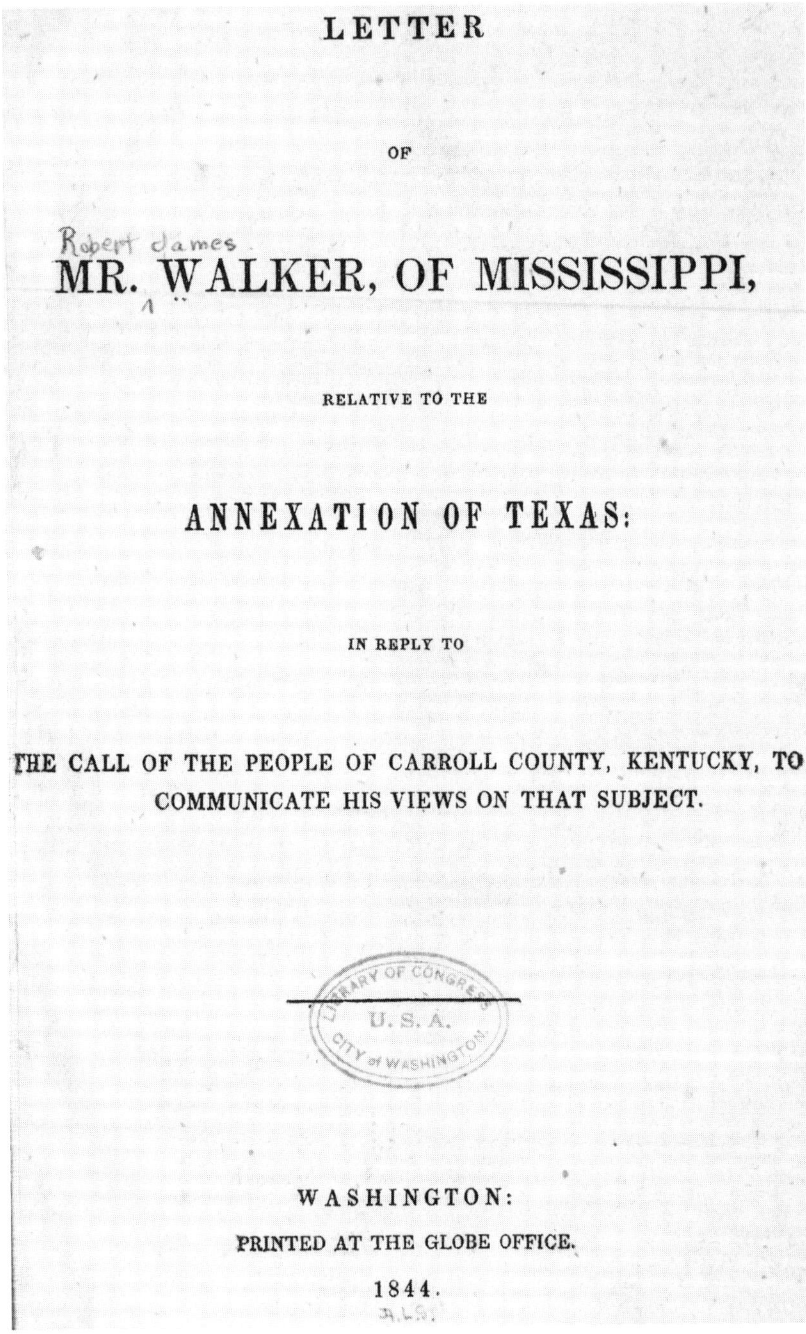

LETTER

OF

MR. WALKER, OF MISSISSIPPI,

RELATIVE TO THE

ANNEXATION OF TEXAS:

IN REPLY TO

THE CALL OF THE PEOPLE OF CARROLL COUNTY, KENTUCKY, TO COMMUNICATE HIS VIEWS ON THAT SUBJECT.

WASHINGTON:

PRINTED AT THE GLOBE OFFICE.

1844.

Figure 4. The front page of Senator Robert Walker's *Letter of Mr. Walker, of Mississippi, Relative to the Annexation of Texas.* (Reproduced courtesy of the Library of Congress.)

in order to open the door for a proannexation Southerner to win the Democratic nomination and drumming up national concern for Texas annexation. That is, Walker was a proannexation ringleader in his own right, a major investor in western lands (including Texas), and a hired propagandist in the pay of the plantation elite. His *Letter,* then, was an attempt to produce a cultural fiction capable of both realigning the power structure of the Democratic party and articulating a unified national response to a series of politico-economic and cultural crises fueled by contradictory regional anxieties.[40]

Walker delivered on his task. In fact, the *Democratic Review* wrote in February 1845 that "the letter has been more extensively read and circulated, and produced a more powerful and decided effect upon the popular mind, than any publication of an American statesman of the present day." The *Review* even claimed that the *Letter* was "the principal cause in . . . the nomination and election of Polk to the Presidency."[41] Indeed, the previously unheralded James Polk (during the campaign disdainful Whigs mocked him by chanting, "Who is James K. Polk?") won the Democratic nomination for president, with Walker's old political guardian and blood relative G. M. Dallas chosen as the candidate for vice president. Polk and Dallas (who were both ardent expansionists) then appointed Walker to head their Washington campaign committee (as I will show, this appointment explains why Walker wrote *The South in Danger*). The problem for Polk and the proannexation Democrats, however, was that although they managed to win the presidency, the combined Northern votes for Clay and the Liberty party's James K. Birney (both of whom ran on nonannexation platforms) surpassed Polk's total by 47,462.[42] In fact, Merk argues that if Birney voters had not fled the Whig party, "Clay would have carried New York and Michigan, and would have won in the Electoral College by a margin of 146-129."[43] Furthermore, the lame-duck Tyler had already presented a Texas annexation treaty to Congress that was soundly rejected in June of 1844.[44] Nonetheless, although there was no sweeping mandate for Polk or for annexation before, during, or after the presidential campaign, Texas annexation was approved by the House on 25 January 1845 and then by the Senate on 27 February 1845, six days before Polk's inauguration.[45] The question then, given this maddeningly complex political situation, is how did Walker's *Letter* achieve its remarkable effect? How, in the face of an extremely tight election and tough Whig opposition, did Texas annexation pass? Why was Walker's *Letter* so persuasive?

Walker begins his *Letter* with a nifty shift of vocabulary, stating that he favors "the *re*annexation of Texas" (223:1, emphasis added). Texas, he says, "was once our own" but was unforgivably "surrendered" as part of the Adams-Onis Treaty of 1819 (225:2).[46] For Walker, then, annexing Texas is "a question of the reestablishment of our ancient boundaries and the repossession of a territory most reluctantly surrendered" (226:2). Thus Texas annexation "is not a question of the extension of our limits, but of the restoration of former boundaries . . . , of reunion" (228:2). These lines shift the question of Texas annexation from the realm of annexation, aggrandizement, and imperialism to that of reclamation, restoration, and reunion. That is, the United States is not robbing and pillaging Mexico but simply and humbly "pursuing [its] ancient and rightful boundaries" (228:1). Adopting this line of rhetorical revisionism, later editions of the *Letter* incorporated the term *reannexation* into the title. For those readers who missed the importance of this rhetorical shift from annexation to reannexation, Walker explained elsewhere, "The term reannexation implies the getting back that which was once ours."[47] Walker of course realized that these boundaries were scarcely old, let alone ancient, and that their custody was the subject of deep political intrigue, which perhaps explains his vehemence when arguing that these so called ancient boundaries were rightfully won in battle against "the usurper Santa Anna" (223:1). Indeed, according to Walker, in 1836 "the people of Texas resolved to resist, and perish upon the battle field, rather than submit to the despotic sway of a treacherous and sanguinary military dictator" (223:1). Walker explains that "short was the conflict, and glorious the issue," and that "the American race was successful" (223:1). Walker concludes his historical introduction by claiming that on winning their freedom from Santa Anna "*The people of Texas,* with unparalleled unanimity, decided in favor of annexation" (223:2).

In his opening arguments Walker thus attempts to unite the diverse and often antagonistic populations of Texas into one homogeneous "people" complete with a unanimous will. Curiously, these new Americans are already citizens of the United States by right of both the ancient boundaries established in the Louisiana Purchase of 1803 and their heroic 1836 victory against the "usurper Santa Anna." These new-yet-old republican warriors for freedom are, as Walker reminds his readers, members of "the American race" (223:1). Framed in this way the issue of Texas annexation reduces to an obvious and unproblematic question: not what to do but rather how most quickly and smoothly to open the nation's arms to its racial, historical, and political brothers and sisters.

Walker's *Letter* was but one part of a viciously orchestrated attack against both Santa Anna in particular and Mexico in general. Indeed, *The Democratic Review* published an essay in September 1844 that dovetailed nicely with Walker's assault on "the usurper," as Alexander Everett argued that "the death of Santa Anna, imperiously and peremptorily demanded by every consideration of humanity and justice, would have been a substantial and permanent benefit to his country."[48] In addition, prior to the rhetorical attacks launched by Walker and Everett, Thomas Walker Gilmer (a former governor of Virginia, an eventual member of Tyler's cabinet, and yet another speculator in Texas land) published a fiery polemic in the *Baltimore Republican and Argus,* claiming, "The fashions of dress are not more capricious in their changes than are the forms of the Mexican government. I apprehend it is destined for some time, to continue in a state of civil chaos, giving no sign of energy, but occasional spasmodic convulsions in a body of bigoted priests and mercenary soldiers."[49] Echoing Gilmer's racism, John O'Sullivan argued in *The Democratic Review* of August 1845 that annexing California (understood as the next logical step, after taking Texas, in fulfilling America's manifest destiny) would actually relieve "imbecile and distracted Mexico" from the unwanted burden of governing a land soon to be overrun by "the irresistible army of Anglo-Saxon emigration."[50] This is not the place for an extended analysis of the sundry rhetorical tropes employed in the long tradition of smearing leaders and nations that stand in the way of U.S. ambitions; I mention the contributions of Everett, Gilmer, and O'Sullivan toward the demonization of Santa Anna in particular and Mexico in general simply to qualify the effect of Walker's *Letter.* Put simply, the *Letter* succeeded largely because it was able to tap into widely accepted racist and nationalist stereotypes that enabled its attack—in this case on Santa Anna—to ring as true as common sense.

Before proceeding into Walker's five main theses, it is important to note that the striking combination of messianic fervor, nationalist aggression, and freewheeling historical revisionism structuring his introduction is deeply embedded within the tradition of American exceptionalism. One key function of this cultural fiction is to reframe treacherous political choices as predestined historical necessities. Indeed, the rhetorical switch from annexation to reannexation repeats a fundamental claim of America's Puritan past. As Sacvan Bercovitch observes, whereas "others might stake their colonial claims on royal patents or racial superiority or missionary rights, for the Massachusetts Bay Puritans it was a matter not of claiming rights but of reclaiming ownership." Bercovitch argues that this reclaiming attitude produced a consensus that "migration was a function of prophesy, and prophesy was an unlimited license to expand."[51] One of Walker's first important rhetorical maneuvers in constructing a cultural fiction capable of luring antislavery Northerners and moderate Southerners into the proannexation movement is thus to invoke a righteous sense of national destiny and mission that will sound familiar to the proud descendants of Puritan New England.

Having constructed the historical groundwork necessary for justifying his rhetoric of Manifest Destiny, Walker proceeds to the body of his argument. For the purposes of analytic clarity, I have organized my comments on the *Letter* according to its five major theses: annexation (1) embodies the will of the Constitution, (2) is a necessary defense against British invasion, (3) will resolve the crises of slavery, (4) will prevent economic collapse, and (5) epitomizes the logic of modernity.

ANNEXATION EMBODIES THE WILL OF THE CONSTITUTION

Early debates surrounding the annexation of Texas often considered whether Congress had the authority to annex an already existing nation (not a territory or state) into the Union. Walker's first thesis accordingly attempts to provide a definitive answer to this question and therefore—like some of the proslavery arguments addressed in chapter 2—is based on a paradoxical form of anti-interpretive interpretation. That is, Walker's first thesis depends on his assumed ability (much like that assumed later by Chief Justice Taney in the Dred Scott case of 1857) to end the possibility of interpretive debate by deciphering the true "intentions of the framers" (224:1). Walker's professed interpretive skills allow him to conclude that the Constitution is equipped with unbounded powers of absorption and that "all the historical facts" attest to this power (224:2). The crucial rhetorical point in this first thesis, however, is not simply that the Constitution is geared for annexation, or that Walker's interpretation of it is meant to foreclose the possibility of all future competing interpretations, but more important, that such actions coincide with the intentions of Presidents Jefferson, Madison, Monroe, Adams, and Jackson, with Henry Clay (secretary of state under Adams and leader of the Whig opposition) thrown in for good measure.

Walker's paradoxically anti-interpretive interpretation is thus based on metonymy. That is, the intentions of a batch of heroes—gleaned through highly selective readings of their diplomatic communications—

are magically conflated with the supposed intention of the Constitution regarding annexation of new states. To put it another way: the essentially inexpressible concept of the Constitution's will is conflated with the more concrete images of recognizable heroes who embody the concept in a simplified, readily comprehensible manner. Hence the Constitution is metonymically condensed into a transparent document expressing the proexpansionist wishes of Jefferson, Madison, and others, while the internecine disputes among these individuals are simultaneously whitewashed into a coherent body of thought that manifests the spirit of a thoroughly proannexationist Constitution. Anyone opposing the annexation of Texas is therefore not only an anti-Constitution troublemaker but also a heretic performing a most unholy dance on the graves of the nation's preeminent statesmen. Thus Walker employs metonymy to conflate Texas annexation, the "intentions of the framers," and the wills of various heroic presidents into one great flaming ball of constitutional righteousness.

Walker uses metonymy exceptionally well, and certainly better than some of his contemporaries do. For example, Thomas Prentice Kettell's *Southern Wealth and Northern Profits* begins by asking the reader for "loyalty to the Constitution" and ends by asking: "Is it not better to stand by the Constitution and the Laws?"[52] The problem here, rhetorically, is that by equating the Constitution with law, Kettell represents the former as what various radicals (both then and now) fear it is: a baffling legal document written by the rich and for the rich in a cunning attempt to persuade the masses to consent to their own disempowerment.[53] Walker, however, employs metonymy to represent the Constitution not as a numbing icon of indecipherable legalese but as the embodiment of the collective will. Michael Warner emphasizes the political use value of such metonymy when he explains that "Americans pictured law justified by its derivation from the will of the people. The legal-political order would be transcendent in its authority but immanent in its source. The trick was to see how law could be given to the people transcendently and received from it immanently at the same time."[54]

My argument then—via Warner—is that Walker uses metonymy with great flair to pull off this trick of textuality and legitimacy, of making the transcendent authority of the law appear to be derived from the immanent source of the "people." Indeed, Walker's use of metonymy takes the various regional conflicts arising from anxieties over slavery and questions concerning who will benefit, politically and economically, from the annexation of Texas and magically conflates them into a national, historical, and ultimately constitutional issue concerning whether the current administration will honor the genuine will of the people.

ANNEXATION WILL PREVENT BRITISH INVASION

One year before Walker published his *Letter,* Thomas Walker Gilmer published an aggressive proannexation editorial entitled "Texas and the United States" in the *Baltimore Republican and Argus.* Smith argues that with the publication of Gilmer's letter on 10 January 1843, "the opening gun of a battle seemed to have been fired."[55] This metaphor of a first shot is somewhat misleading, however, for although Gilmer's letter may have initiated a new round of interest in annexing Texas, one of his central rhetorical ploys was to argue for annexation in terms that returned to perhaps the single most pervasive fear of all patriotic Americans: the dreaded encroachment of Britain. Indeed, Gilmer argues that "England, whose possessions and jurisdiction extend over so large a portion of the globe, whose influence is felt every where, will either possess or control Texas, if it does not come under the jurisdiction of the United States."[56]

Walker was an astute student of American politics and (as I will show while discussing *The South in Danger*) a remarkably thorough reviewer of the popular press. He therefore would have been both fully steeped in America's thriving anti-British mythology and familiar with Gilmer's letter, especially considering that he and Gilmer were friends, power brokers in the same extreme proannexation faction of the Democratic party, and eventually fellow members of Tyler's cabinet. It therefore comes as no surprise that the second major argument of Walker's *Letter* addresses both the threat of imminent British reinvasion and the annexation of Texas as a defense against this possibility. Echoing Gilmer, Walker states that "the present boundary is the worst which could be devised," for "it surrenders the Red River, and Arkansas, and their numerous tributaries, for thousands of miles, to a foreign power." Furthermore, "it brings that power upon the Gulf . . . too near New Orleans . . . [,] within a day's sail of the mouth of the Mississippi" (227:2). Walker then reminds his readers that Britain's government is "controlled by her aristocracy, the avowed enemies of republican government," and that "though saturated with blood, and gorged with power, she yet marches on her course to universal dominion" (239:1). The escalatory tone of the argument then turns toward cataplexis (the rhetoric of threats) as Walker grumbles: "and here, upon our own borders, Texas is next to be her prey" (239:1). Walker then reminds his readers of Britain's various heinous acts in the War of 1812, lists its vanquished international enemies—now all servile colonies—and guarantees his readers that "to refuse to accept the reannexation is to resurrender the Territory of Texas . . . into the hands of England" (236:2–237:1, 229:1).

Such incendiary rhetoric echoes Andrew Jackson's warning that failing to annex Texas would cost massive amounts of money and blood, but this threat faces two obvious problems. First, Jackson describes the question as a specifically western problem, thus articulating the issue as a regional rather than national crisis. Second, Jackson includes a crass reference to the millions of (presumably) tax dollars that reclaiming these western lands will cost, thereby confirming the suspicions of both Northerners and moderate Southerners that their tax dollars have become little more than a defense fund for the Southwest's cotton elite. Jackson's threat is thus fundamentally rooted in pro–Slave Power concerns, therefore dramatically limiting the cultural fiction's scope and appeal. Walker, however, drapes his prophesies of imminent disasters looming in the West within rhetoric that is both nationalist and biblical. For example, he concludes his necessary defense thesis by issuing a remarkably biblical warning: "Let all who have aided in producing this dread catastrophe flee the wrath of an indignant nation, which will burst forth like lava, and roll in fiery torrents over the political graves of all who shall thus have contributed to the ruin of their country" (239:2).

Walker's invocation of biblical imagery clearly echoes a strategy Bercovitch describes as growing from a fundamental tenet of Puritan symbology and hence one of the new nation's founding cultural fictions: "to give the country a past and future in sacred history, and to render its civic institutions a fulfillment of prophesy."[57] These mightily exaggerated passages do not just strive for historical and cultural legitimacy by borrowing familiar biblical rhetoric and Puritanlike cultural fictions; their more obvious purpose is to expand the question of Texas annexation into a national concern. This maneuver is politically astute, for although the North's rural farmers, members of the working classes, and bourgeoisie might not have given a damn about the demise of the Southwest's plantation elite, the return of King George's troops would have been entirely another matter. Furthermore, Walker would have been fully aware that Northerners opposed to abolitionist activities placed much of the blame for such agitation on the meddling influence of Britain. Indeed, Leonard Richards argues in his study of antiabolitionist mob violence that "the ultimate symbol of concerted [abolitionist] action, systematic agitation, and centrally imposed conformity was the [myth of a] British plot."[58] Walker's hyperbolic description of the imminent threat from Britain therefore enables him to turn the shimmering cotton-field dreams of the Southern plantation elite into a chilling national-defense nightmare complete with biblical, antiabolitionist, and anti-British overtones.

Considering the rhetorical gymnastics involved in constructing this argument, it perhaps comes as no surprise to realize that Walker may have known that England had no plans for colonization or abolition. In a letter dated 19 June 1844, George Bancroft bluntly tells Walker: "England has no desire to colonize Texas or to abolish slavery there; but does desire a monopoly of the Texas market under a virtually exclusive treaty. The issue then is, Texas for the British manufacturers and ship owners . . . or Texas for us by reannexation."[59] Bancroft's letter arrived four-and-a-half months after the first publication of Walker's *Letter* (but before its numerous reprints and the first publication of *The South in Danger*), so perhaps Bancroft's measured analysis shocked Walker into realizing that his original claims were overblown (although Walker did not accordingly change his argument in later reprints of the *Letter*), or perhaps Bancroft's views simply did not correspond to Walker's reading of the situation. At the same time, their mutual friendship and long-standing correspondence suggests that prior to publishing the most important document of his career, Walker would have consulted his friend, a world-class historian, intellectual, and diplomat, regarding England's intentions. If this is the case, then Bancroft's letter may amount to a forceful restatement within an ongoing debate between the two men. The Bancroft letter might be read, then, as further evidence suggesting that Walker's heated representation of England's intentions was not only rhetorical (in the worst sense of seeking to persuade an audience with powerful language, regardless of the facts) but even willfully misleading.

This more damning conclusion is supported by the fact that Lord Aberdeen had clearly stated British interests in a 26 December 1843 document later dubbed "the Pakenham letter": "With regard to Texas, we avow that we wish to see slavery abolished there . . . [, but] Great Britain does not desire to establish in Texas . . . a dominant influence. . . . Her objects are purely commercial."[60] The Bancroft and Pakenham letters are complicated and subtle documents steeped in diplomatic intrigue, yet they both suggest that Walker viewed hyperbolic threats of colonization and abolition, regardless of their validity or even plausibility, as more likely to trigger politically expedient chest thumping than were guarded discussions of market shares.

However conscious his subterfuge, Walker's *Letter* succeeded in constructing this anti-British necessary defense argument because it tapped into and was reinforced by a series of related cultural fictions. For example, it received considerable support from the *Democratic Review,* which echoed the necessary defense argument in its July 1844 edition. Editor O'Sullivan barked: "To abandon Texas now is to invite for her British Protection and British Policy. It is to close round us the circle of British

Power."[61] Furthermore, during the summer directly preceding publication of the *Letter,* it was widely publicized that on 18 August 1843 in the House of Lords, Lord Aberdeen (the foreign secretary) and Lord Brougham openly debated how England might influence the Texas situation. Reports of this debate reached America via the packet ship *Victoria* on 19 September 1843.[62] Particularly when coupled with the fact that the controversial World Antislavery Convention convened in London that same summer, word of this debate could easily be twisted to support Walker's hyperbolic claims that Britain was conniving to lure Texas from the fold.[63] Indeed, news of the antislavery convention and the House of Lords debate contributed substantially to the widely accepted (although not necessarily accurate) notion that Britain was secretly maneuvering for the abolition of slavery in Texas and that immediate U.S. action was therefore required to prevent Texas from drifting further into the dreaded path of British imperialism. Thus, although Walker's *Letter* was certainly the most widely distributed pamphlet attempting to spark the sense of an impending national crisis, it could not have succeeded in this task without a series of interlocking and mutually reciprocal factors, such as the support of the *Democratic Review,* Walker's Democratic colleagues in Congress, and the frantic rumor mill regarding Britain's supposed abolitionist and imperialist intentions.

ANNEXATION WILL RESOLVE THE CRISES OF SLAVERY

As I discussed in chapter 2, Northern workers feared that large numbers of freed slaves migrating into their already unstable communities could jeopardize their precarious economic situations. Walker was no doubt aware of these fears. He accordingly warns that ex-slaves migrating northward "might earn a wretched and precarious subsistence, by competing with the white laborers of the North, and reducing their wages to the lowest point in the sliding scale of starvation and misery" (232:1). Walker then launches an extended reading of the controversial report of the 1840 U.S. census, in which he claims to prove that free blacks are ten times more likely than whites to end up in poorhouses, jails, asylums, hospitals, and so on. The report's conclusions had been thoroughly repudiated as early as 1843, when Edward Jarvis reported in the *Boston Medical and Surgical Journal* that the census was a rigged, "fallacious and self-condemning document."[64] Despite this contrary evidence, Walker repeats one of the central arguments of antebellum proslavery cultural fictions by claiming these findings as incontrovertible scientific fact—not unlike the "sociology" marshaled by Fitzhugh and others—to prove that freed slaves would be incapable of surviving in a free labor market. Indeed, according to Walker, the census proves that abolition would be catastrophic for the "millions of the negro race whom wretchedness and crime would drive to despair and madness" (232:1). This tidal wave of despairing, mad, criminal ex-slaves would swamp the happy North, driving down wages and driving up crime, hence threatening the possibility of democracy itself. Walker's *Letter* thus participates vigorously in the rhetoric of impending doom.

Such rhetoric was sufficiently prevalent that abolitionists felt bound to counter it in their own materials. For example, the *American Anti-Slavery Almanac* laments that "if ghosts were flesh and blood, and flew in flocks, the spectres of beggary and crime conjured up by '*We Shall be overrun with them*' would darken all our northern air."[65] This remarkable passage indicates not only that claims such as Walker's had become ubiquitous but also that at least some Northern whites escaped the supposedly universal fear that freed slaves would overrun the North. Walker was no doubt aware that the impact of freed slaves on the North was a subject of much debate and mostly speculation, so having played his racial card—the claim that freeing the slaves would create starvation and misery—he proceeds to address a much less rhetorical and simply factual crisis: the Slave Power was dominating congressional politics so completely as to undermine the democratic process.

Indeed, many Northerners feared that the push for Texas annexation indicated runaway Southern control of national politics. For example, in 1837 William Channing (a Unitarian minister from Boston) wrote to Henry Clay that Texas annexation was little more than an attempt "to extend and perpetuate slavery."[66] Such fears had been expressed the year before in Benjamin Lundy's widely distributed *War in Texas; A Review of Facts and Circumstances, Showing that this Contest is the Result of a long Premeditated Crusade Against the Government set on foot by Slaveholders, Land Speculators, etc., with the View of Re-establishing, Extending, and Perpetuating the System of Slavery and the Slave Trade in the Republic of Mexico.* This supposed crusade's calamitous effects on democracy are denounced even more vehemently in Theodore Sedgwick's pamphlet *Thoughts on the Annexation of Texas* (1844), where he argues, "The annexation of Texas is but another name for the *perpetuity of slavery;* and we who now enjoy the rights and hold the soil of the Union, must bid farewell for ever to the hope of relieving ourselves from the danger, the odium, and the disgrace inseparable from this pernicious institution."[67] Charles Francis Adams's *Report of the Massachusetts Committee to Prevent the Admission of Texas as a Slave State* (1845; see figure 5) is equally adamant in its charge that the combination of slavery and expansionism was destroying the democracy. Circulated throughout New

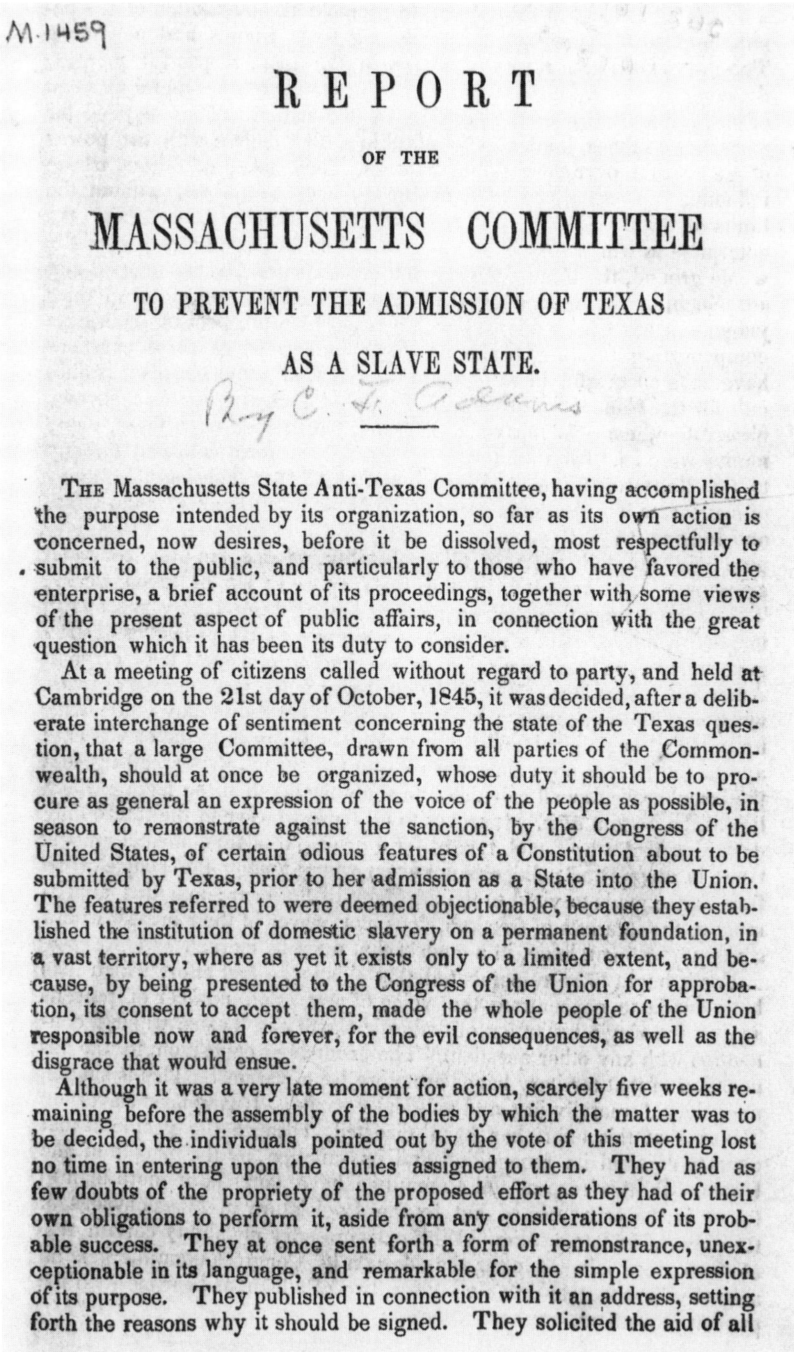

REPORT

OF THE

MASSACHUSETTS COMMITTEE

TO PREVENT THE ADMISSION OF TEXAS AS A SLAVE STATE.

By C. F. Adams

THE Massachusetts State Anti-Texas Committee, having accomplished the purpose intended by its organization, so far as its own action is concerned, now desires, before it be dissolved, most respectfully to submit to the public, and particularly to those who have favored the enterprise, a brief account of its proceedings, together with some views of the present aspect of public affairs, in connection with the great question which it has been its duty to consider.

At a meeting of citizens called without regard to party, and held at Cambridge on the 21st day of October, 1845, it was decided, after a deliberate interchange of sentiment concerning the state of the Texas question, that a large Committee, drawn from all parties of the Commonwealth, should at once be organized, whose duty it should be to procure as general an expression of the voice of the people as possible, in season to remonstrate against the sanction, by the Congress of the United States, of certain odious features of a Constitution about to be submitted by Texas, prior to her admission as a State into the Union. The features referred to were deemed objectionable, because they established the institution of domestic slavery on a permanent foundation, in a vast territory, where as yet it exists only to a limited extent, and because, by being presented to the Congress of the Union for approbation, its consent to accept them, made the whole people of the Union responsible now and forever, for the evil consequences, as well as the disgrace that would ensue.

Although it was a very late moment for action, scarcely five weeks remaining before the assembly of the bodies by which the matter was to be decided, the individuals pointed out by the vote of this meeting lost no time in entering upon the duties assigned to them. They had as few doubts of the propriety of the proposed effort as they had of their own obligations to perform it, aside from any considerations of its probable success. They at once sent forth a form of remonstrance, unexceptionable in its language, and remarkable for the simple expression of its purpose. They published in connection with it an address, setting forth the reasons why it should be signed. They solicited the aid of all

Figure 5. The front page of Charles Francis Adams's *Report of the Massachusetts Committee to Prevent the Admission of Texas as a Slave State.* (Reproduced courtesy of the Newberry Library, Chicago.)

England, New York, Pennsylvania, Indiana, and Ohio and then submitted to Congress with over 100,000 signatures endorsing its arguments, Adams's *Report* argues that annexing Texas would be "an alarming encroachment upon the rights of the freemen of the Union, a perversion of the principles of republican government, and a deliberate assault upon the compromises of the Constitution."[68] Channing, Lundy, Sedgwick, and Adams each demonstrate aspects of the widespread belief that the annexation of Texas was little more than an excuse for the untrammeled advance of slavery into new territory and hence for the Slave Power's final hijacking of democracy.

Proannexationists were clearly aware of such sentiments. They responded by claiming that Texas annexation was not a covert means of extending slavery and Southern political power but rather the most prudent way for the Union to rid itself of slavery. Indeed, in his 10 January 1843 letter to the *Baltimore Republican and Argus,* Thomas Walker Gilmer writes that "the culture of cotton and sugar in the United States has done more to withdraw slavery southward, than all the expedients which the wisest of this or other generations could devise."[69] Gilmer then restates this thesis in a 15 May 1843 editorial in *Niles' Register,* where he argues that the biological lure of warm weather "may induce the slave population now in the United States to advance southward in the event of annexation."[70] Walker's *Letter,* again elaborating on themes previously addressed by Gilmer, supports this thesis by citing a series of figures demonstrating that slavery is slowly migrating westward and that—if left to its own internal economic and biological logic and aided by Texas annexation—it will "disappear from Delaware in ten years, and from Maryland in twenty, and have greatly diminished in Virginia and Kentucky" (233:2). Indeed, Walker argues that annexing Texas will not only accelerate this trend but culminate in the eventual removal of all Africans from the United States, for "they would be diffused gradually through Texas into Mexico, and Central and South America" (234:1). Walker's primary assumption here, again repeating one of the central themes of proslavery cultural fictions, is that slaves will be drawn southward for innate, biological reasons: "As regards the slaves, the African being from a tropical climate, and from the region of the burning sands and sun, his comfort and condition would be greatly improved, by a transfer from northern latitudes to the genial and most salubrious climate of Texas" (234:1).

Hence, given the geopolitical and economic tendencies of cotton production and the innate drives of those laborers who hail from tropical regions, Walker arrives at the claim that Texas could function as a magical safety valve providing "the only practicable outlet for the African population . . . into Mexico and Central and South America" (234:1). Texas annexation is thus turned into a cultural fiction that promises the maintenance of white working-class wages in the North, the gradual demise of slavery in the South, and the eventual removal of all Africans from the United States, complete with the added Manifest Destiny bonus of softening up Mexico and Latin America for the imminent imperialist excursions to follow in the wake of the slaves' migration.

Such Manifest Destiny arguments exerted considerable influence. Only a decade earlier, in the Virginia legislature's debates regarding slavery, Charles Faulkner had protested the political and cultural effects of slavery's move south- and westward. Predicting that before long "the black population will exceed the white population" in much of the South, Faulkner warns, "We will not that you shall make our fair domain the receptacle of your mass of political filth and corruption."[71] By 1844 Faulkner's warning may have sounded like little more than an anachronistic complaint of a western Virginian fearful of Tidewater elites. Alternatively, perhaps the sheer force of Manifest Destiny persuaded Americans that such demographic changes were a small price to pay on the road to empire. In any event, the popular press widely supported Walker's safety-valve thesis, thus reinforcing the arguments of his *Letter* while subtly pushing concerns such as Faulkner's to the outskirts of political consideration.

Senator George McDuffie was not the only person to support Walker's argument that annexation would draw slaves to the West. O'Sullivan's *Democratic Review* continued its generous support of Walker's *Letter* when it published an essay in July 1844 claiming that "Texas will open before it as an outlet, and slavery, retiring from the Middle and Southern States of the present confederacy, will find for a time a resting place there. But only for a time, for the irreversible law of population . . . will emancipate Texas in her turn, and the negro will then pass to a land of political freedom and social dignity under a congenial sky. He will pass without civil convulsion, and leave no domestic ruin in his path."[72] Pursuing this same safety-valve argument the following July, O'Sullivan argues that annexing Texas will "produce the effect of draining off that labor southwardly, by the same unvarying law that bids water descend the slope that invites it." Whereas abolitionist agitation causes "civil convulsion" and "domestic ruin," annexing Texas, following the gentle, preordained laws of nature, will lead to both "the eventual voluntary abolition of slavery" and "the ultimate disappearance of the negro race" within the nation's borders.[73] President Tyler, addressing the Senate in autumn 1844, expanded such safety-valve rhetoric into a white supremacist's ultimate fantasy in which annexing Texas would "pave the way for a gradual but speedy removal of that population to the Mexican States, where they will meet with a population with which they may amalgamate, and through which they may improve."[74] Hence annexing Texas is turned into an opportunity not only to rid the nation of slavery but also, via amalgamation with Mexicans, to begin the long-awaited task of eliminating the Africans entirely.

Whether any of these promised results were even remotely likely is not the point. What is important is that by projecting the annexation of Texas as a nonconvulsive and nonruinous step within history's predestined unfolding, Walker, along with McDuffie, O'Sullivan, and President Tyler, created a rhetorical space for consensus in which proslavery Southerners would not feel immediately attacked, antislavery Northerners could imagine a progressive resolution of the issue in the not-too-distant future, white supremacists everywhere could imagine a pure, lily-white America, and everyone concerned could avoid difficult domestic problems by latching onto the intoxicating promise of the United States' realizing its manifest destiny as a hemispheric empire.[75]

ANNEXATION WILL PREVENT ECONOMIC COLLAPSE

Walker's most lengthy passages support the thesis that failing to annex Texas will destroy the economies of both the South and the North. For example, Walker states:

> The products of the slave-holding States, in 1840, amounted in value to $404,429,638. These products, then, of the South, must have alone enabled it to furnish a home market for all the surplus manufactures of the North. . . . Strike down these products by the immediate abolition of slavery, and the markets of the South, for want of the means to purchase, will be lost to the people of the North; and North and South will be involved in one common ruin. Yes, in the harbors of the North the vessels would rot at their wharves for want of exchangeable products to carry; the building of ships would cease, and the grass would grow in many a street now enlivened by an active and progressive industry. . . . One universal bankruptcy would overspread the country. (231:2)

As was detailed in chapter 2, the North was making a fortune from its trade with the South, yet universal bankruptcy was obviously unlikely as long as the North could continue trading favorably with Europe. This is where Walker again plays the nationalist trump card, for he dives into a lengthy analysis showing how the failure to annex Texas would not only hurt the North but also bolster trade for the Unites States' most dreaded

European competitors. For example, Walker claims that in 1839 Texas consumed nearly one-fourth of U.S. "domestic manufactures," worth some $1,687,082 (243:2). Texas opened diplomatic relations with France that same year, however, and with both Holland and England in 1840, hence opening the door for these European economic rivals to siphon off trade. Accordingly, the impressive trade figure for 1839 dwindled to a paltry $190,604 by 1843 (243:2). Walker thus asserts a direct and ominous correlation between falling U.S. profits and increased relations between Texas and other foreign economic powers. This trend, if left unchecked, will surely result in "Texas becoming a commercial dependent of England" (236:1). Thus Walker argues that not annexing Texas will throw the entire nation into economic collapse, pave the way for accelerated European trade with Texas, and eventually cause the downfall of the United States.

It is instructive to note that Walker's nightmarish vision of universal bankruptcy foreshadows the apocalyptic claims of economic disaster presented in such proslavery manifestos as David Christy's *Cotton Is King* (1855), Thomas Prentice Kettell's *Southern Wealth and Northern Profits* (1860), and Stephen Colwell's *Five Cotton States and New York* (1861), each of which argues that abandoning the cause of the Southern Slave Power elite will produce nationwide economic collapse. Walker's *Letter* presents a more persuasive rhetorical appeal than do these later documents, however, because its initial question of economic collapse is buried within the even more deeply resonant historical rhetoric of American unity vis-à-vis the threat of European economic competition and even military hostility. This economic argument is persuasive, then, precisely because Walker frames it within nationalist rhetoric that articulates a cross-class, cross-party, and cross-regional alliance of Americans against perceived outsiders.

In addition to constructing a rhetorically united American people who stand strong in the face of perceived threats from outsiders, particularly the much-loathed British, such broad nationalist claims also obscure the fact that, despite the prevailing Jacksonian rhetoric of democracy and equality, Texas was based on a profoundly inequitable economic system. Again, only 2 percent of the white population in Texas owned twenty or more slaves, so that Texas's economic elites, the "planter class," occupied (as did their contemporaries in the rest of the South) a position of remarkably antidemocratic politico-economic power.[76] Hence William Freehling's typically wry characterization of proannexation extremists as "the minority of despots living within a majoritarian republic" dovetails with his biting assertion that "slave holder republicanism was not very republican when it came to debating slavery."[77] So Texas lingered as a miraculous politico-economic dream of the capitalist elite—whether Southern slaveholders or Northern merchants, manufacturers, and speculators who stood to make a killing off of increased Texas trade—yet Walker portrays the issue as a national crisis of transcendent importance.

Consistently ignoring economic inequalities in favor of overarching nationalist rhetoric constitutes what Benedict Anderson refers to as the "magic of nationalism," which strives "to imagine a community or nation as deep, horizontal comradeship, regardless of actual inequality and exploitation."[78] Furthermore, using nationalist rhetoric to mask economic inequality reflects a fundamental tenet of Jacksonian politics. Indeed, Alexander Saxton summarizes the key Jacksonian practice of plastering over economic inequality with nationalist rhetoric as follows: "Egalitarianism, posed as high principle, requires either a policy of leveling . . . or else a denial that differences in wealth carry any invidious significance. . . . While making no direct effort to eliminate the economic base of class difference, they [Jacksonians] consistently rejected the concept of class hierarchy as applicable to the American Nation."[79] In a fashion consistent with one of Jacksonian politics' overriding cultural fictions, then, Walker's thesis about the economic disasters that nonannexation would create exudes righteous nationalist rhetoric but never specifies whose economy is at stake. More specifically, his plea for annexation is made from the perspective of a wealthy (and apparently crooked) land speculator who is either unconcerned with or simply ignorant of the fact that such Jacksonian rhetoric is essentially fictional. Nevertheless, speaking in terms of some assumptive egalitarian national economy is more appealing and rhetorically persuasive than admitting (as Tyler's secretary of state, Abel Upshur, was fond of doing) that Texas annexation is primarily the work of the Southwest's slaveholding elite.[80] Thus Walker's *Letter* reproduces one of the principal cultural fictions of the antebellum era, for its author avoids any discussion of class conflict by masking the economic agenda of the slaveholding capitalist elite within the glowing egalitarian rhetoric of the nation.

ANNEXATION EPITOMIZES THE SPIRIT OF MODERNITY

Walker's most subtle rhetorical ploy is to portray Texas annexation as part of a grand, preordained historical epoch stretching into the beckoning future. Walker begins this argument by noting that Texas is easily accessible by steam engine, which means that "he who would say that Texas is too large or distant for reannexation to the Union must have been sleeping since the application of steam to locomotion" (231:1). He thus enlists the latest scientific and industrial technology to portray Texas annexation as a logical element in the imminent unfolding of history itself. Walker does not use the word *modernity* in his argument, yet his propensity to link progress to the political aspirations of the United States clearly indicates that he is attempting to portray Texas annexation as an integral and unavoidable element in the long march of modernity. Indeed, in passages that provide stellar examples of the rhetoric of Manifest Destiny, Walker portrays Texas annexation, with the help of the mighty steam engine, as foreshadowing the day when the United States will "embrace a continent" (230:1). The natural pull of both scientific and historical progress will not stop there, however, for "the reannexation of Texas would strengthen and fortify the whole Union, and antedate the period when our own country would be the first and greatest of all the powers of the earth" (235:2). Walker goes on to explain the political and historical implications of this heroic growth, stating that the debate over Texas annexation is "one of the mighty movements in deciding the great question between monarchy and republicanism" (238:2). To support such grand rhetoric, the *Letter* closes with seven pages of elaborate tables detailing the unstoppable rise in U.S. economic relations with over sixty-five foreign regions, including the South Pacific, Peru, Trieste, Manila and the Philippines, Russia, Australia, the British West Indies, France's Atlantic coast, and even the mysterious destination Walker labels "uncertain places" (250–51). Thus Walker situates his *Letter* within a thoroughly modernist discourse that links the fate of America's national sovereignty and cultural authority to an expansive capitalist energy that literally spans the globe.

Indeed, Walker reduces several phenomena, including the mechanical power of the steam engine, the heroic expansion of the United States as a continental and even global power, the capitalist domination of faraway hinterlands, and the republican battle against European-style monarchies, to mere tokens of modernity's preordained logic. That is, annexing Texas is not so much a question of geopolitical expedience and the legitimacy of national sovereignty as an integral and even inescapable link in the boundless rush of history itself. This sense of an imperial and millennial modernity is conveyed nicely in a 20 April 1844 letter Richard Rush wrote to Walker to celebrate the achievements of his *Letter.* Rush gushes: "The question, as you handle it, presents the highest considerations belonging to our foreign policy now and hereafter, in combination with all that is most urgent and permanent." This vocabulary of permanence leads Rush to conclude that Walker's *Letter* has answered questions that will affect "the destiny of ages."[81]

Along with eliciting such private celebrations of the rapidly approaching dawn of a permanent American empire, Walker's *Letter* also received ample public support in its creation of a cultural fiction linking U.S. imperial claims to the "natural" pull of history. For example, in April 1844 the *Democratic Review* published an essay entitled "The Texas Question," in which it prophesied: "Our system of government is one which, rightly administered—on the principle of State-Rights Theory—will bear indefinite extension; nor do we doubt but that in the fullness of time it is destined to embrace within its wide sweep every habitable square inch of the continent."[82] This is a remarkable passage, for while supporting Texas annexation, it also offers an endorsement for the essential proslavery argument of states' rights, two references to an already known future, and an ostensibly indubitable prophecy that the United States will annex not only Texas but, eventually, all of Mexico and Canada. Similar arguments were forwarded by O'Sullivan, President Tyler, Senator Buchanan, and others.[83] Compared to such aggressive proslavery and proimperialist claims, Walker's thesis regarding the relation of Texas's fate to the larger sweep of modernity seems almost moderate. Walker's *Letter,* then, was not acting alone, as a stray voice in the wind; rather, it was a carefully crafted element in a larger barrage of propaganda claiming progress, Providence, and modernity as the foundations of America's manifest destiny.

Walker's Letter, The South in Danger, *and Print Capitalism*

Michael Warner observes that "by the Revolution . . . the business of governing relocated itself from the context of town meetings and market-street conversations to the realm of a public constituted in writing and print. The political discourse that ensued was not just a new way of carrying on the same old power relationships: it marked a critical shift in the arena of power."[84] Walker's *Letter* exemplifies the mature form of the dialectic Warner describes; that is, it shows the arena of power's expansion from local, personal, and oral levels of political conversation into more properly national, cultural, and written debates engaged predominantly through mass-produced material. With this in mind, I conclude this chapter by offering some brief observations regarding the relationships among Walker's *Letter,* his curious counterargument to the *Letter* in his anonymously authored pamphlet *The South in Danger,* and the political economy of print capitalism. Taken as a whole, these closing comments illustrate yet again that the discursive possibilities of modernity within antebellum America were negotiated collectively through the competing means of democratic dissent that new modes of production and distribution made possible.

One primary legacy of the Jacksonian era was the initiation of what we now call the culture industry. For example, Alexander Saxton notes that in 1830 there were 65 daily newspapers in the United States, with an average circulation of 1,200 and an average cost of six cents a copy. By 1840 the number of dailies had risen to 138, and by 1850 this number had ballooned to 254 dailies, with an average circulation of just under 3,000 and an average cost of a penny a copy.[85] Like Saxton, Ronald Zboray demonstrates how these remarkable changes resulted from the increasingly streamlined "reorganization of labor in the workplace"; the development of the steam-driven flatbed press; the explosion of transportation possibilities accompanying the expansion of canals and railroads; and a host of new technologies relating to paper production (moving from cotton- and linen-based paper to wood- and pulp-based paper), stereotyping and electrotyping (which are faster than traditional modes of typography), nighttime illumination (via better lamps), and even the early phases of optometry.[86]

Saxton reminds us, however, that these new technologies of mass production and increasingly national distribution required massive capitalization. Hence he observes that "at one end of this sequence lay a minimal price of entry and a prohibitive unit cost; at the other, a unit curve approaching zero and an investment curve rising almost vertically: mass illiteracy at one end, oligopolistic or monopolized control of communication at the other." There may have been a halcyon period in which these two curves met in democratic equilibrium, but Saxton concludes his analysis with the sobering realization that as the growing requirements of capital accumulation rendered the political economy of print capitalism increasingly undemocratic, "egalitarian rhetoric, which for the artisan editors had served as a weapon against the oligarchy, became for their successors a means of obscuring newly developing class separations." Indeed, the movement toward modern print capitalism paralleled the general politico-economic trajectory of antebellum America, tracing what Zboray has described as "a distinctly undemocratic trend."[87]

There is a crushing and fundamentally modern paradox here: the same technologies of mass production that enable the rising capitalist elite to cloak their economic power in the disguising rhetoric of democracy simultaneously provide the tangible, visible, and infinitely reproducible evidence, in the form of mass-circulation dailies, that one's friends, neighbors, and fellow citizens are sharing the same social, cultural, and historical space, hence providing the lived sense of here and now that makes the very concept of mass democracy possible. The radically new means of mass production and distribution associated with the first phases of modern print capitalism thus enable a strange act of *ironic synecdoche.* That is, instead of leading to a sense of alienation and displacement—by demonstrating the sheer multitude of autonomous, contingently related consumers linked by little more than their shared newspaper—such mass-circulating texts apparently enabled readers to imagine themselves, via their participation in the shared world conveyed in the same commodity/text, as members of some larger imagined community. This is ironic synecdoche, then, because one imagines oneself (the individual part) as being organically linked to a larger national culture (the collective whole) by experiencing a mass-produced text or other commodity that stands not for community but for profit, not for democracy but for capitalism, not for collective action but for individual consumption. Indeed, as Anderson describes this process, "each communicant is well aware that the ceremony he performs (in reading the paper) is being replicated simultaneously by thousands (or millions) of others of whose existence he is confident, yet of whose identity he has not the slightest notion. . . . What more vivid figure for the secular, historically clocked, imagined community can be envisioned?"[88]

The paradox of such mass-produced imagined communities and their resulting ironic synecdoche is that while modern print capitalism enables an unprecedented expansion of communal (and national) boundaries and constituencies, it simultaneously renders the representational bonds that unite these communities increasingly tenuous. As the part-for-whole transference of legitimacy and authority between the people (the individual parts who grant legitimacy to a given order) and the government (the collective whole that embodies political authority) expands beyond the realm of the local and the immediately knowable, the possibility that the synecdochic convertibility between legitimacy/part and authority/whole may become circuitous, or perhaps even incomprehensible, is accelerated.[89] Thus, even while the newly expansionist democracy relies for its sense of legitimacy and cohesion on the dissemination of the mass-produced texts made possible by the print-capital revolution, it simultaneously suffers from the inevitable crisis of democratic representation that follows from building a nation where political obligations and allegiances are increasingly confusing and even incomprehensible. In short, who represents whom, and how can you tell when the claim to represent someone or some people is legitimate?

It comes as no surprise, then, to learn that a common political tactic of the period was to charge one's opponents with misrepresenting their constituencies. For example, President Tyler, amid a fiery proannexation polemic, attacked Congress's rejection of his first Texas annexation treaty as the work not of democracy loving representatives of the popular will, but rather of the "sordid, grasping and rapacious spirit of our legislation." In fact, Tyler claimed that "under the epithets of *'general,' 'national,' 'American,'* they embrace only the interests of the small and favored classes."[90] Of course, this charge of claiming to speak for the whole while merely conniving for the benefits of some exclusive part could be applied just as accurately to the Democrats' chief proannexationist spokesperson, Robert Walker. The early phases of modern print capitalism therefore indicate a dramatic transformation in American history, as the chasm between politicians and people, between the assumed whole of America and its rapidly multiplying parts, widened into a yawning canyon that replaced questions about ethics, possibilities, and communities with concerns about the veracity of one's claims to speak for any constituency larger than oneself and one's mutually invested backroom cronies.

This crisis in democratic representation reached new levels of complexity with Walker's *The South in Danger: Read before You Vote* (figure 6). Published originally on 25 September 1844 as a four-page address to the Democratic Association of Washington, D.C., mailed liberally and exclusively throughout the South, and initially attributed to the pen of James Towles, the document was written by Walker (whom Polk had by then picked to chair his campaign committee) in a last-ditch preelection attempt to scare up proannexationist Polk votes among waffling Southern Whigs.[91] The document's target audience raises serious questions about Walker's *Letter,* for although the *Letter* is a remarkably nuanced attempt to position Texas annexation as a moderate, prudent, historically preordained step toward America's manifest destiny, and hence as a palatable option to wary Northerners, *The South in Danger* is a frantic, almost hysterical explosion of antiabolitionist dogma that, strangely, appeals to precisely those stereotypically base Southern interests (white supremacy, antiabolitionism, virulent regionalism, and so on) that the *Letter* went to such lengths to dismiss. *The South in Danger* is therefore a curious self-refutation of the arguments Walker forwarded seven months earlier in his *Letter.*

The first sentence of the pamphlet establishes a tone of crisis. Walker foregoes the subtle historical posturing of the *Letter* to argue bluntly, "There never was a period when the South was in so much danger as at this moment" (1). This unprecedented danger is the result of Northern Whigs' going soft on slavery. In fact, Walker charges that "their views are identical with those of the abolitionists" and that "the abolition of slavery will be more certainly effected by the election of Clay [the Whig candidate] than that of Birney [the explicitly abolitionist candidate of the

THE SOUTH IN DANGER.

READ BEFORE YOU VOTE.

ADDRESS OF THE DEMOCRATIC ASSOCIATION OF WASHINGTON, D. C.

There never was a period when the South was in so much danger as at this moment. To procure the Abolition vote for Henry Clay, we will show that the Whig party of the North, their leading presses, legislative bodies, and statesmen, have denounced the South, they have held up slavery as a crime, they have promised a speedy union to effect its overthrow with the Abolitionists, and have joined with them in holding up the South to obloquy and reproach. The means used by this new coalition are to represent the people of the South to their sister States and to the world as disgraced and degraded by the institution of slavery, and as unworthy of Christian communion and social intercourse. Already this demoniac feeling has dissolved the Methodist church, and other American churches are threatened with a similar fate. The object is to *taboo the South*, to render us infamous, to put the mark of Cain upon our forehead, and to deprive us of character first, as the means of despoiling us of our property afterwards. Men of the South, the effort is to disgrace and degrade you and your children forever. That such a party exists in the North, is conceded. They denounce you in their presses, petitions, and speeches, as man-stealers, as robbers, as flesh-jobbers, as slave-breeders, as convict criminals, as vile and infamous, as unworthy of Christian or social communion, and, finally, as existing only by sufferance as a part of the Union. Now if, as we shall demonstrate, the party which thus denounces the South is courted by the Whig party of the North, if they are assured, as we shall show, by the Whigs of the North, that their views are identical with those of the Abolitionists, that they are only using different means to accomplish the same object, and that the abolition of slavery will be more certainly effected by the election of Clay than that of Birney, surely you cannot continue united as a party with the Whigs of the North, who thus join with your enemies to disgrace and degrade you. If the leading Whig statesmen of the North denounce you as culprits and criminals, and, immediately succeeding this denunciation, these your avowed enemies are nominated and elected as Governors, as members of Congress and of the State Legislatures, by the Whig party of the North, can you continue united with such a party; and if you do, are not your own votes joined with those of your enemies in subjecting you to disgrace and degradation? But let us to the proof; and we extract from the National Intelligencer, republished in the Liberty Legion, the following address on the subject of Texas, by twenty-one members of Congress, *all* friends of Mr. Clay, *all* of whom, since their condemnation of you, have been sustained by the united vote of the Whigs of the North:

"We hesitate not to say, that annexation, effected by any act or proceeding of the Federal Government, or any of its departments, would be identical with dissolution. It would be a violation of our national compact, its objects, designs, and the great elementary principles which entered into its formation, of a character so deep and fundamental, and would be an attempt to eternize an institution and a power of a nature so unjust in themselves, so injurious to the interests and abhorrent to the feelings of the people of the free States, as, in our opinion, not only inevitably to result in a dissolution of the Union, but fully to justify it; and we not only assert that the people of the free States 'ought not to submit to it,' but we say, with confidence, they would not submit to it. We know their present temper and spirit on this subject too well to believe for a moment that they would become *particeps criminis* in any such subtle contrivance for the irremediable perpetuation of an institution which the wisest and best men who formed our Federal Constitution, as well from the slave as the free States, *regarded as an evil and a curse*, soon to become extinct under the operation of laws to be passed prohibiting the slave trade, and the progressive influence of the principles of the Revolution."

"John Quincy Adams, of Massachusetts; Seth M. Gates, of N. York; William Slade, of Vermont, William B. Calhoun, of Massachusetts; Joshua R. Giddings, of Ohio; Sherlock J. Andrews, of Ohio; Nathaniel B. Borden, of Massachusetts; Thomas C. Chittenden, of New York; John Mattocks, of Vermont; Christopher Morgan, of New York; Joshua M. Howard, of Michigan; Victory Birdseye, of New York; Thomas A. Tomlinson, of New York, Staley N. Clarke, of New York; Charles Hudson, of Massachusetts; Archibald L. Linn, of New York; Thomas W. Williams, of Connecticut; Truman Smith, of Connecticut; David Bronson, of Maine; George N. Briggs, of Massachusetts; and Hiland Hall, of Vermont.

"WASHINGTON, *March* 3, 1843."

Of the Whig members of Congress who signed this address, (for it was scorned and denounced by the Democrats,) each one was elected by the Whig party, each of them is still a Whig, an ardent friend of Henry Clay, and each of them has been sustained since this denunciation of the South by his Whig constituents of the North, thus endorsing these libels upon us and our institutions. These Whig members of Congress denounced slavery "as an evil and a curse," as an institution "unjust, injurious to the interests and *abhorrent* to the feelings of the people of the free States;" and, finally, they declared that the attempt to sustain it by the annexation of Texas would "fully justify a dissolution of the Union." If these charges are true, they disgrace and degrade the South. Yet they were made by 21 leading Whig friends of Mr. Clay in Congress, and endorsed subsequently by their Whig constituents. Nearly all of these twenty-one members were sustained for re-election by their Whig constituents, or those who did not return again to Congress they elevated to higher stations. Thus, Mattocks, in Sept. 1843, and Slade, in Sept. 1844, were elected by the Whigs as Governors of Vermont, and Briggs, in Nov. 1843, as Governor of Massachusetts. Such are the allies with whom the Whigs of the South are asked to co-operate in the election of Henry Clay. Such is the party in the North, whom the Whigs of the South are asked to place in power—thus sustaining the enemies who denounce, instead of their friends, the Democracy of the North, who sustain and defend the South and their institutions.

Mr. Giddings, of Ohio, one of the twenty-one Whig members of Congress who issued the above address, in his speech in Congress on the 1st May, 1844, against the annexation of Texas, says:

Figure 6. The front page of Senator Walker's *The South in Danger: Read before You Vote.* (Reproduced courtesy of the Library of Congress.)

Liberty party]" (1). Walker's rhetorical strategy, then, regarding both Polk's candidacy for the presidency and Texas annexation, is to push Clay and the Northern Whigs into the dreaded abolitionist camp, rendering Polk and annexation a prudent alternative to a Clay (and therefore abolitionist) victory, which, so Walker prophesies, will "disgrace and degrade you and your children forever" (1). Having thus established this escalatory tone within the first paragraph of the opening page, Walker spends the next three pages adducing an overwhelming string of examples in which Whigs make provocative antislavery and antiannexation promises, not the worst of which comes from an infamous 3 March 1843 "Conscience Whig" circular (signed by John Quincy Adams, Joshua Giddings, and nineteen additional outspoken antiannexationist Whigs who are "ardent friends of Mr. Clay") featuring the ill-chosen threat that annexing Texas will "inevitably result in a dissolution of the Union" (1).

The question of representational legitimacy is therefore crucial to Walker's *South in Danger.* Although Clay was actually ambivalent on the annexation issue, and the Whig party, particularly in the North, was in turmoil over it (just as the party was divided into so called Conscience Whigs and Cotton Whigs, with the former against and the latter for slavery), Walker uses extreme comments from speeches, pamphlets, newspapers, and circulars to portray Clay and the Northern Whigs as, respectively, an unwavering candidate and a united party bonded primarily by their shared hatred of both slavery and the South. Despite this clear misrepresentation of the facts, much of the pamphlet's vitriol follows from the fact that Walker charges Clay and the National Whig leadership with rhetorical dishonesty. In fact, Walker suggests that Clay's nationally publicized speeches and letters carefully avoid both the more radical ideas espoused by various regional Whig leaders and Clay's own more aggressive statements on the subject. To expose the depth of this duplicity, Walker cites Clay arguing in Congress on 20 January 1827 (eighteen years prior to the debates at hand) that slavery is "THIS DEEPEST STAIN . . . THIS FOUL BLOT" (4). National Whig moderation, then, when considered in the light of Walker's eye-popping examples, appears to be a politically expedient attempt to mask the Whigs' and Clay's radical abolitionist principles in more palatable tones of moderation.[92] In short, Walker charges the Whigs with acting as a Trojan Horse for abolitionism and hence with committing a grievous act of representational deception.

That Walker cites an overwhelming number of printed sources from a geographically sweeping sample to cobble together a geographically specific how-to-vote pamphlet illustrates my point regarding print capitalism and the representational paradoxes of modern democracy. Specifically, *The South in Danger* represents the transition of American politics into a modern mass-media-based monster democracy of mass-produced deception. The Whigs were, of course, outraged by Walker's circular; they accordingly republished 40,000 copies of *The South in Danger* throughout the North, complete with a short, scalding commentary entitled "Locofoco Honesty," in which they refuted Democrats' charges that the Whigs had faked the original document to portray Polk and the Democrats as rabid proslavery advocates. Charge, countercharge, counter-countercharge, and so on, all in the form of mass-produced documents claiming to provide the single missing piece of evidence that reveals the whole truth behind the confusing barrage of conflicting claims. Not surprisingly, *The South in Danger* triggered a messy controversy regarding not only Walker's authorship but also the questions of (1) whether Walker abused his franking privileges in distributing the document, (2) whether Walker's original thesis bore any relation to the truth or was rather an irresponsible cobbling together of extreme statements taken out of context, (3) whether the Whigs' violated proprietary standards of political decorum in republishing the document, and (4) whether any of these campaign histrionics had anything to do with the nation's real concerns and needs.

American politics have always been sensational; with *The South in Danger* they become sensational in a dramatically new, thoroughly modern, mass-produced manner. Indeed, these four questions regarding *The South in Danger* may be understood, in a more expansive historical mode, as addressing (1) how modern bureaucratic privileges and the practices of democracy may coexist, (2) how a nation as large as the United States may conduct politics without falling prey to mass-produced trickery and slander, (3) how mass-parties may operate on a national scale without compromising the spirit of democracy, and (4) how national campaigns may proceed without obliterating any sense of representational veracity within the synecdochic structure of American democracy. In this sense, then, both Walker's *Letter on Texas Annexation* and his *South in Danger* need to be understood as wonderfully illustrative examples of a crucial turning point in antebellum democracy. Specifically, the *Letter* and *The South in Danger* both mark the point at which the new mass-production technologies that prompted the growth of print capitalism converged with the nationalist imperative for imperial expansion. Indeed, if we accept the premise that modernity is distinguished from previous historical moments by its use of technologies of mass representation to launch "imagined communities" beyond the barriers of geography, language, and ethnicity, then it follows that these two texts unmistakably announce the rise of modernity in antebellum America.[93] In short, both documents signal a dramatic new convergence of political power in which the technologies of mass production fueling print capitalism, the geopolitical aspirations of the slaveholding elite, nearly universal anxieties regarding race, and the nation's rapidly accelerating romance with empire find common cause in the rhetoric of Manifest Destiny.

Walker's *Letter* and *The South in Danger* illustrate the possibilities and pitfalls of mass representation in an expanding empire fueled by slavery, racism, and print capitalism, but other antebellum Americans found themselves wondering about the aesthetic and political opportunities that followed from this crisis in democratic representation. Indeed, while individuals such as Walker, Tyler, McDuffie, Buchanan, and O'Sullivan scanned the far horizon, looking outward for the new lands and resources necessary to fulfill the nation's manifest destiny, other antebellum Americans contemplated the local, looking laterally for the new styles and forms of representation necessary for building a new poetics of self-making. The daguerreotype was among the most important tools in this new poetics of self-making, and Walt Whitman was both the daguerreotype's champion and one of the period's most fascinating and ardently democratic self-stylers. In the following chapter I turn to Whitman's poetry, his love of both the daguerreotype and democracy, and the larger cultural milieu of modern image making as an art form, commodity fad, and tool for a new poetics of self-making. Whereas I have portrayed Walker and his supporters as manipulating new means of representation to advance the cause of an imperialist and slavery-driven empire, I will portray Whitman and his fellow self-stylers as exploring new means of representation to advance a variety of causes, chief among them the construction of a new democracy of self-making strong enough to resist what many antebellum Americans perceived to be the deadening pull of capitalism and modernity. Before turning to Whitman and daguerreotypes, the chapter opens with a discussion of Ralph Waldo Emerson, who, as much as any American of the period, was deeply concerned with what I call the dialectics of commodification, self-making, and democracy.

4 *Whitman's Pose, the Daguerreotype, and the Dialectics of Commodification, Self-Making, and Democracy*

> Is it not the chief disgrace in the world, not to be an unit;—not to be reckoned one character;—not to yield that peculiar fruit which each man was created to bear, but to be reckoned in the gross, in the hundred, or the thousand, of the party, the section, to which we belong; and our opinion predicted geographically, as the north, or the south? Not so, brothers and friends—please God, ours shall not be so.
>
> —Ralph Waldo Emerson, "The American Scholar"

Thus Emerson pleads with his God to help him and his brothers and friends succeed in their search for a civic pedagogy that will enable the American scholar to achieve a properly spiritual, intellectual, vigorous, independent, and nationalist character.[1] Ostensibly a speech about the institutionalization of knowledge in the new nation, "The American Scholar" foregrounds two fundamentally modern questions. First, how can the individual character survive amid the mass-produced culture of modernity? Second, how does capitalism affect democracy? Emerson is disingenuous, however, when he pleads for supernatural guidance regarding these historical and political questions, for he clearly believes that achieving a properly American character is a simple process of applying honest labor to life's problems. Hence he exhibits a confident, off-hand tone when promising that, "of course, he who has put forth his total strength in fit actions has the richest return of wisdom" (93). Emerson thus describes the heroic pursuit of wisdom in terms that suggest the mathematical logic of banking: invest your labor in fit actions and, like clockwork, like compoundable interest, a rich return will accrue. Rendered in the midst of a 31 August 1837 lecture to Harvard's Phi Beta Kappa Society, Emerson's reassuring banking metaphor surely struck a chord of smug familiarity with the elite gathered in what was then—as now—one of the nation's premier conduits of power and privilege.

Given that the summer of 1837 found America stumbling through its worst economic depression to date, with perhaps 90 percent of the factories in the East having closed, Emerson's confidence sounds naïve and idealistic, if not entirely deluded. For while Emerson reassuringly claimed that fit actions would reap rich returns, America's new capitalist markets were in such turmoil that Sean Wilentz has characterized 1836 as "the year of the strikes." Some of these strikes appeared so threatening to the wealthy whose children would soon be listening to Emerson speak at places such as Harvard that New York City's elite, for the first time in that city's history, called in the military as strikebreakers. One response to this unfortunately precedent-setting use of military power to enforce hardening class divisions was an outpouring of peaceful political activism that culminated in a June 1836 rally of over 30,000 angry New Yorkers. This remarkable example of democratic dissent was, as Wilentz describes it, "the largest protest gathering in American history" to date and "represented about one-fifth of the entire adult population of New York City."[2] The likelihood of fit actions reaping rich returns was thus very much in doubt in 1837, for the country seemed less likely to ascend to some glorious Emersonian transcendence than to continue descending into economic depression and class-based violence.

From this perspective, Charles Sellers's recent description of Emerson's speeches from the period as engaging in "a romantic orgy of self-indulgent evasion" is not entirely unwarranted. Nevertheless, Emerson's avoidance of such bothersome facts has traditionally been celebrated as a sign of his unflagging optimism, his characteristically American sense that things will work out, and his refusal to compromise cosmic spiritual aspirations by acknowledging the petty realities of political and economic life. Such a view explains the glowing tone of F. O. Matthiessen's canon-shaping masterpiece *American Renaissance,* which happily proffers the claim that Emerson "had not a trace of skepticism in his being."[3]

In retrospect it appears that both Sellers and Matthiessen push Emerson toward some unnecessarily caricatured extreme—either silly bourgeois lackey or the nation's heroic cheerleader, respectively—for the epigraph indicates clearly that Emerson was well aware of the nation's precarious state in the tumultuous summer of 1837. Indeed, although Emerson's "American Scholar" speech eschews explicit discussion of the strikes and protests described by Rezneck and Wilentz, it nonetheless contains enough cautionary passages regarding the dangers of modern capitalism to have left its young listeners trembling in fright. In fact, one is hard-pressed not to read the speech as a tortured warning that even the young man of the best character may soon find himself swamped not so much by the ravages of the depression then sweeping the land as by a new world of mass-produced banality.

In fact, although Emerson relies throughout his speech on happy images of economic wealth, scholarly intelligence, historical progress, and spiritual renewal, he returns again and again to the fundamentally modern threat of what Marx would soon label "reification": the dehumanizing treatment of things as people and people as things. For example, Emerson warns that the "One Man" of old, the individual organically linked to a larger, holistic community, "has been so distributed to multitudes, has been so minutely subdivided and peddled out, that it is spilled into drops, and cannot be gathered. The state of society is one in which the members have suffered amputation from the trunk, and strut about so many walking monsters,—a good finger, a neck, a stomach, an elbow, but never a man." Hence, "man is metamorphosed into a thing" (84). This is a remarkable passage, especially since another eleven years would pass before Marx would argue in *The Communist Manifesto* that "owing to the extensive use of machinery and to division of labor, the work of the proletarians has lost all individual character. . . . He becomes an appendage of the machine." In a passage that sounds as if he were cribbing from Emerson's "American Scholar," Marx then laments the fact that for the disempowered laborer, modernity's transformations in labor practices, notions of the self, and community culture amount to "a mere training to act as a machine." These are terrifying, almost gothic images in which the rapidly modernizing countrysides of both Emerson's America and Marx's Europe are littered with dehumanized monsters ripped from their once-bucolic worlds and thrust, limb by bloody limb, into the mechanized meat grinder of modern capitalism.[4]

Although Emerson's tone throughout much of the essay is every bit as nostalgic as that of Fitzhugh and his fellow proslavery advocates (see chapter 2), it is clear that as would Marx, Emerson is looking ahead, scanning the horizon of the not yet, the about to be. Whereas Marx's gaze into the future leads him to prophesy imminent political revolution, however, Emerson responds more temperately, warning his listeners that in a world increasingly besieged by the mass-produced products of print capitalism, where strangers emigrating from unheard-of places are swelling cities at exponential rates and the earliest forms of factory life are slowly eroding centuries-old work habits and life patterns, even the best Phi Beta Kappa Harvarder will be desperately challenged to maintain self-identity. Emerson, then, like almost all the antebellum figures I have addressed in this study, recognized that modernity was realigning old political orders, changing old work habits, and shattering old notions of community and self. On the one hand, Emerson saw these transformations as opportunities, which explains his hopeful plea for the creation of a radically new form of American scholar. On the other hand, Emerson saw these transformations as catastrophes, which explains his terrible warnings of the disgrace produced by reification. Emerson thus realized that both the opportunities and the catastrophes of modernity were forcing fundamental reappraisals concerning how the self is constructed, how the self and society interact, how the rule of the many threatens the integrity of the self, and ultimately, how the practices of the market threaten the promises of democracy. As this chapter's title suggests, then, one may approach Emerson's work as a sustained examination of the dialectics of commodification, self-making, and democracy.

Emerson struggled with these questions throughout his career, yet he never tried to answer them in a form other than the high-minded political sermon. Walt Whitman, however, realized that pursuing Emerson's troubling questions required new forms of expression, new ways of seeing, new means of representation. Moreover, although Whitman is known as one of the period's great poets and journalists, he was also fascinated by and deeply involved in the aesthetic and political possibilities of the period's new means of visual representation, particularly the daguerreotype. Whitman's work, then, whether poetry or promotion of the daguerreotype, may be approached as a more aesthetically adventurous attempt to address Emerson's two driving questions: how does modernity affect the status of and relationships among selves and society, and how does modern capitalism affect the promises of democracy? Like Emerson, Whitman believed that one way to answer these questions was to plumb the depths of character. Nonetheless, whereas Emerson saw character as an almost spiritual essence threatened most immediately by the anonymity-producing and compromise-inducing blur of mass culture—which he saw as "the smooth mediocrity and squalid contentment of the times," a culture sinking in "a spirit of cowardly compromise"—Whitman was concerned (and perhaps even obsessed) with the ways character can be represented in public.[5] How do you know character when you see it? How do you know when it is real? What I described at the end of chapter 3 as a crisis in democratic representation thus confronted Whitman as a series of interrelated dilemmas: How can you represent the character of the self while speaking of the democracy without succumbing to the vague generalities that litter Emerson's sermonizing? How can you speak of the grand whole while honoring each inviolable part? How can you be a man or woman of the people yet still celebrate your individuality? How can you make art in a culture that cherishes commodified banality? Like Emerson, then, Whitman found himself struggling to make sense of (and conquer, as was his tendency) the dialectics of commodification, self-making, and democracy.

To a remarkable degree Whitman sought answers to these questions in daguerreotypes. Indeed, like many of his fellow antebellum Americans, Whitman believed that daguerreotypes were so intensely transparent, so radically honest, so unimpeachably obvious as evidence, that the crisis of democratic representation launched by the rise of modernity might be solved by seeing the world—and writing poetry—through the lens of a camera. For example, consider the fact that the first page of Whitman's original 1855 *Leaves of Grass* features an engraving by Samuel Hollyer based on a daguerreotype of Whitman made by Gabriel Harrison—and no name. This curious omission means that the author of the volume of poetry called *Leaves of Grass*, who identifies himself in the preface simply as "an American," is introduced to the reading public initially as a visual image. One possible explanation for this curious use of a daguerreotype-based etching instead of a name is that such mechanically produced images carried the weight of truth in antebellum America. For example, in 1840 Edgar Allan Poe gushed that "the closest scrutiny of the photogenic drawing discloses only a more absolute truth, a more perfect identity of aspect with the thing represented. The variations of shade, and the gradations of both linear and aerial perspective are those of truth itself in the supremeness of its perfection."[6] Walter Whitman was an avid fan of the daguerreotype, wrote frequently about the aesthetic magic of New York's daguerreotype galleries, and was close friends with many of the leading figures in the burgeoning daguerreotype movement, so it is fair to assume that there is a purposeful, rhetorically productive relationship between the poetic claims made in *Leaves of Grass* and the truth-bearing visual image of the nameless author who appears on its first page. Thus Whitman may have hoped that the etching would demonstrate, better than the traditionally written name ever could, the absolute truth concerning the character of the man who wrote the curious and controversial poems that followed.

Nevertheless, Whitman was clearly aware that mechanical means of representation and mass production allow a wide array of staging, costuming, and lighting effects, all of which can dramatically alter the truth of a given visual image. Indeed, as Walker's *South in Danger* illustrates, the nascent modern culture of print capitalism opened America not only to new forms of public debate but also to the dangers of mass-produced deception and mass-distributed propaganda. Hence, although Roland Barthes famously warned in 1964 that "the more technology develops the diffusion of information (and notably of images), the more it provides the means of masking the constructed meaning under the appearance of the given meaning," he was by no means the first viewer of images (or reader of texts) to realize that mass-produced means of representation enable producers to engage in any number of dubious practices.[7] In fact, it appears that Whitman was fully aware that photography's apparent veracity had its uses even while he practiced the sort of visual masking that later worried Barthes. For example, Whitman's pose on the 1855 frontispiece (figure 7) is both defiant and inviting: the open shirt collar, the hand perched on hip, the hat casually leaning to one side, the pants worn with no suspenders, and the shirt worn loosely with no vest—these are the markers of a magnificent "loafer," a proud workingman who stands free from the entangling web of commodities and stuffy propriety that Emerson feared were choking antebellum American culture. The volume's poems are heroic and grand and cosmic, literally transcendent, written alternately from the perspectives of the many, a god, and nature itself, yet here is a man, in the flesh, looking the reader saucily in the eye.[8] No matter how one reads the poems, viewers will no doubt agree that the image is rich with character, precisely the thing Emerson feared was slipping away from antebellum America.

So the etching clearly functions as a disarmingly personal statement of presence and honesty—*here is a man's man; here is an author to trust and believe in*—but at the same time, the image has obviously been constructed carefully and deliberately as an aesthetic object. Daguerreotypes could not be transferred directly to the printed page, which is why printers used lithographs made from daguerreotypes; these lithographs could be quite crisp and clear, yet they lacked the aesthetic power of daguerreotypes. In response to this reproductive quandary, printers began commissioning artists to make engraved steel plates that copied images from daguerreotypes. Such plates typically strove for as much sheer mimetic

Figure 7. The frontispiece of Walt Whitman's *Leaves of Grass,* Samuel Hollyer's engraving, from Gabriel Harrison's July 1854 daguerreotype. (Reproduced courtesy of the New York Historical Society.)

accuracy as possible, yet as Ed Folsom has observed, Whitman asked Hollyer "to engrave Harrison's daguerreotype in a way that did not *disguise* but rather *emphasized* the artificial and constructed nature" of the image.[9] Indeed, the curiously blank background and the fading out of Whitman's legs just above his knees both indicate conscious aesthetic choices regarding a strategy of representation. Hence, even though Whitman relied on the image's power to tap into the truth that daguerreotypes could offer, his pose demonstrates his own manipulation of that truth for aesthetic purposes. In this sense, then, Whitman's pose embodies the paradoxes of a culture obsessed with veracity and transparency yet simultaneously transfixed by the new representational possibilities of modern print capitalism. I accordingly use Whitman's carefully constructed visual image of himself (or his poetic persona, which I discuss later) to address the convergence of a series of important cultural fictions regarding the paradoxes of representation and the dialectics of commodification, self-making, and democracy in antebellum America.[10]

The rest of the chapter unfolds in four stages. The first section discusses the meteoric rise of the daguerreotype as a significant new form of representation, focusing on the cultural implications of the technological transformation in which images of the self changed from expensive hand-painted portraits to cheap, mechanically produced daguerreotypes. This is the story, then, of a cultural shift from elite art (portraiture) to populist commodity (daguerreotype). The second section addresses the strategic utilization of daguerreotypes as a form of evidence for two of the more important disciplinary political movements in antebellum America: phrenology and penology. This is the story, then, of the rapid expansion in the nascent middle class's ability both to consume images of itself and to produce images of select groups of "others." Indeed, as I will demonstrate, the new means of visually representing the self and others played crucial roles in the complex historical circumstances surrounding the construction of antebellum notions of class, race, nationality, and even democracy itself. The third section engages in two maneuvers. First, it offers a detailed rhetorical analysis of some of Whitman's "catalogue poems" from *Leaves of Grass,* which I read as humbly ironic examples of the paradoxes of democratic representation. Second, it discusses Whitman's position within the midcentury culture of New York's daguerreotype galleries, artists, and patrons. This is the story of Whitman's efforts to answer Emerson's questions regarding the relationships among the self, society, capitalism, and democracy by exploring both new poetic forms and visual means of self-making. The fourth section concludes the chapter by returning to the political implications of antebellum America's transformation into a modernist mass-market economy saturated with mechanically produced images of the self and the other. Ultimately, then, *Leaves of Grass* and the rise of the daguerreotype serve as opportunities for speculating on both the paradoxes of representation and the dialectics of commodification, self-making, and democracy in antebellum America.

The Emergence of the Daguerreotype

Much modernist art criticism addresses the confusions resulting from the technological reproduction of aesthetic objects. That is, what happens when the "real" or "auratic"—what Poe called "absolute truth"—encounters the mass-produced "fake"? Contemporary postmodern theories of aesthetic production argue that this neat dualism between the real and the fake, the aura of originality versus what Walter Benjamin called the "phony smell of the commodity," is grounded in romantic notions that naively privilege art as some unsoiled expression of genius.[11] This critical sophistication was not prevalent among the art-consuming public of 1855, however, particularly as concerns the daguerreotype. As Cathy Davidson notes, the daguerreotype was part of a wider cultural and aesthetic "obsession with accuracy" in which the daguerreotype held a privileged position mediating the nebulous space between science and magic.[12] For example, the 1847 edition of *Webster's Dictionary* offers a definition of the daguerreotype that incorporates lengthy scientific descriptions of its various physical and chemical properties yet concludes with the stunned explanation that "the image appears as by enchantment." Such appeals to the magical properties of the daguerreotype were dropped from the 1864 version, thus highlighting the progression of the commonly held belief that daguerreotypes are scientific presentations, not aesthetic representations, of the natural world.[13]

The notion that the daguerreotype constitutes a truthful and scientific presentation of the facts and not a deceptive aesthetic representation was influenced by antebellum debates regarding the relationship between art and class. It was widely understood at the time that painted portraiture, then a process available almost exclusively to the wealthy and powerful, was concerned less with representational accuracy than with pleasing fickle patrons. As Gustave de Beaumont mockingly observed in 1835, "in the United States there is one type of painting that flourishes—portrait painting; but its prosperity is due not to love of art but to self-love."[14] Unlike such flights of visual fancy made to please the upper crust, the daguerreotype was perceived as a practical and populist art form. As

Naomi Rosenblum observes, daguerreotypes "accorded with the taste of a society that distrusted handmade art as hinting of luxuriousness" while being "enamored of almost everything related to practical sciences."[15] In short, whereas traditional painted portraiture was viewed as a flattery-based aristocratic art of representation, the daguerreotype was widely viewed as a truth-based democratic science of presentation.

Furthermore, the daguerreotype's rise to popularity coincided with the crushing depression of the late 1830s and early 1840s, thus leading many citizens to associate daguerreotypes with the cultural practices of the hard-hit working classes. For example, on 24 February 1843 a New York City stringer wrote his editor in Washington, D.C., , saying, "I presume you would like to know who makes money in New York in these Jeremiad times? I can hear but two classes—the beggars and the takers of likenesses by daguerreotype. After begging, daguerreotyping is the next most profitable vocation. It will soon be difficult to find man or woman who has not his likeness done by the sun."[16] The tone here is playfully satirical, yet the portrayal of making daguerreotypes as a profitable vocation, not an art form, and of having them made as a popular cultural practice of the decimated working classes crawling through the depression's difficult times indicates that the daguerreotype was considered a populist form of direct presentation. Rendered by the sun, not an artist beholden to some patron's whims, daguerreotypes thus avoided the snooty assumptions about class and privilege associated with traditional painted portraitures.

To explicate the daguerreotype's cultural role, the historian must therefore pursue broad questions regarding dialectical relationships among antebellum advances in technology and changing notions of class consciousness, both of which affected the political economy of representation. For example, prior to the technological breakthroughs and economic downturns of the late 1830s and early 1840s, having one's self or family represented as an aesthetic object was the privilege solely of the elite. David Jaffe observes that the early portrait artists were expensive hired brushes whose clients were exclusively "the provincial elite. . . . Those able to afford the services of a Chandler or a Moulthroup were the magistrates and ministers: the established gentry in village society who found in such family icons the means to display their personal possessions and social status."[17] The portrait was thus a tangible sign of privilege that spoke simultaneously of an economy of abundance, national pride, and unbridled optimism for a future unfolding in waves of elegant plenitude. As James Thomas Flexner describes things in his giddy characterization of the period, *"Everyone felt that dynasties were descend-*

ing from them, and they could not bear the thought that their followers would never see their features."[18]

Consider Winthrop Chandler's 1770 portrait of the Reverend Ebeneezer Devotion (figure 8). The painting represents Devotion in all his righteous Protestant glory: stern, haughty, in the costume of his profession, surrounded by the tangible markers of both his learning and his class status. The Devotion family originally settled in Massachusetts in 1645, and Ebeneezer graduated from Yale in 1732; the minister therefore embodies the righteous legacy of New England's traditional elite. Chandler was accordingly commissioned to paint a portrait of Devotion's wife, Martha, as well. In that portrait she appears holding a leather-bound book in her left hand, with an exquisite fan in her right hand and a properly restrained bonnet on her head, her entire being framed by pillowy bunches of green silk curtains.[19]

Although such haughty yet austere elitism appears to confirm Beaumont's charge regarding the narcissistic function of portraiture, these images appear downright pedestrian compared to the work of John Singleton Copley. Originally a friend and neighbor of Boston's elite, Copley

Figure 8. Winthrop Chandler, portrait of the Reverend Ebeneezer Devotion (1770). (Reproduced courtesy of the Brookline Historical Society, Brookline, Massachusetts.)

painted stunningly lush, elegant portraits of the period's leading figures, including the siblings Nicholas and Rebecca Boylston (1767), Paul Revere (1768), Samuel Adams (1772), and Mr. and Mrs. Thomas Mifflin (1773). The painting *Boy with a Squirrel* (1765; figure 9) garnered Copley instant international fame, for its introduction to London's gallery society in 1766 secured Copley election into Britain's elite "Society of Artists." The unnamed boy in the painting is Copley's half-brother, Henry Pelham (the son of Copley's mother and her second husband, Peter Pelham), who in later years helped Copley produce portraits more quickly by "laying in backgrounds." Hence, despite the image's heady appeal to a world of shimmering satin and velvety leisure, of glassy surfaces and childish innocence, in which nature itself has been domesticated as a plaything for the New World elite, Copley and Pelham would soon be forced to labor side by side, producing images as quickly as possible to survive the uncertainties of the fickle portraiture market. Copley's painting thus exemplifies a dreamy bourgeois vision compromised by the artist's own troubled relationship to ever-changing market desires.

Copley's stunning vision of a world of abundance and leisure was

Figure 9. John Singleton Copley, *Boy with a Squirrel* (1765). (Reproduced with permission of the Museum of Fine Arts, Boston. © 2000 Museum of Fine Arts, Boston. All rights reserved.)

further compromised by his complicated political adventures. Copley lived next door to John Hancock and was friends with Paul Revere (who made some of Copley's frames), Samuel Adams, and many of Boston's leading citizens, yet by the time of the Revolution his politics had become questionable. In 1769 he married Susannah Clarke, daughter of Richard Clarke, an agent for the dreaded East India Trading Company and "one of the leading Tories of Boston," thus positioning himself squarely in the enemy camp. Perhaps to escape such political difficulties, or perhaps to improve his social standing by exhibiting and working alongside the great European masters, Copley left America for the Continent in 1774. He never returned, thus constructing the legend of Copley as America's first expatriate artist to ascend the heights of European culture.[20] As much as does any figure from the period, then, Copley as both a loathed political figure and a respected artistic star demonstrates that painted portraits were the wish-laden province of the elite, that they were closer in tone and vision to European-style monarchy than American-style republicanism, and that they were of questionable political value in a democracy supposedly based in large part on transparency.

This correlation between class privilege and portraiture began to erode in the early 1830s, when entrepreneurial folk artists such as Erastus Salisbury Field and Rufus Porter broadened the market for portraits by offering cheaper renditions of their subjects.[21] Field and Porter accomplished this feat by relying on two dramatic changes in the means of aesthetic production. First, they used stock poses that enabled them to paint a subject quickly simply by filling in the particular customer's head and hands. Second, they customized their portraits by using easily interchanged and reusable stencils of furniture, curtains, and other commodities that could be placed around their subjects, hence adding the appearance of uniqueness. These two techniques enabled Field and Porter to reduce labor time and therefore costs, hence making portraiture available to a much broader art-consuming public.[22] According to Jaffe, this early move toward mass-produced images of the self enabled Field "to portray the rural bourgeoisie's expectations of elegance at a low price," although the results were hardly unique. For example, the supposedly individualized and unique portraits of Paul Smith Palmer and Nathaniel Cook (titled *Man with a Tune Book*) (both ca. 1835–38; see figures 10 and 11) are clearly based on the same stock pose, with Field filling out the image by using stencils of various props and backgrounds meant to signify the respective subject's class standing.[23] Field's primary biographer, Mary Black, notes that such labor-saving techniques enabled Field to sell single portraits for around five dollars; on one occasion he painted eleven portraits

Figures 10 and 11. Erastus Salisbury Field, portraits of Paul Smith Palmer and Nathaniel Cook (entitled *Man with a Tune Book*) (ca. 1835–38). (Reproduced courtesy of the National Gallery of Art. Gifts of Edgar William and Bernice Chrysler Garbisch. © 2001 Board of Trustees, National Gallery of Art, Washington, D.C.)

of the Hubbard family for only twenty-nine dollars. Field's breakthrough, then, was in offering the appearance of individuality while beginning the paradoxical process of producing *homogeneously unique* images of the self. Hence the poetics of self-making enters the process of modern commodification, in turn changing forever what it means to be the subject of representation.[24]

Despite his crucial role in transforming the ways Americans consumed images of the self, Field and his painted portraiture business were eventually displaced by the faster, cheaper, more realistic art of the daguerreotype. Faced with ever-advancing technologies for producing images of and commodities based on the self, Field turned to painting imaginative renditions of biblical scenes, which remained the province of painting until the advent of motion pictures. Faced with these same modern transformations in the means of production, modes of consumption, and methods of representation, Porter experimented with a camera obscura that "could make rather good portraits in fifteen minutes" (some critics credit him as having invented this device).[25] Like Field, then, Porter sought to increase consumer accessibility to portraits by decreasing both the time required to make them and the cost required to commission them. Field and Porter thus mark an early stage of the transition from a premodern world of prohibitively expensive and time-consuming painted portraits of the traditional elite into an increasingly modern world of affordable and relatively quickly made portraits of the masses.

Both the daguerreotype and its earliest practitioners may be approached, then, as rich historical opportunities for studying changing antebellum notions of the dialectics of commodification, self-making, and democracy. Indeed, unlike any art form before it, the daguerreotype provided a truly mass-commodity-buying public the privilege of consuming themselves as agents of aesthetic consumption. The fact that this consumption was based on new technologies of reproduction that made homogeneity look unique renders the daguerreotype an even more powerful symbol of the modern cultural transformations that terrified Emerson and fascinated Whitman. Carol Schloss argues that the daguerreotype was a "potentially democratic art, giving to middle class and poor people the permanent images that had previously been an elite prerogative, for at $2 per sitting, almost anyone could afford a daguerreotype."[26] Thomas Easterly's daguerreotype *Unidentified Black Man* (1850; figure 12) provides a fine example of this democratization. As one of the frontier's boomtowns, one of the Mississippi's most important trading ports, and a town uniquely situated regarding slavery, St. Louis was home to a large and sometimes prosperous community of free blacks. The pictured

Figure 12. Thomas Easterly, *Unidentified Black Man with a Goatee,* undated daguerreotype. (Reproduced courtesy of the Missouri Historical Society, St. Louis.)

gentleman, whose clothes seem to place him among this free black working class, would have hence been among the first generation of African Americans to enjoy seeing himself as a visual image that could be shared with friends and family. To St. Louis's working-class free blacks of the antebellum period, this must certainly have felt something like what was understood as freedom.

Viewing daguerreotypy less enthusiastically, Flexner observes that traditional painted portraiture was ruined by "the disastrous intervention of photography."[27] The interesting historical question here, however, is not about the comparative fate of dueling aesthetic genres but about the way transformations within these genres—painting and daguerreotypy alike—indicate deeper cultural transformations in means of production, modes of consumption, and methods of representation. For example, the daguerreotype dramatically altered the economics of representation. Early "picture factories" organized the daguerreotyping process along strict divisions of tasks among teams of laborers, each fulfilling specific production roles (unlike the slower "artistry" of a single daguerreotypist). Such teams of laborer-artists produced 3¼" × 2¾"sixth-plates for fifty cents, and "miniatures," measuring roughly 1¾" × 1¼ ", for a quarter. Beaumont Newhall notes that the more highly streamlined daguerreotype studios could turn out as many as 1,000 images a day, an unprecedented capacity to mass-produce images of the self.[28] Trachtenberg even employs a phrase usually reserved for much later historical developments in Taylorized production when he refers to these portraiture studios as "mini-assembly lines."[29] This phrase may be somewhat hyperbolic in strict economic and historical terms, yet it demonstrates that the daguerreotype launched a new phase in the commodification and industrialization of image making.

Indeed, the combination of accelerating production rates and lowering prices clearly enabled a new class of consumers to enter the marketplace of images—hence Easterly's 1850 daguerreotype of his fellow St. Louisian. Trachtenberg reports that at the national level, daguerreotype production grew from 2 million in 1853 to over 3 million in 1860. Although these numbers clearly indicate a thriving industry—Newhall reports that there were eighty-six daguerreotype galleries in New York City alone in 1853—it is not immediately clear how this amounts to democratization.[30] Indeed, the low cost of daguerreotypes clearly enabled a new class of Americans to participate in the process of consuming themselves as images, but this appears to indicate an expansion in the realm of consumerism, not democracy.

Finding oneself confused by the subtle dialectics of commodification, self-making, and democracy illustrates a fundamental paradox of antebellum America. That is, the daguerreotype's spectacular success suggests that by midcentury notions of individuality were increasingly influenced by the same homogenizing, technological means of production and distribution that fueled the emerging modernist, capitalist marketplace. Hence, while the daguerreotype clearly enabled an expansion of the commodity-buying public, it also marks two crucial historical transformations in the poetics of self-making. First, it indicates that commodity consumption was becoming one of the key activities by which Americans recognized themselves as both citizens of the state and members of a particular class. Second, it demonstrates that the consuming individual increasingly found him- or herself represented in mass-produced images, symbols, and commodities that appear to call the very notion of individuality into question. For example, images made at any of John Plumbe's fourteen galleries (in New York, Boston, Louisville, Philadelphia, Baltimore, St. Louis, and Cincinnati, among others) were stamped with the imposing corporate moniker "PLUMBE," regardless of which worker made the image.[31] Hence the individual in the image, while enjoying the historically and aesthetically unprecedented privilege of consuming a generally accurate image of him- or herself, was simultaneously entwined within a streamlined, proto-Taylorized production process driven by principles of capitalism, not democracy.

Exploring the paradoxical contradictions of this dialectic, in which new productive technologies fostered an increased ability to envision oneself as a self-consuming autonomous individual while simultaneously producing cultural homogeneity and versions of citizenship dependent on consumption, was not one of the burning issues for midcentury daguerreotype-consuming Americans. Instead, as Poe's stunned exclamation indicates, Americans were primarily fascinated by the daguerreotype's uncanny accuracy. For example, in 1841, just two years after François Gouraud (Louis-Jacques-Mandé Daguerre's agent) introduced the daguerreotype to America, Anson Clarke wrote that daguerreotype portraits were "produced by the unerring operations of physical law" and that "human judgment and skill have no connection with the perfection of the picture," which thus creates "the exact image of the object."[32] The daguerreotype therefore enjoyed a privileged place in antebellum American culture, for it was coveted as both a commodity that signified a certain class status (working and middle class, but not "uppity") and a scientifically true presentation of the chosen subject. This paradoxical duality of a technologically produced commodity that is nonetheless perceived as the truth incarnate perhaps explains the meteoric rise of the daguerreotype as a commodity fad, for it allowed masses of citizens to engage in the rapidly expanding capitalist economy of commodity and image exchange without feeling like they had sacrificed either their individuality or their morality to the temptations of modernity.

More specifically, many citizens perceived the ripping capitalist bedlam of antebellum America as a hellish bazaar of sinners, shysters, crooks, and hoodlums. This is, after all, the circuslike world of P. T. Barnum; of the double-speaking riverboat freeloaders who sneak through the incomprehensible pages of Melville's *Confidence Man;* of the gambling dens, drinking houses, and backroom prostitution rings made famous in George Foster's urban exposés; of the courtroom double crosses and dirty dealings that litter the outrageous pages of Joseph Baldwin's *Flush Times;* and of the deceptions, cheats, scams, and scandals of George Lippard's *Quaker City.*[33] The literature of the period is full of such tales of deceit, subterfuge, and chicanery, all chronicling America's boggled transition into the world of modern capitalism. Indeed, as the previous three chapters have detailed, the transition from a predominantly rural barter economy into the rough-and-tumble world of industrializing urban capitalist marketplaces left many Americans reeling from the explosion of dubious activities that brought a quick buck at the expense of some country bumpkin. As my earlier quotations from Emerson and Whitman indicate, the anxieties following these cultural transformations were expressed in large part as concerns regarding the honesty and transparency of character.

One response to this crisis in democratic representation was to celebrate the inescapable constructedness of the self and its various appearances. According to Karen Halttunen, "by the 1850s . . . the American middle classes . . . were learning to place confidence not in the sincere countenance but in the social mask; to trust not in simple dress but in elaborate disguises." That is, Americans had shifted from "a sentimental demand for transparency and sincerity to a worldly Victorian demand for a skillful social performance."[34] The daguerreotype offered an alternative response rooted in the desire for transparency, certainty, and at least the appearance of honesty. Indeed, antebellum America's romance with the "absolute truth" of daguerreotypes needs to be understood as part of a larger cultural response to modern capitalism's tendency to unsettle values and norms. Trachtenberg thus claims that "the quasimagical mirror of the daguerreotype miniature seemed to offer an amulet against the menace hidden within the Broadway spectacle, the threat of counterfeit transactions at the market center of the Empire City."[35] This reading presents the daguerreotype's truth value as a visual amulet against modernity's anxieties and uncertainties.

In addition to fueling a major consumer fad—as witnessed in the simultaneous market enlargement and cultural appeasement of a fraud-conscious yet image-consuming public—the remarkable popularity of daguerreotypes enabled a series of what economists refer to as "backward" and "forward linkages," both of which contributed to the dramatic expansion of America's productive technologies and international market power.[36] A backward linkage occurs when a commodity prompts a transformation in the production techniques of the materials necessary for its completion. For example, as early as 1839 the J. M. L. & W. H. Scovill Company of Waterbury, Connecticut, anticipating a boom market, began producing the silver-plated copper needed for daguerreotypes. At the time French plates sold for $2 each, yet within six years the Scovill Company was selling comparable American-made plates for $3.50 per dozen, undercutting the French and contributing to the rise of American industry as an international force.[37] A forward linkage occurs when a commodity prompts a revolution in the production and marketing techniques of additional commodities that enhance or piggyback on its initial popularity. For example, Samuel Peck and Halver Halverston, in searching for new means of producing daguerreotype "union cases" that would last longer than simple wood cases, developed a shellac-and-wood compress system that led them to become "one of the first plastic-molding plants in the U.S."[38] The backward and forward linkages entwined with the economics of the daguerreotype thus created new production and marketing possibilities for aligned industries, hence contributing to the period's radically expansive and experimental energy.

Along with enabling these modern economic transformations, the daguerreotype also became widely popular as a means of engaging in stridently nationalist debates. For example, at London's 1851 Crystal Palace Exhibition, as part of the Exhibition of the Works of Industry (not art but industry), Americans John Wipple, Martin Lawrence, and Mathew Brady won three of the five available daguerreotype awards. Horace Greeley then used the occasion to boast that the booming U.S. daguerreotype industry was further evidence that America had surpassed its European rivals in scientific progress, commercial energy, and aesthetic creativity.[39] Concerning the complex relationships among economics, technology, daguerreotypes, and nationalism, it is worth noting that the daguerreotype was sufficiently popular that the first U.S. journals dedicated to photography, Samuel Dwight Humphrey's *Daguerreian Journal* (launched 15 November 1850) and Henry Hunt Snelling's *Photographic Art-Journal* (launched January 1851), attracted widespread support. Hence the daguerreotype was also enmeshed in the midcentury rush toward new means of print capitalism and, in this case, in the nascent attempts to construct a sense of a national art culture complete with its own journals.[40]

The most famous of the early daguerreotypists, Mathew Brady, combined the consumerist, nationalist, artistic, and political possibilities of the daguerreotype in a dizzying outpouring of both visual images and written texts. In 1844 Brady opened the first of what was to be a long string of daguerreotype galleries in New York City. Realizing that America's strident love of its leaders held startling marketing possibilities, Brady opened a branch office in Washington, D.C., in 1850.[41] One result of Brady's work in Washington, his *Gallery of Illustrious Americans* (1850), demonstrates the merging of consumerism, nationalist pride in America's daguerreotyping skills, and the pressing political crises of the antebellum period. For example, in his editor's "salutation" to the reader/consumer, Charles Edwards states that "there is nothing sectional in the scope of this work, it will be comprehensive in its spirit; and it is hoped that it may mark an era in the progress of American Art, and bind the Union still more firmly together."[42] Published amid scalding debates regarding the fate of slavery, westward expansion, and what many observers thought to be the ultimate fate of the Union, if not democracy itself, Edwards's promise that the *Gallery of Illustrious Americans* would foster national unity clearly states Brady's hope that daguerreotypes could play explicitly political roles.

Indeed, Brady's images of Zachary Taylor and Lewis Cass are representative of the new genre of daguerreotype as politician's tool (figures 13 and 14). Notice that these austere leaders are not surrounded by commodities, as are Palmer and Cook in their portraits by Field. These statesmen are not simply citizens of good taste and upstanding class but rather men of transcendent abilities who, unlike Whitman with his inviting gaze, do not need to make eye contact with the viewer. Such heroic images clearly intend to convey to the image-consuming public a vision of great individuals, leaders who stand above the messy fray of politics, heroes capable of guiding the nation through its difficult times with policies "comprehensive in spirit." Even while engaging in such explicitly political gestures, Brady was ever the salesman. For example, in a fine play of words, the cover of his *Gallery* announces itself as the "Gift Book of the Republic," hence positing itself as a gift of healing made to a nation torn by brutal political crises. The *Gallery* also functions as a gift of unquestionable commodity value that, as an elegant display book of uncommon size and beauty, speaks to cultural sophistication, modern urbanity, and national pride. Despite such rhetorical sophistication, both linguistically and visually, Brady's *Gallery* apparently failed as a commodity: although the book promises to deliver twenty-four images, it contains but twelve; presumably the other twelve images were scheduled for inclusion in a second volume that was never completed.

While producing such patriotic prose, stunning imagery, and consumerist candy, Brady was also quickly climbing the social ladder. In fact, one of his later New York galleries sat across the street from P. T. Barnum's American Museum of Oddities and next to the elegant Astor House, and Brady himself lived in the Astor House Hotel. To summarize my opening arguments regarding the historical importance of daguerreotypes and the dialectics of commodification, self-making, and democracy in antebellum American, then, consider the following four interrelated observations. First, Brady's *Gallery of Illustrious Americans* signals a forthcoming society of deception in which politicians achieve status not as legislators and statesmen but as subjects of pretentious publicity shots. Second, while Brady was pushing to turn the daguerreotype into a tool of political showmanship, across the street Barnum was mastering the art of hoodwinking a public spending its leisure time by consuming

Figures 13 and 14. Mathew Brady, daguerreotypes of Zachary Taylor and Lewis Cass, from *Gallery of Illustrious Americans.* (Reproduced courtesy of the New York Historical Society.)

mass-produced spectacles. Third, as Brady and Barnum expanded the possibilities of visual representation and commodity consumption, the Astor House loomed next door as a great monument to midcentury conspicuous consumption and the power of the new urban bourgeoisie. Fourth, these three transformations each encouraged the nascent urban working and middle classes to learn to express themselves by consuming commodities. Rather than indicate an enhanced democracy, these four observations suggest modern capitalism's stunning ability to absorb both technological and aesthetic breakthroughs as the high-energy fuel for the next frantic stage of commodification.[43]

The Daguerreotype and Disciplinary Politics at Midcentury

The daguerreotype thus played a key role in transforming antebellum notions of representation and capitalist practices of production and commodity exchange. As Davidson describes it, the daguerreotype was the most important factor in the gradual "technologizing of sight and self." Daguerreotypes were such ubiquitous signs of both modernity and capitalism that Oliver Wendell Holmes described them as being "like greenbacks."[44] Given that the daguerreotype was among the first modern objects of accelerated consumer fascination and therefore (much like greenbacks) an important breakthrough in both the production of commodities and the accelerated distribution of mass-circulating images, it comes as no surprise that the daguerreotype's supposed veracity was employed in antebellum attempts to discipline sexuality and gender roles, to prove the genetic bases of glaring social inequalities, and to legitimize slavery. As Davidson suggests, then, the daguerreotype was ideally positioned to serve as visual technological evidence for supporting political claims about social others.

As previous chapters show with respect to various contexts, the 1840s and 1850s saw intense social dislocation in which the new-found class fluidity and geographic mobility of the emerging modern capitalist empire fostered a frantic scramble for and rearrangement of prestige, wealth, and power. These chapters demonstrate that this cultural and political repositioning took place largely through the rhetorical production of categories of race, nationality, class, gender, morality, and criminality. Whereas forward-looking Americans such as Northup, Child, Whitman, and Brady understood these transformations as wonderful opportunities for remaking the world, tradition-bound Americans such as Fitzhugh, George Barrell Cheever, and Abel Upshur believed that the loosening of traditional social norms called for a concerted effort to discipline culture. David Rothman accordingly positions the historically unprecedented expansion of America's prisons and asylums in late-Jacksonian America as part of a larger cultural backlash against the social crises produced by this newfound social instability. This reading places the frantic construction of the category of the criminal "other" within a desperate attempt by traditional elites, conservative elements of the nascent bourgeoisie, and segments of the disorder-fearing middle classes to "establish a new system for stabilizing the community."[45] As I will show, the daguerreotype played a significant role in this stabilizing process.

Indeed, given this framework of profound social upheaval, and recognizing that such upheaval called forth a variety of disciplinary responses, it is not surprising that the dramatically real and truthful quality of daguerreotypes was attractive to citizens who sought to provide visual evidence supporting attempts to reconstruct cultural boundaries of taste, political lines of inclusion and exclusion, and even concrete walls behind which to discipline a new generation of undesirables. The "absolute truth" of daguerreotypes thus tempted both traditional conservatives and liberal reformers to offer visual images as evidence of correlations between class, sociability, and stereotypical physical characteristics. Alan Sekula accordingly argues that the disciplinary possibilities of the daguerreotype's truth value—what he calls early photography's "new juridical realism"—enabled both traditional cultural conservatives and liberal reformers to merge the premises of phrenology and penology, using photography "to establish and delimit the terrain of the *other,* to define both the *generalized look*—the typology—and the *contingent instance* of deviance and social pathology."[46] In rhetorical terms, Sekula's point is that daguerreotypes enabled their manipulators to pursue synecdochic arguments in which any "contingent instance of deviance" (part) could be converted into a representative example of "the generalized look" (whole) of otherness. Such arguments are viciously circular, for preformed assumptions drive the search for local examples (parts) that illustrate larger cultural prejudices (wholes), which for validation need to point back to supporting examples (parts), and so on. Daguerreotypes were useful for visualizing such arguments because Americans believed that they were neither staged nor plotted but factual and transparent.

For examples of the synecdochic use of daguerreotypes as visual evidence for converting specific examples into a generalized look of otherness, consider the fact that Mathew Brady made daguerreotypes of prisoners at Blackwell's Island in 1846 for illustrations in Marmaduke Sampson's *Rationale of Crime and Its Appropriate Treatment; Being a Treatise on Criminal Jurisprudence Considered in Relation to Cerebral Organization.* Sampson originally published *Rationale of Crime* in England in 1840. Eliza Farnham, a young reformer appointed matron of New York's Mount Pleasant State Prison (the women's prison at Sing Sing) in 1844, decided that Sampson's treatise was so important that she prepared a second edition for publication in America in 1846. To spice up the second edition, Farnham commissioned Mathew Brady to take a series of daguerreotypes of prisoners at New York City's infamous Blackwell's Island Jail, with each prisoner serving as a visual archetype of some aspect of criminality.[47] The noted phrenologist Lorenzo Fowler pointed out representative characters, whom Brady photographed; the resulting images were then rendered in the text as drawings by Edward Serrell, an artist who worked in the chaplain's office at Sing Sing. Serrell's sketch of "S.R." (figure 15) thus demonstrates the convergence of daguerreotypes, phrenology, and penology in a reformist manifesto that, while calling for the progressive reform of America's prisons, argues primarily that those who "stagger in the wild intoxication of crime" need "by general instruction and example, a knowledge of the Divine Laws" (65–

S. R.

Figure 15. Edward Serrell, sketch of "S.R." (1846), based on Mathew Brady's daguerreotype, in Marmaduke Sampson's *Rationale of Crime and Its Appropriate Treatment.* (Reproduced courtesy of the Department of Special Collections, Stanford University Libraries.)

66). Even in the face of such appeals to traditional notions of the divine, Brady's daguerreotypes and Serrell's drawings function as tools in the visual and phrenological construction of new notions of class, race, and criminality.[48]

Working along these same phrenological and penological lines, Sir Francis Galton used photographs supplied by the United Kingdom's chief inspector of prisons to develop a "system of composite photography" by which to study "whether different facial features were associated with different types of crime."[49] A similar project was undertaken in America, where noted proslavery eugenicist Louis Agassiz commissioned South Carolina daguerreotypist J. T. Zealey to produce over two thousand daguerreotypes of slaves for his eugenics experiments regarding the relationship between "facial types" and "mental abilities"; the set includes Zealey's 1850 portrait of "Renty" (figure 16). In a culture predisposed to judge innate abilities and the promise of democratic citizenship according to the color of someone's skin or facial structure, daguerreotypes such as this one proved useful for corroborating preexisting prejudices. What

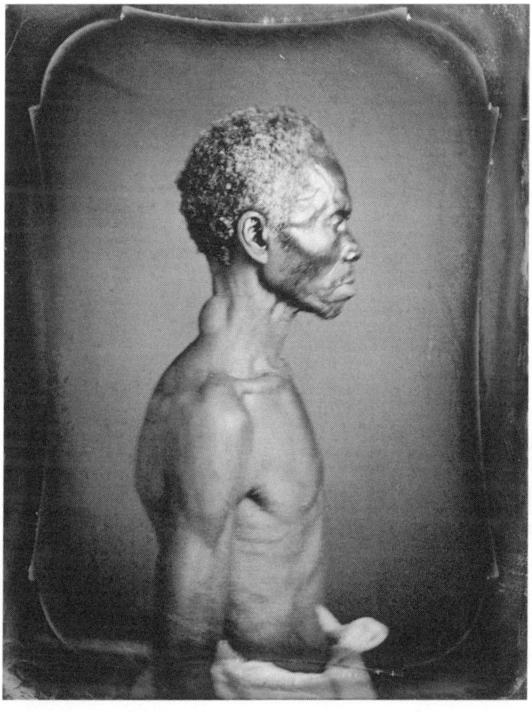

Figure 16. J. T. Zealey, daguerreotype of "Renty" (1850). (Reproduced courtesy of the Peabody Museum of Archaeology and Ethnology, Harvard University.)

better proof of someone's absolute otherness than the graphic realism of the daguerreotype?

In addition to facilitating proslavery cultural fictions, Zealey's daguerreotypes demonstrate a familiar midcentury form of racially tinged voyeurism. In the North, where daguerreotypes of blacks were extremely rare, Zealey's images of Drana and Delia, slave women who appear in a variety of nude poses, brought essentially strange, foreign, even invisible images to light while simultaneously shrouding the complex politics of desire within the rhetoric of "science." Indeed, even while revealing the naked bodies of slaves, Zealey's images look loosely scientific because they depict expressionless subjects seen from multiple perspectives. For example, Zealey includes frontal and side shots of Drana and Delia, both nude from the waste up; Alfred appears in full-length back and side nudes; Jem appears in full-length frontal and back nudes.[50] These chilling, clinical images, which clearly foreshadow mug shots from the late twentieth century, demonstrate again the interweaving of daguerreotypes with sexual desire, phrenology, penology, and racial assumptions. As Robyn Weigman observes: "The visible must be understood as giving way to the authority of the invisible recesses of the body, to organs and functions. The full force of this production of racial discourse was nonetheless contingent on the status of an observer, whose relation to the object under investigation was mediated and deepened by newly developed technologies for rendering the invisible visible."[51] Zealey's daguerreotypes, commissioned by one of the period's leading scientists, illustrate Weigman's thesis precisely.

It is important to remember that these examples demonstrate not only attempts to use daguerreotypes as evidence for larger social movements but also the confusing complexity of these social movements. On the one hand, Sampson's *Rationale of Crime* ranks among the period's major phrenological and penological documents; its heavy-handed merging of Christian dogma and supposedly scientific reasoning reflects more a priori assumptions than carefully researched evidence. On the other hand, the text is one of the period's most powerful indictments of both the death penalty and the horrific conditions of many of America's early prisons, jails, asylums, and workhouses. In fact, Sampson's arguments were so progressive at the time that in her preface to the American edition, Farnham warns readers that they may find Sampson's reasoning "wholly subversive of many deeply-rooted ideas" (ix). Likewise, England's *Phrenological Journal* noted: "We welcome Mr. Sampson as a most valuable accession to the band of phrenological advocates of sound criminal jurisprudence."[52] Thus, while contributing to the period's attempts to define and characterize the criminal other, Sampson's text simultaneously constitutes a milestone in early attempts to humanize the treatment of criminals. Aggasiz's situation was equally complicated, for though his study of race and intelligence via Zealey's daguerreotypes provides a chilling example of politically conditioned assumptions driving the scientific process, much of his research was undertaken as part of his long-standing battle with strident Christian dogmatism regarding creationism. Indeed, while using daguerreotypes as visual evidence to support racist stereotypes, Aggasiz was simultaneously contributing to the slow advance of secular humanism—in this case attacking religious mythology by forwarding new theories of human evolution.[53] I offer these complicating caveats by way of demonstrating that Sampson's and Aggasiz's use of daguerreotypes as visual evidence in their ostensibly reform-minded texts—much like the larger social movements they represent—cannot be explained easily by reference to contemporary political sensibilities.

The supposed truth of the daguerreotype was therefore employed to confirm a wide variety of social agendas, for in a world where intelligence, grace, and the promise of civil participation in the democracy were linked to skin color, skull shape, and facial characteristics, what better proof of someone's otherness could there be than a daguerreotype graphically portraying the other's ineluctable difference? The question-begging structure of this proof is of little consequence for the simple fact that daguerreotypes were perceived not as constructed, aesthetic images but as unmediated, scientific evidence of the truth itself. For example, James Ryder argued that the "all-seeing eye" of his camera could automatically determine that "a rogue was a rogue" and that "the honest man, when found, was recognized and properly estimated." In terms of such confident mid-century claims to judge character on the basis on visual observation, it is noteworthy that the entrepreneurial Fowler brothers, Lorenzo and Orson (the founders of the *American Phrenological Journal*), were so convinced of the veracity of daguerreotypes that they occasionally performed astounding phrenological character readings based on them.[54] The modern nexus of daguerreotypes, phrenology, and penology thus played a central role in both defining and popularizing public images of race, class, intelligence, and criminality.

This is not the place for an extended analysis of the complex politics of the early phrenology and penology movements; my point here is that each of these examples (the daguerreotype as consumer fad, as a technology of nationalism, as phrenologist's evidence, as politician's aid, and as penologist's tool) points toward a public that grants the daguerreotype a remarkable quality of representational legitimacy. Indeed, in each of the instances I have cited thus far, one finds antebellum Americans seeing the daguerreotype, as Poe claimed, as "the truth itself." The proponents of the previously cited disciplinary and reform movements were not alone in attempting to deploy this veracity to support their desired political objectives, however, for Whitman too sought to enhance his vision of the ideal nation via the representational power of the daguerreotype.

Whitman and the Rhetorical Politics of Democracy

Whitman's decision to include an etching from a daguerreotype on the opening page of the 1855 version of *Leaves of Grass,* but to omit his name there, shows the extent to which he recognized the daguerreotype's persuasive power. Given the profound hyperbole of the book's poetic claims, I suggest that Whitman used the famous image instead of his written name to certify the otherwise questionable authenticity of the author. Ed Folsom has proposed a similar thesis; he writes that Whitman's visual image "stood as a kind of surrogate identification, as if the authorizing presence of the volume was more effectively represented by an illustration than by the more conventional linguistic sign."[55] My purpose in this section is threefold, with each step expanding the thesis first advanced by Folsom into a more culturally wide-ranging and historically concerned argument regarding the dialectics of commodification, self-making, and democracy. First, by reading Whitman's 1855 preface and his "catalogue poems," I demonstrate the strong affinities between consistent rhetorical structures in Whitman's written work and the aesthetic logic of daguerreotypes. Second, by situating Whitman within New York City's emergent daguerreotype community, I demonstrate the important relationships among Whitman's poems and images and the period's dominant notions of both aesthetic and properly political representation. Third, by examining the early reviews of *Leaves of Grass,* I address the metonymic conflation that led Whitman's first critics to identify Walter Whitman the author, Walt Whitman the visual poet, and the poem's cosmic (and cosmically confusing) persona as the same "essential being."

It is important to note that Whitman was drawing on a long-standing tradition of publishing works anonymously. After all, many of Ben Franklin's essays were published pseudonymously, the Constitution bears no mark of authorial credit, and Thomas Jefferson's *Notes on the State of Virginia* appeared initially with no name. In fact, Cathy Davidson reports that "of approximately sixty-five novelists who published [in the United States] before 1820, less than a third were named on the title pages of their books." Among antebellum works, David Christy's wildly popular proslavery manifesto *Cotton Is King* was, like *Leaves of Grass*, initially credited as the work of "an American."[56] What makes *Leaves of Grass* such a noteworthy case, then, is not the fact that Whitman chose to omit his name from the title page and cover but rather that he chose to substitute an anonymous image for it. Furthermore, the attempt to condense the unmanageable poetic complexities and political contradictions of the written text into the singular physicality of the visible self presented in the daguerreotype repeats one of the central rhetorical paradoxes of Whitman's poetry, for he claims repeatedly to embody the spirit of presence, immediacy, and physicality while simultaneously claiming an oceanic and all-knowing position that illustrates absence, mediation, and totality.[57] Understanding Whitman's use of the frontispiece image thus requires understanding what the ensuing poems claim about representation.

Whitman claims to produce words that, like daguerreotypes, are transparent, truthful, and unimpeachably realistic. For example, consider his blustery preface, where he promises: "What I tell I tell precisely for what it is. . . . What I experience or portray shall go from my composition without a shred of my composition. You shall stand by my side and look in the mirror with me."[58] Whitman thus asks readers to approach this work as if it were a daguerreotype, a noncompositional composition, a verbal snapshot of the truth itself. Along these same lines, Whitman claims that his poetry will "enter the essences of real things" (iv), that it will "go directly to the creation" (vi), and that it will "reject none" but "permit all" (xii). Such grand claims for an all-inclusive poetics that is unmediated and noncompositional, that is as precisely accurate as a mirror, that drives through the false appearance world toward an all-encompassing democracy of essences, clearly indicate Whitman's desire to write poetry that carries the supposed absolute truth of a daguerreotype.

At a deeper structural level, these claims indicate a poetics that eschews the argumentative practices of epistemology. Whitman promises to write poetry that is prepolitical, that is so obviously and genuinely real as to transcend the messy problematics of explanation, argumentation, and verification. Indeed, when he states that he will "possess the Origin" (14) and "see the huge first nothing" (50), Whitman is assuming that his daguerreotype-like sense of presence, immediacy, and physicality will enable him to crash through the feckless stockpiling of commodities and the ossification of perception and back into the natural world, where things simply are what they are. The antiepistemological imperative of these claims, which abandon justifying arguments and explanations for blasts of organic, self-evident truth, has been characterized sympathetically by Roy Harvey Pearce, who notes that "Whitman demanded of his readers not just the willing suspension of disbelief, but belief itself."[59] Apparently, then, one of Whitman's fundamental impulses was to write poetry that, much like the accepted truth of daguerreotypes, is so real, so unavoidably believable, that it embodies the spirit of presence, immediacy, and physicality. Whitman's representational strategy thus relies on a subtle form of metonymy, in which the complex spaces between cause and effect and between self and society are collapsed into a tangible sign. As I discussed in chapter 1, Kenneth Burke conceives of metonymy as a form of reduction that strives "to convey some incorporeal or intangible state in terms of the corporeal or tangible."[60] Clearly Whitman's poetics of presence strives for this sense of the material. Additionally, speaking in terms of scale manipulation, Whitman promises to capture the infinite sweep of life itself, of "the huge first nothing," and to share it with us in his poetry; this too amounts to a classic example of what Burke refers to as the metonymic function of conflating incomprehensible forces with tangible signs. Whitman's representational strategy—the pursuit of a sense of presence, immediacy, and physicality—therefore relies largely on the trope of metonymy. Again, the frontispiece image embodies this metonymic process.

Nonetheless, Whitman appears to be driven just as powerfully by the desire to write poetry that is oceanic, cosmic, and all-knowing. Thus, while claiming that his poems embody the absolute immediacy and physicality of the moment, he strives to hover above the world as a godlike figure of total consciousness. For example, in the preface he argues that "the greatest poet hardly knows pettiness or triviality. If he breathes into any thing that was before thought small it dilates with the grandeur and life of the universe. He is a seer" (v). Or consider Whitman's claims that "the American bards . . . shall be kosmos" (vii) and that "an individual is as superb as a nation when he has the qualities which make a nation superb" (xii). Hence, Whitman wants not only to inhabit the ontological bedrock certainty of the material present but also to write a universalizing, overarching poetry able to gather up the fragments of the moment into a grand cathartic totality that indicates the poet's absence from any specific here and now, his godlike mediation of life's complexities, and his cosmic ability to grasp the secret meaning unifying the world's infinitely small physical particulars. The representational strategy here amounts to a utopian form of synecdoche, for Whitman promises to reveal the brilliant master plan that unites all individuals (parts) in a kind and generous nation (whole).

The original version of *Leaves of Grass* is thus structured by two competing rhetorical strategies: a particularizing, metonymic rhetoric of presence, immediacy, and physicality and a universalizing, synecdochic rhetoric of absence, mediation, and totality. The play of these competing rhetorical strategies appears most clearly in Whitman's "catalogue poems," where he strings together remarkably long, disjointed lists in which citizens are meant to stand both as moments of radical individuality and as representatives of the cosmic totality that is America.[61] For example, in what is perhaps Whitman's most famous catalog, from what later became section 15 of the poem now called "Song of Myself," he rambles off on a dizzying list of more than seventy-five characters.[62] Here are the first few lines:

> The pure contralto sings in the organloft,
> The carpenter dresses his plank . . . the tongue of his foreplane
> whistles its wild ascending lisp,
> The married and unmarried children ride home to their thanksgiving
> dinner,
> The pilot seizes the king-pin, he heaves down with a strong arm,
> The mate stands braced in the whaleboat, lance and harpoon are
> ready. (21)

Despite the fact that there is no apparent narrative or rhetorical thread linking these characters, the passage ends: "And such one and all tend inward to me, and I tend outwards to them, / And such as it is to be of these more or less I am" (23). Whitman thus claims that each particular part of life stands in as a promise of the whole, yet despite this self-proclaimed synecdochic intention, these passages provoke above all else the sense that each line amounts to a snapshot of life, that each character, much like the supposedly self-evident and truthful daguerreotype, is so immediate and familiar that it reveals its full and rich humanity in quick one-line descriptions. At the same time, however, the appeal to the larger sense of a finely ordered "one and all" suggests that the catalog is meant to indicate the cosmic totality of America. Hence, amid the metonymic particularity of these apparently unrelated characters, Whitman celebrates his power to synecdochically reunite the particulars in a magnificent whole. This is not the place to engage in a lengthy discussion of the various critical debates regarding the literary and rhetorical merits of such catalog poetry.[63] Rather, I mention Whitman's duality of purpose simply to indicate that it amounts to a poetic version of Brady's famous daguerreotype galleries. Indeed, the long catalogs feel much like a poetic and more democratic (or at least less elitist) gallery of "illustrious Americans" in which Whitman, having appointed himself the nation's bard, assumes he can plumb the underlying structure and meaning of the otherwise secret connections among all the images, citizens, and moments of time.

The gigantic heroism (and delusion) of pursuing such synecdochic unification via his metonymic catalogs has struck readers and critics alike as both the utopian beauty and self-canceling contradiction that make Whitman's early work fascinating, maddening, and at times downright funny. For example, recall D. H. Lawrence's wickedly sarcastic review of these poems, in which he laments "all those lists of things boiled in one pudding-cloth! . . And what then? It's all empty, just an empty Allness." Nancy Ruttenburg argues that what Lawrence called "empty Allness" is produced through a "miracle of simultaneity," a "balletic equilibrium of power and possibility" amounting to a curiously antidemocratic conflation of impulses that, ultimately, "would supercede the oppositional encounter crucial to the production of democratic personality." Whitman's award-winning biographer David Reynolds puts it more simply by noting Whitman's paradoxical pursuit of a poetic vision that is both "universal and microscopic."[64] Whitman may or may not have been aware that his synecdochic/universal and metonymic/microscopic impulses were leading him in such apparently contradictory directions, yet he clearly realized that his poetry would strike the reading public of 1855 as nothing less than strange. In fact, he penned at least three anonymous reviews of his work in which he offers tips on ways to approach both the text and its author.[65] Since Whitman realized that his poetry would cause the reading public difficulty, particularly regarding his claims to achieve what are obviously contradictory representational goals, his use of both the frontispiece etching and the overall representational strategy of appealing to a daguerreotype-like sense of immediate realness can be understood as a rhetorical attempt to ameliorate the conflict between the metonymic trope of presence and immediacy and the synecdochic trope of mediation and cosmic totality.

Again, readers and viewers in the 1850s were unlikely to ask whether the daguerreotype represents the poet/author or the persona of the poems, instead conflating the subject of the daguerreotype, the author of the text, and the persona of the poems into one being. In short, Whitman's contemporaries were likely to accept his carefully constructed visual representation as an immediate, truthful presentation revealing the character of both the poet and the poems' persona. Accepting this metonymic conflation of the poet, the poems' persona, and the character portrayed in the frontispiece in turn prepares the reader/viewer for a more sympathetic reading of the text's obviously outrageous claims. In fact, Graham Clarke contends that throughout his poetic career Whitman employed daguerreotypes to "establish a portrait of precisely the poetic self Whitman wanted and, as pictures, construct, rather than reflect, an imagined ideal."[66] It may be difficult to believe that Whitman actually planned this out, that he somehow consciously manipulated the daguerreotype to fulfill this rhetorical function. Before proceeding then, I delve into Whitman's familiarity with the ostensibly absolute truth of the daguerreotype.

Whitman's writings for the *Brooklyn Daily Eagle* demonstrate that he was intimately familiar with the representational power of daguerreotypes as early as 1846, for on 2 July of that year he published an enthusiastic account of a visit to Plumbe's New York gallery. Whitman exclaims: "What a spectacle! In whatever direction you turn your peering gaze, you see naught but human faces! There they stretch, from floor to ceiling—hundreds of them. Ah! what tales might those pictures tell if their mute lips had the power of speech! How romance then, would be infinitely outdone by *fact.*"[67] Interestingly, beyond conveying a sense of frenzied enthusiasm through a barrage of exclamation points, this passage grants daguerreotypes the power of conveying the truth itself. Indeed, Whitman clearly juxtaposes the facts that spring forth from daguerreotypes against the bogus romanticism traditionally found in portraiture. He then celebrates the daguerreotype's uniquely democratic energy by listing an honor roll of Americans whose portraits appear in Plumbe's gallery, including: John Quincy Adams, James K. and Mrs. Polk, Senator Benton, the radical New York politicians Mike Walsh and Robert Owen, and the well-known newspaper editor and activist Horace Greeley. Much like Brady in his *Gallery of Illustrious Americans,* Whitman apparently provides this who's who of respected citizens to convey a sense of the daguerreotype's distinctly nationalist, American qualities and to express his own wonder at the beauty and vibrancy of American democracy.

Whitman then links the nationalist potential of daguerreotypes and the wonder of democracy with the culture's overwhelming obsession with truthfulness, for he assures his readers that the portraits are so "natural" that in them, "time, space, both are annihilated, and we identify the semblance with the reality" (117). Thus Whitman found in Plumbe's gallery a collection of daguerreotype portraits that fulfilled the visual equivalent of the sweeping representational burden he would later assign to *Leaves of Grass.* Indeed, in much the same manner as Whitman would later want readers to approach the freestanding characters of his "catalogue poems," he reads Plumbe's daguerreotypes—"stretching from floor to ceiling, hundreds of them" piled one atop another, discrete images that require no narrative implicature—as unfettered, direct, real representations of heroic citizens. In a classic demonstration of synecdoche, Whitman argues that these daguerreotypes, like his cataloged characters, stand individually as unique parts that simultaneously embody the holistic totality of America's democratic energy.[68]

Of course, the fact that Plumbe, like many Americans of his generation, was unable to maintain his class standing, commercial solvency, or artistic vision within the turbulent marketplace of pre–Civil War America makes it painfully ironic that Whitman's visit to Plumbe's gallery prompted such an outpouring of democratic idealism. Ed Folsom writes: "In 1847 Plumbe, whose attention had been more on railroad schemes than on his studio, sold his New York Gallery and soon went bankrupt; in 1849 he followed the gold rush to California. He committed suicide in Dubuque in 1857."[69] Hence the utopian vision of democracy that Whitman found stimulating in Plumbe's gallery was, at least in this case, crushed beneath the weight of modern capitalism's harsh realities.

Nonetheless, while Whitman was loafing around Plumbe's gallery, he met Gabriel Harrison, a rising young daguerreotypist and fellow disenchanted radical Democrat circulating among New York City's Locofoco crowd. Ruth Bohan describes Harrison as a "painter, poet, short story writer, and actor" who, "during the Free Soil campaign of 1848–49, served as a delegate at the Utica convention and as President of Manhattan's fourteenth ward Free Soil League." Harrison was thus an exemplar of the enlightened American later envisioned in Whitman's poetry, for he was both an artist and a politically engaged citizen. In fact, both Whitman and Harrison attended the Free Soil Nomination Convention, a hotbed of Locofoco activism, in Buffalo in August 1848.[70] It is no surprise, then, that Whitman and Harrison became close friends or that Harrison took numerous daguerreotypes of Whitman, including the famous July 1854 image that became the frontispiece for *Leaves of Grass.* In short, through his friendship and both political and artistic relationships with Harrison, Whitman was immersed in the culture of daguerreotypy and daguerreotype artists. He therefore would have been acutely aware of a well-posed daguerreotype's ability to convey the kind of electric immediacy and truthfulness that a printed name alone could not achieve.[71]

Furthermore, Whitman's intuitions regarding the likelihood that his readers would metonymically collapse his poetic persona, visual image, and authorial being are supported by the early reviews of *Leaves of Grass.* In fact, of the seventeen known reviews of the 1855 version, twelve explicitly refer to the frontispiece, thus demonstrating the attention-grabbing power of Whitman's visual image.[72] For example, in what is believed to be the first published review of *Leaves of Grass* not written by Whitman himself, Charles Dana observes that "from the unique effig[y] of the anonymous author of this volume which graces the frontispiece, we may infer that he belongs to the exemplary class of society sometimes irreverently styled 'loafers.' He is therein represented in a garb, half sailor's and half workman's, with no superfluous appendage of coat or waistcoat, a 'wide-awake' perched jauntily on his head, one hand in his pocket and the other on his hip, with a certain air of mild defiance, and an expression of pensive insolence."[73] Dana approaches the text, then, having yet to read a single word but already imagining exactly the character that Whitman's poems seek to establish.

Another of Whitman's early reviewers likewise metonymically conflates the daguerreotype's subject, the book's author, and the poem's persona: Charles Eliot Norton observes that, "as seems very proper in a book of transcendental poetry, the author withholds his name from the title page, and presents his portrait, neatly engraved on steel, instead. This, no doubt, is upon the principle that the name is merely accidental; while the portrait affords an idea of *the essential being* from whom these utterances proceed."[74] The trope of an essential being is echoed in another of the early reviews, where the anonymous author (perhaps Whitman) observes that the "author is Walter Whitman. . . . his name is not on the frontispiece, but his portrait, half length is. The contents of the book form a daguerreotype of his inner being."[75] Dana, Norton, and this anonymous reviewer's descriptions of the frontispiece epitomize the representational process I have been describing in this section. That is, the image's technologically constructed meaning is automatically accepted as the poet's essential being, hence influencing the reader's approach to the following poems.

In an anonymous review in the *National Intelligencer,* 18 February 1856, the critic notes the odd substitution of the frontispiece image for a name and then proceeds to refer to the book's author alternatively as "Walter," "Mr. Whitman," "Walter Whitman," and "Mr. W."[76] It is as if the author's name is not nearly as important as his more truthful visual image. This remarkable faith in the veracity of visual images clearly affects the way readers approach the text, for Whitman's promises to fulfill rhetorically contradictory functions are both so baffling and so hyperbolic that they render any sense of his self problematic. The auratic version of the self on the frontispiece therefore makes the poem's outrageous persona less troubling, for it offers readers visual evidence concerning the true identity of the author. The ultimate paradox here is that the competing poetic tropes of absence/totality/synecdoche and immediacy/presence/metonymy are mediated by a visual image that presents "the truth itself" in a form that nonetheless suggests the oncoming possibility of the endless mechanical reproduction (and hence manipulation) of such supposedly truthful visual images. Making these connections between the political economy of representation and Whitman's use of the daguerreotype points to one of the fundamental paradoxes of American democracy. That is, Whitman's attempt to launch himself into the utopian realm of absolute truth while simultaneously striving for a sense of unmediated presence finds him employing the very modes of mechanization and reproduction that will increasingly thwart such possibilities. The 1855 etching thus embodies nicely the paradox of representation in American democracy.

The Paradox of Representation in American Democracy

I have been arguing that Whitman's use of a visual image to provide physical immediacy and veracity to the otherwise highly suspect self presented as the omnivorous persona of *Leaves of Grass* provides an excellent example of some of the representational paradoxes produced by the rise of the daguerreotype, print capitalism, and modernity in general. I have in turn argued that these representational paradoxes indicate the larger cultural, political, economic, and historical complications at play in the dialectics of commodification, self-making, and democracy. I accordingly close this chapter by turning more directly to the question of democracy's paradoxical representational legitimacy.

As noted by philosophers of democracy from Jefferson, Madison, Emerson, and Whitman through Hannah Arendt, Edward Morgan, James Morone, Robert Hariman, Michael Warner, and Sacvan Bercovitch, a democracy is legitimate only insofar as the immense powers wielded by representative individuals are perceived to derive from the popular will.[77] For Jefferson, Madison, and Morone (among others), this process is essentially institutional and political: how does political representation work as regards elected officials and questions of citizenship? For Emerson, Whitman, Hariman, and Warner (among others), this process is essentially aesthetic and cultural: how do citizens and noncitizens alike address questions of political representation in public, aesthetic forums of debate? For Arendt, Morgan, and Bercovitch (among others), this process is simultaneously political and aesthetic, institutional and cultural. Regardless of which perspective one privileges, the question of democracy's legitimacy always returns to the same dilemmas: how can the few speak for the many, and why do the many grant respect and fealty to a government made up of but a minute fraction of the people? In short, why does the cultural fiction of democracy work?

Using Arendt's terms, one could say that there must be a popularly accepted understanding of the honesty and transparency of the process by which the people, the source of *political legitimacy,* are represented both in and by the government, the organizing force of *political authority.* As I demonstrated in chapter 3 with respect to Walker's *Letter on Texas Annexation* and *The South in Danger,* however, the rise of modern print capitalism seriously complicates this synecdochic convertibility from part to whole and from people to government. Indeed, the rise of mass-produced texts and images means that the process of democratic representation may fall prey to any number of means of manipulation, both at the aesthetic, representational level and at the properly institutional, political level, hence calling the legitimacy of democratic representation into serious question. Nevertheless, as I demonstrated in chapter 1 when I examined the abolitionist arguments of North, Child, and Douglass, this same system of mass-produced texts enabled Americans to engage in heartfelt political debates that transcended the narrow confines of space and tradition, hence allowing the rhetorical give-and-take of democracy to thrive in a historically unprecedented fashion. *Leaves of Grass* is an exceptional example of both these possibilities working simultaneously, yet Whitman's drive to speak as the nation's bard ends up demonstrating not so much his healing, unifying power as his desire to embody a process that cannot be embodied in any one voice, image, or text. Hence Michael Warner observes that "the republican statesman is in some measure a contradiction in terms: he is the embodiment of that which cannot be embodied."[78]

Again, in publishing his image Whitman needs to be understood as attempting to practice a similarly paradoxical act of embodying what cannot be embodied. That is, the frontispiece image is meant to conflate the auratic and immediate selves that promote and produce the poems (Walter Whitman, promoter, and Walt Whitman, author) with the self-proclaimed universalizing poet of the democracy ("an American," Walt the giant persona), yet the complex dynamics of antebellum democracy cannot be condensed into one all-embracing moment or poem. The one unavoidable fact of modernity is that by midcentury the "public" had become too big geographically, too divided economically, and too fractured politically to find harmonious voice in a single poet's vision. The synecdochic part-for-whole structure of democratic representation, particularly when complicated by the various aspects of modernity, therefore cannot be collapsed into one all-revealing text. Indeed, although Whitman wants to speak as both an auratic, independent self and the overarching, godlike voice of the nation, the sheer complexity of modern life refuses to let the fluid, ever-changing part-for-whole transference that makes democracy possible collapse metonymically into one cosmic moment of unity. Whitman's "catalogue poems," then, while specifically celebrating the multiplicity and wonder of American democracy, point not so much toward the rich unity and cohesion of social space as toward the inherently thwarted desire for community in the face of modernity's jarring dislocations.

As Hariman notes in *Political Style,* however, the attempt "to achieve aesthetic and political coherence across speaker, text, and audience" is among the foundational characteristics of "the republican mind." Perhaps it is because Whitman struggles openly with this paradox of the republican mind, enthusiastically pursuing what Hariman calls "the trope of civic embodiment," that American readers find him endearing.[79] This would mean, then, that we love Whitman specifically because of his audacity in trying to realize the fiction of democracy, to embody both poetically and visually a form of representative legitimacy and immediacy that we know to be impossible.

The consistent friction between Whitman's metonymic trope of presence, immediacy, and transparency and his synecdochic trope of absence, mediation, and totality appears to render the poetry technically ironic. Indeed, recalling my comments on Burke in the introduction, one may postulate that *Leaves of Grass* is subtly and humbly ironic, for it amounts to a series of perspective-revising self-negations that nonetheless posit an overwhelming faith in our collective ability to muddle through. On the one hand, Whitman's drive to bridge the representational gap between part and whole, self and society, word and world, amounts to a unilateral and decidedly undemocratic decree in which the shuttling space of instability and change (the representational space between part and whole, legitimacy and authority) has been collapsed into one transparent, fixed moment of truth. On the other hand, Whitman simultaneously begs the reader to think and act independently, free of all restraining norms and customs. If one is willing to think of Whitman as a practitioner of humble irony, then this tension may be read not as a crippling contradiction but as an enabling opportunity for thinking about the endless dialectical possibilities for the self and society to live and grow together—precisely the Emersonian question with which this chapter opened.

Arendt reminds us in *On Revolution* that the cultural space of legitimacy, roughly understood as the source of democratic power (the people), and the institutional space of authority, roughly understood as the force of law (the government), must exist in dialectical tension to circumvent the rise of authoritarian power.[80] Thinking along Arendt's terms, one might say that the rhetorical structure of Whitman's lists demonstrates a fundamentally utopian desire for direct, transparent relations among equals throughout all branches of society while simultaneously showing us that this desire must—as Arendt argues—always remain ambiguous and tenuous within democratic culture. Whitman thus offers us an America that is both utopian and ironic, heroic and humble, inexpressibly mediated and immediately physical. Whitman's use of an etching based on a daguerreotype as the frontispiece to *Leaves of Grass* can then be read not only as indicating a specific historical moment's fascination with new technological means of producing images of the self but also as symbolizing the larger cultural paradoxes that lay at the heart of representation in antebellum America.[81]

It is important to recall, however, that antebellum America was struggling not only to address these paradoxes of democratic representation but also to discover how to pursue democracy's promises amid capitalism's predatory practices and the nation's slow transformation from radical republicanism to modern liberalism.[82] Whitman was not exempt from these questions. Indeed, Whitman's relationship to what we call today the state tellingly shows how the paradoxes of democratic representation in antebellum America were complicated by both capitalist and liberal bureaucratic imperatives. More specifically, while I have already detailed the many political, aesthetic, and cultural aspects of Whitman's use of a visual image instead of his name, with the author referring to himself in the preface simply as "an American," I have not yet discussed whether Whitman's poetic identity is complicated by the banal economic requirements of the state. That is, on the bottom of the book's third sheet (the frontispiece constitutes the first sheet, and the second sheet—the title page—has "Leaves of Grass. Brooklyn, New York: 1855" printed in large letters across it), printed in small block letters, the following notice appears: "Entered according to Act of Congress in the year 1855, by Walter Whitman, in the Clerk's Office of the District Court of the United States for the Southern District of New York."[83] Hence Whitman's metaphysics, his poetic pyrotechnics, his transindividual, cross-gendered, suprahistorical desires are preceded by the legal, economic requirements of a state committed to protecting private property. The visual poet, later identified in the poems only as an American, is here named (and not even as Walt, his familiar public persona, but as Walter); the cosmic seer is here situated as simply another citizen enmeshed in the growing bureaucratic labyrinth of the modernizing capitalist state; the heroic visionary of a better, more righteous democracy is here authorized by the same Congress whose profligate moral compromises his poetry assails. The copyright notice thus adds another layer of complexity and compromise to Whitman's transcendent and utopian vision, for it demonstrates that this book—like all other books manufactured in the new world of print capitalism—circulates under the auspices of market-inspired bureaucratic machinery.

Considering the complicated interrelationships among the frontispiece, the daguerreotype fad, and the humbly ironic rhetorical structure of the heroic poetic claims that follow the mundane copyright notice, it is hard not to see the original *Leaves of Grass* as embodying the dizzying tensions carrying America forward into the more industrialized, institutionalized, and commercialized world of modernity. Indeed, Whitman, like America, demonstrates both the pitfalls and possibilities of mass-produced individuality and obliquely representative democracy. Nonetheless, it seems that much of the fascination with this volume, as both written text and daguerreotype image, derives from the fact that it hopefully yet humbly attempts to live playfully within these representative paradoxes. Whitman's attempts both to live amid these representational paradoxes and to glide above the period's daunting historical crises as the universal seer are obviously problematic, yet his utopian longing for a synecdochic democracy of kind and generous equals strikes me as a welcome corrective for a world obsessed with mass-produced individuality, hyperconsumption, and the petty narcissism of minor differences.

CONCLUSION: THE PARADOXES OF DEMOCRATIC REPRESENTATION

Faced with the daunting cultural and political complications stemming from antebellum America's slow transformation toward modernity, many Americans sought to participate in the democratic process not so much by engaging in formal governmental actions as by stepping into public cultural spaces, by taking advantage of the new possibilities, made available by print capitalism, to speak amid and write for mass audiences of equally concerned citizens. The American Lyceum was one such attempt to use these new means of democratic dissent to return to, revise, and otherwise reenergize the nation's founding cultural fictions. For example, in the first bound volume of *Proceedings of the American Lyceum,* published in 1832, the Honorable Theodore Frelinghuysen contributed a wondrously strange essay entitled "Study of Our Political Institutions." Ostensibly a clarion call to "the youth of the United States" to engage more thoroughly in "the study of political institutions . . . and especially ours," the essay opens with a Bancroft-like paean to the Founding Fathers' "manly spirits." "They dreaded less the haunts of savage men," Frelinghuysen boasts, "than the despotism which invaded the rights of conscience." These brave warriors for freedom were triply blessed, for their own qualities of "fortitude" and "love of country" were supplemented by "the benignity of Providence" and "propitious circumstances." Frelinghuysen thus clearly points toward both the then widely accepted cultural fiction that America has been divinely blessed and what historians have come to label "exceptionalism," the cultural fiction that circumstances somehow freed the young nation from many of the complicating historical burdens and obligations then haunting Europe. Thus, on Frelinghuysen's model, America is a nation of manly patriotism, divine Providence, and new beginnings.[1] One can hardly imagine an essay articulating more fully some of the dominant cultural fictions then popular in antebellum America.

Like many of the cultural-fiction-building texts I address in this study, however, Frelinghuysen's essay is riddled with paradoxes. For example, regarding the complicated relationships among the masses and the nation's official political institutions, Frelinghuysen argues that "the confidence reposed in them [the masses] has been elevating in its influence; the people have felt the duty of self-government, and risen up to the high responsibilities of their condition." This passage seems to indicate that the government has somehow placed faith in the masses, who have responded to this honor by elevating themselves, becoming better, kinder, more noble beings worthy of such benign leadership. Three sentences later, however, Frelinghuysen argues that "the intelligence and virtue of the American community imparted all that energy and wisdom to their political systems" (31). Here he says not that the government improved the masses but that the masses have improved the government. So which one is it? Do the elite few guide the pedestrian many, or do the honorable masses guide duly responsive political systems? As if this question were not confusing enough, the next sentence explains that "it is a corollary, as certain as any mathematical deduction, that to attain or perpetuate such noble ends, the fountain and treasury of political power must itself be enlightened and pure. The people must be taught to understand their rights, duties, and powers" (31). One wonders not only who will tackle this task but also how and why a supposedly intelligent and virtuous people would elect someone else to teach them what Frelinghuysen—and no less an authority than Jefferson—has told us they already know?[2]

The whole point of Frelinghuysen's argument, however, like the hundreds of similar essays and speeches given by his fellow Lyceum activists, is to produce that delicate position of cultural authority from which one can talk about teaching fellow citizens how to understand their rights, duties, and powers without sounding like a monarchist. Frelinghuysen is jockeying here not so much for official political power as for cultural power, the right to articulate authoritatively what the people need or do not need to know and do to be good citizens. Indeed, Frelinghuysen is speaking about class power, the ability to determine values and norms as if they were in everyone's—not just his and his friends'—best interest. The heroic preamble to this power play, with its celebration of the Founding Fathers, is therefore rhetorically necessary because it masks Frelinghuysen's class-based appeal for new cultural authority behind tried-and-true cultural fictions. That is, invoking heroic cultural fictions regarding the founders serves rhetorically to cloud Frelinghuysen's claim to rank among a new class of professional intellectuals. In short, he speaks of the mythology of nationalism while constructing class privilege.

Nonetheless, Frelinghuysen's subtle claim to class privilege and authority within a speech that celebrates the founders of American democracy is curiously self-compromising. From one perspective he tells us that the government teaches the people to rise to "the high responsibilities of their condition"; this is a traditionally elitist conception of politics as a top-down process of management. "High responsibilities" here means paying taxes and not causing an inordinate amount of trouble. From another perspective he states that the masses teach the government to honor their will; this is a radically new populist conception of politics as democratic. "High responsibilities" here means honoring the progressive promises of the Enlightenment. From yet a third perspective he warns that someone—Frelinghuysen? the Lyceum movement?—must teach the people to understand their rights, duties, and so on; this is what I call the new bourgeois conception of cultural power. "High responsibilities" here means working hard, buying hard, and knowing one's place in the rapidly ossifying social hierarchies created by modern capitalism. The fact that Frelinghuysen embraces all three perspectives within the same paragraph illustrates the paradoxes of democratic representation.

Indeed, Frelinghuysen happily incorporates a traditional sense of elitism, a radical new sense of populism, and an even newer sense of bourgeois cultural leadership without ever considering that these perspectives might be mutually contradictory. Forwarding such self-canceling perspectives is obviously paradoxical, if not downright befuddling, for one cannot be a traditionally elitist, radically populist, class-building bourgeois reformer. Nonetheless, the form of Frelinghuysen's appeal—first given as a public speech and then distributed through the new means of print capitalism—is fundamentally democratic. Whatever disciplinary class overtones one may attribute to it, the Lyceum movement was understood at the time as an enlightened, progressive, locally organized, open forum of public instruction, entertainment, and debate. What better example is there of the people coming together to empower themselves by discussing the issues of the day? Printing the proceedings of such gatherings is but the logical extension of their democratic force, enabling an even larger audience to consider the arguments at hand. The paradoxical content of Frelinghuysen's text thus seems less important than the fact that it embodies the possibilities of modern democracy's new communicative forms. Much as do works by Northup and Adorno, whom I discussed in the introduction, Frelinghuysen's text revolves around the subtly ironic tension generated by the contradictions between the content and form of its rhetoric.

Understood in this manner, Frelinghuysen's ironic adventure into the paradoxes of democratic representation may be seen to parallel both Emerson's confusions in "The American Scholar" and Whitman's dilemmas in *Leaves of Grass.* In fact, all three texts confront similar questions about democracy and modernity: How can one make unilateral declarations about democracy? How can one celebrate the form of democracy's rhetorical give-and-take, its dialectical play of powers, while speaking alone? How can one live amid many clamoring voices yet still cling to a sense of self? Frelinghuysen in 1832, Emerson in 1837, and Whitman in 1855 are each unable to answer these questions, yet interestingly, all three men ask them in forms that privilege open public debate. Democracy, then, at least as practiced by Frelinghuysen, Emerson, and Whitman, entails the ironic pursuit of paradoxical questions that, even in their unanswerability, enable citizens to come together in public debate. What matters here is not the heroic pursuit of answers so much as the humble posing of good questions under fair conditions of debate. The title of this study, *Democratic Dissent,* is meant to capture this subtle irony, for every case studied here indicates that living in a democracy means dissenting. In short, democracy is nothing more than the institutionalization of a culture that cherishes public dissent; public dissent is nothing more than the cultural process of celebrating democracy. It is a paradox, but it works. Cultural fictions may be understood simply as the enabling narratives and edifying rhetorical conventions by which we come to learn how to live this paradox.

Nevertheless, many antebellum cultural fictions were complicated mightily by two related factors: slavery and capitalism. Chapter 1 described how some abolitionists dissented from slavery by assenting to what they saw as the enlightening, modernizing, progress-enhancing powers of capitalism; chapter 2 described how some proslavery advocates supported slavery because it was, in their fundamentally nostalgic worldview, less barbarous than modern capitalism. I need not recount those rhetorical battles, but it is worth repeating that all the many subtle shades of different positions within these battles over slavery and capitalism recognized the efficacy of democratic means of dissent: marshal your evidence, mix liberally with pathos, speak publicly, print your materials, attack your critics, and repeat until exhausted or satisfied. In fact, it is significant that the factors perhaps most responsible for turning the tide against slavery were the 1836 "Gag Rule," the rising tide of mob violence against abolitionists, and the 1850 Fugitive Slave Act. As my readings of Ben Franklin, Tom Paine, and Abraham Lincoln illustrate, many Northern whites feared the serious evils that might result from abolition, yet even this appeared less threatening than the South's acts in silencing petitions to Congress, its perceived endorsement of democracy-endangering violence, and its extension of slave-catching duties to the North, all of which crossed the line from simply disagreeing over ideas to trampling on the communicative forms of democracy itself. This explains the success of John Quincy Adams, Robert Rantoul, and those other antislavery activists who based their rhetoric less on the horrors of slavery than on the threat the Slave Power posed to the communicative possibilities of democracy. In this sense, the Civil War was fought not over the contents of ideas but over the forms of their expression.

The best example of this thesis remains Congressman Preston Brooks's 22 May 1856 assault on Charles Sumner in the U.S. Senate (figure 17). On 19 and 20 May, responding to proslavery aggression surrounding the 1854 Kansas-Nebraska Act, Sumner read a fiery antislavery speech that came to be known as "Crimes against Kansas." Originally elected to the Senate as a Massachusetts Free Soiler in 1851, Sumner had converted to the new Republican party around 1855. His polemic was thus a rhetorical blast announcing what many Americans feared most: a radically activist antislavery party of national proportions. Brooks took offense at, among other things, what he believed were slurs Sumner had directed against both Brooks's home state, South Carolina, and the state's

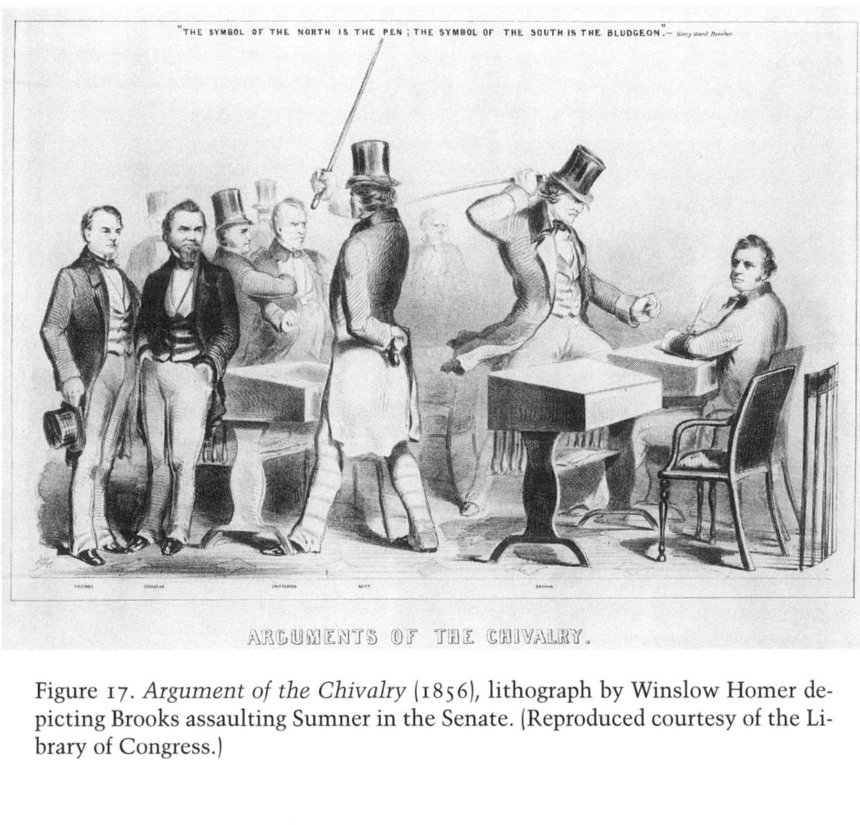

Figure 17. *Argument of the Chivalry* (1856), lithograph by Winslow Homer depicting Brooks assaulting Sumner in the Senate. (Reproduced courtesy of the Library of Congress.)

senator (and Brooks's cousin), Andrew Butler. Hence, on 22 May, in an act that quickly came to stand as a synecdoche for the South's attempt to silence all debate on the subject, Brooks viciously assaulted Sumner on the floor of the Senate. Brooks attacked Sumner from behind and repeatedly smashed him over the head with a cane as Sumner sat at his desk writing notes—Sumner never saw him coming. The beating was so brutal that Sumner never recovered full health. Perhaps even more than did the three previously adduced factors, this physical assault came to symbolize a violence-prone South curtailing the very possibilities of democratic dissent in the name of protecting slavery. As the damning caption atop figure 17 indicates: "The symbol of the North is the pen; the symbol of the South is the bludgeon."[3]

The capitalist-driven reverse of this thesis was true as well, for many antebellum Americans believed that arguing in any form either against or over slavery was too dangerous, not because of what such democratic dissent might mean for the communicative possibilities of democracy itself, but because of what it might mean for the market. Again, the fast road to do-nothingism, which relied on the rhetoric of paralysis, was greased with the fear that democracy might get in the way of dollars. However one may feel regarding the ways in which modern capitalism's economic opportunities came to substitute for the struggle for political equality, Gustave de Beaumont was painfully insightful when he observed in 1835, "It seems as though greed were blowing a deadly wind upon America."[4]

Nonetheless, at its best democratic dissent transcends this deadly wind of greed, or at least the compromising logic of the marketplace. It has become an American cultural fiction as old as any other that the founders put their lives and fortunes on the line for liberty, yet we do ourselves a disservice when we forget that this cultural fiction is true. The abolitionists as well put the pursuit of dignity and honor above dollars, for they fought a battle so radical politically that it cost many of them—such as Lydia Maria Child—their careers, jobs, families, and friends. Even while putting their lives on the line, however, the abolitionists understood that part of what makes democratic dissent possible and sometimes successful is its commitment to humble irony. For example, consider *The American Anti-Slavery Almanac* for 1839. The first page of the almanac, essentially a second title plate, includes a harrowing image printed above the question "What has the North to do with slavery?" (figure 18). The next page tells us that the image depicts "a woman, who, having been punished for her misfortunes by being kept in jail in Philadelphia, is torn from her child, born in jail [the child is hidden in the dark to middle left of the image], and delivered, by a northern constable, to the exasperated slave-

Figure 18. "What has the North to do with Slavery?" from the 1839 *American Anti-Slavery Almanac.* (Reproduced courtesy of the Gilder Lehrman Collection, Pierpont Morgan Library, New York City, GLC 5826.)

holder." This explanation adds that the scene in the background on the right depicts the fate of "a respectable colored citizen" who, upon trying to enter a "public exhibition," "was not only refused, but BEATEN WITH A CANE." The supposedly free North is thus portrayed here as a land of hypocrisy swarming with state-sanctioned violence. This image thus graphically depicts the North's role with respect to slavery, with pages 5, 7, 9, 11, and 13 covering, in grueling detail, Northern complicity in slavery's economic, political, legislative, judicial, and cultural aspects. Such materials are damning, yet the abolitionists position themselves as part of the very thing they attack: they are just as fully *of* and *in* this culture as anyone else. The almanac's tone of horror and shame is thus also intertwined with a humble sense of the abolitionists' own complicity with the cultural practices slavery requires.

In addition to serving as a magnificent and humble manifesto attacking slavery, the publication is also a true almanac, complete with tables chronicling each month's lunar phases, high tides, astronomical characters, hours of daylight, and so on. Look closely under the columns entitled "miscellaneous," however, and you will find buried in each month's table of astronomical information little phrases such as "Slaves suffer much," "Slaveholders growing more calm," "Squalls in Congress," and so on.[5] In contrast to the surrounding pages of graphic details illustrating the horrors of slavery, these cheeky meteorological jokes suggest reimagining the abolitionists in a new light. Less the work of pretentious and righteous moralizers, these goofy yet deadly serious asides demonstrate pranksters experimenting with their printing press, playing around with the new means of textual production, basically having fun—even while assailing the machinery of death—with the possibilities of democratic dissent. Indeed, these passages are ironic not only because they ask readers to rethink the very function of almanacs, now seen not simply as a farmer's best tool but also as a political manifesto, and not only because they ask readers to rethink the status of the weather, now seen not simply as a fact of nature but also as an enabling element of slavery itself, but because they invite readers to rethink the abolitionists as well, now seen not simply as Bible-thumping Yankees but also as playfully ironic and humble citizens struggling to forge their own cultural fictions with whatever tools available to them.

Chapter 3 demonstrated how the nation's expansion into an empire further complicated the paradoxes of democratic representation and the possibilities of democratic dissent, most directly by forcing the nation to decide whether to allow slavery into new lands. Walker's safety-valve thesis regarding Texas annexation was seen as rhetorically persuasive precisely because it decided the issue by forestalling it. That is, Walker argued that annexing Texas now would create geopolitical and economic opportunities for dealing with slavery later. As the outraged responses by Sedgwick, Adams, Lundy, and others indicate, many Americans understood that this mischievous, apparent compromise meant take the land now but postpone, defer, put off and do nothing on slavery. Nonetheless, Walker's, O'Sullivan's, and Buchanan's rhetoric of Manifest Destiny carried the day, leading America to annex Texas, start a war with Mexico, bully England regarding Oregon, and even consider invading Cuba and much of Latin America. Indeed, antebellum Americans seem to have been particularly susceptible to persuasion by cultural fictions invoking the grandeur of empire—as contemporary Americans still are. The fact that Walker's power in producing these cultural fictions derived from his mastery of the new means of print capitalism is deeply significant, for it shows that the same means of mass production and distribution that enabled abolitionists to engage the nation in an unprecedented debate about ethics in turn enabled people such as Walker to engage the nation in an unprecedented barrage—as best illustrated in *The South in Danger*—of mean-spirited propaganda. The paradox of democratic representation, then, as seen in the case of Senator Walker's career as a proslavery advocate of Manifest Destiny, is that expanded forms of communication did not lead to improved means of communication. Rather, the nation simply found itself confronted with more and more printed matter of increasingly less verifiable authorship full of ever more shrill calls to defend slavery and expand the empire.

All this goes a long way toward explaining Whitman's frontispiece to *Leaves of Grass,* where he used a visual image and no name. In the face of this rising tide of printed matter, which I positioned in chapter 4 as the communicative corollary to a culture increasingly flooded with strangers, crooks, shysters, and the other unfathomable characters modernity produced, Whitman clearly understood that his culture was becoming obsessed with veracity. So how could he better demonstrate his own veracity, his own transparent authenticity, his own sheer physical presence, than by portraying himself on the frontispiece via an etching based on the antebellum period's favorite means of visual representation, the daguerreotype? In this sense, Whitman's love of what Poe called the daguerreotype's "absolute truth" may be understood as almost the exact opposite of Walker's love of rhetorical subterfuge. Indeed, Whitman dedicated his life to trying to make the promises of democracy more real, more obvious, more immediate, whereas Walker dedicated his life to trying to make the promises of democracy more obtuse, more veiled, more mediated. Despite these obvious political differences, both men stand now as examples of the ways in which our antebellum forebears struggled to give voice to their competing visions of American democracy as it could and should be. Thus Walker and Whitman not only teach us about the political, cultural, and aesthetic complexities that emerged as antebellum America learned to live with and by the new forms of mass communication made possible by print capitalism; they also teach us both to respect the dignity and drama of public self-expression and to honor our obligations to their efforts by speaking in and writing for our own chosen publics.

In closing, I turn again to Emerson. Speaking in the New York City Tabernacle on 7 March 1854, almost four years to the day after the passage of the much-loathed Fugitive Slave Act, Emerson begins his speech by claiming, "I do not often speak to public questions. They are odious and hurtful and it seems like meddling."[6] Coming from the man widely considered to have given more speeches to more people in more places about more public questions than just about anyone else in the nation at the time, this opening must surely have left listeners chuckling—they would not have missed the irony of this claim.[7] Emerson then offers this blessing on democratic dissent: "Ah! Great is the privilege of Eloquence. What gratitude does every human being feel to him who speaks well for the right—who translates truth into language entirely plain and clear!" (77). Lest listeners think that Emerson is praising himself, he then spends the next few minutes assailing Daniel Webster for his support of the Fugitive Slave Act. "Nobody doubts that Daniel Webster could make a good speech," Emerson admits, but the real question was whether Webster would "stand for Right or for Might" (78). As everyone now knows, "Mr. Webster decided for slavery"; hence, under the guise of free discourse, "immense mischief was done" (79). What makes Emerson's attack on Webster so curious is that Emerson never discusses the Fugitive Slave Act in any detail. Rather, he assails Webster for the crime of abusing eloquence in the defense of slavery. Nonetheless, even while thumping Webster (who had died two years earlier), Emerson employs the same rhetorical strategy Webster had made famous: the political jeremiad, the high-minded harangue. It is certainly ironic, then, to find Emerson trying to persuade an audience that Webster is posthumously guilty of having persuaded his earlier one.[8]

Thus, even when asked to speak on the anniversary of the law that finally—as my reading of Douglass's Rochester speech shows—revealed slavery to be national, not sectional, in character, Emerson embodies the paradox of democratic dissent. Although Emerson asks his listeners to choose between "*may* and *must:* the sense of right and duty, on one hand; and the material necessities, on the other" (81), his speech illustrates the inescapable fact that this choice is likely to be made on the basis of the lure of eloquence. The paradox of democratic representation, then, as embodied here so powerfully by Emerson's speech, is that there are no grounds for deciding about rhetorical claims other than more rhetorical claims. Dissenting from Webster's proslavery version of democracy thus requires Emerson to forward his own transcendentalist version of democracy, with both men struggling less to proffer something like the truth than simply to find a persuasive argument, some eloquence, a cultural fiction capable of carrying the day. As did Emerson and Webster, we, too, face this dilemma: to author cultural fictions persuasive enough to persuade our fellow citizens to accept our version of democratic dissent.

NOTES

Introduction

1. One genre of persuasion not examined here is music. On the various uses of songs in American public culture, see Robert Branham and Stephen Hartnett, *Sweet Freedom's Song: "My Country 'Tis of Thee" and Democracy in America* (Oxford: Oxford University Press, 2002); Vera Brodsky Lawrence, *Music for Patriots, Politicians, and Presidents: Harmonies and Discords of the First Hundred Years* (New York: Macmillan, 1975); Philip Foner, *American Labor Songs of the Nineteenth Century* (Urbana: University of Illinois Press, 1975); and Vicki Eaklor, *American Antislavery Songs: A Collection and Analysis* (New York: Greenwood, 1988).

2. Kenneth Burke, no title, contribution to "What Is Americanism? A Symposium on Marxism and the American Tradition," *Partisan Review* 3, no. 3 (Apr. 1936): 11; Marion S. Barry Jr., "Statement to the 1960 Democratic Party Platform Committee," in *Public Address in the Twentieth-Century South: Evolution of a Region*, ed. W. Stuart Towns (Westport, Conn.: Praeger, 1999), 90.

3. For more along these lines, see Sacvan Bercovitch, *The Rites of Assent: Transformations in the Symbolic Construction of America* (New York: Routledge, 1993); James Morone, *The Democratic Wish: Popular Participation and the Limits of American Government* (New York: Basic Books, 1990); and Stephen Hartnett and Ramsey Eric Ramsey, "'A Plain Public Road': Evaluating Arguments for Democracy in a Post-Metaphysical World," *Argumentation and Advocacy* 35, no. 3 (Winter 1999): 95–114.

4. Throughout the study I use the terms *forebears* and *ancestors* in their secular, intellectual, and political senses, not in their more restrictive familial and progenitive senses.

5. The philosophical critique of epistemology has been articulated most clearly (albeit with troublesome political implications) in Richard Rorty's *Consequences of Pragmatism* (Minneapolis: University of Minnesota Press, 1982) and *Contingency, Irony, and Solidarity* (Cambridge: Cambridge University Press, 1989). The reascent of rhetoric as a response to this philosophical crisis has been explained succinctly in the following texts: Calvin Schrag, "Rhetoric Resituated at the End of Philosophy," *Quarterly Journal of Speech* 71, no. 2 (May 1985): 164–75; Gerard Hauser, "Between Philosophy and Rhetoric: Interpositions within Traditions," *Philosophy and Rhetoric* 28, no. 3 (1995): iii–xvii; and Thomas Farrell, *Norms of Rhetorical Culture* (New Haven, Conn.: Yale University Press, 1993). The critique of macrological histories has been forwarded in a number of important texts, including Michel de Certeau, *The Writing of History*, trans. Tom

Conley (New York: Columbia University Press, 1988 [French original, 1975]); Robert Berkhofer, *Beyond the Great Story: History as Text and Discourse* (Cambridge, Mass.: Harvard University Press, 1995); Hans Kellner, *Language and Historical Representation: Getting the Story Crooked* (Madison: University of Wisconsin Press, 1989); and H. Aram Veeser, ed., *The New Historicism* (New York: Routledge, 1989). I have been influenced by many excellent explanations of the manner in which rhetorical historians may proceed within this postepistemological, postmetanarrative moment, especially Steven Mailloux, "Rhetorical Hermeneutics," *Critical Inquiry* 11, no. 4 (June 1985): 620–41; idem, "Rhetorical Hermeneutics Revisited," *Text and Performance Quarterly* 11 (1991): 233–48; and Robert Hariman, *Political Style: The Artistry of Power* (Chicago: University of Chicago, 1995). For an attempt to synthesize these various theories while rereading the cultural fictions surrounding Daniel Boone, see Stephen Hartnett, "Michel de Certeau's Critical Historiography and the Rhetoric of Maps," *Philosophy and Rhetoric* 31, no. 4 (Fall 1998): 283–302.

6. One could obviously enrich this critical perspective by considering the question of gender formation. I have published work on this subject elsewhere; see Stephen Hartnett, "*'It Is Terrible to Possess Such Power!'*: Early Modernity, Phrenology, and Alienated Desire as Class and Gender Warfare in Hawthorne's 'The Birth Mark,'" *Prospero* 5 (Fall 1998): 5–26; idem, "Fanny Fern's 1855 *Ruth Hall*, the Cheerful Brutality of Capitalism, and the Irony of Sentimental Rhetoric," *Quarterly Journal of Speech* (forthcoming).

7. For wonderful examples of this methodology, see David Reynolds, *Beneath the American Renaissance: The Subversive Imagination in the Age of Emerson and Melville* (Cambridge, Mass.: Harvard University Press, 1988); and Karen Halttunen, *Confidence Men and Painted Women: A Study of Middle-Class Culture in America, 1830–1870* (New Haven, Conn.: Yale University Press, 1982). Although it is not as broad in methodological scope as the books by Reynolds and Halttunen, also see Kenneth Cmiel, *Democratic Eloquence: The Fight over Popular Speech in Nineteenth-Century America* (Berkeley: University of California Press, 1990).

8. For a study that pursues this contextualist imperative within the tradition of the history of ideas, see Jay Fliegelman, *Declaring Independence: Jefferson, Natural Language, and the Culture of Performance* (Palo Alto, Calif.: Stanford University Press, 1993). The best materialist account of the period is Charles Sellers, *The Market Revolution: Jacksonian America, 1815–1846* (Oxford: Oxford University Press, 1991). For a study that combines these qualities, see Sean Wilentz, *Chants Democratic: New York City and the Rise of the American Working Class, 1788–1850* (Oxford: Oxford University Press, 1984).

9. For example, I am condensing here what was at one point a rather hotly contested debate (at least among rhetorical and communication scholars) regarding the relationships among texts and contexts. For statements from the thick of the battle, see Robert Branham and W. Barnett Pearce, "Between Text and Context: Toward a Rhetoric of Contextual Reconstruction," *Quarterly Journal of Speech* 71 (1985): 19–36; and Stephen Lucas, "The Renaissance of American Public Address: Text and Context in Rhetorical Criticism," *Quarterly Journal of Speech* 74 (1988): 241–60. For more recent examples of the state of rhetorical criticism and theory, see Steven Mailloux, ed., *Rhetoric, Sophistry, Pragmatism* (Cambridge: Cambridge University Press, 1995); Ian Angus and Lenore Langsdorf, eds., *The Critical Turn: Rhetoric and Philosophy in Postmodern Discourse* (Carbondale:

Southern Illinois University Press, 1993); and Paul Hernadi, ed., *The Rhetoric of Interpretation and the Interpretation of Rhetoric* (Durham, N.C.: Duke University Press, 1989).

10. Kenneth Burke, "Four Master Tropes," *A Grammar of Motives* (Berkeley: University of California Press, 1969 [1945]), 514.

11. I am thus reading Burke's notion of humble irony through his earlier notion of a comic frame of acceptance; see Kenneth Burke, *Attitudes towards History,* 3d ed. (Berkeley: University of California Press, 1984 [1937]), esp. 42, 170–71.

12. Along these lines, see Robert Gunderson, "The Oxymoron Strain in American Rhetoric," *Central States Speech Journal* 28 (Summer 1977), where he discusses "fighting Quakers . . . conforming individualists . . . transcendental opportunists . . . honest grafters . . . repressive champions of liberty . . . courageous conformity . . . [and] lustful moralism" (95).

13. Kenneth Burke, "Revolutionary Symbolism in America" (speech before the American Writers' Congress given in New York City on 26 April 1935), in *American Writers' Congress,* ed. Henry Hart (New York: International, 1935), 87–94; responses by Michael Gold and Joseph Freeman from "Discussion and Proceedings," *American Writers' Congress,* 166, 168–69. For a fictional portrayal of the event, see James T. Farrell, *Yet Other Waters* (New York: Vanguard, 1952), 123–24, where "John Keefe" is Burke. Farrell was on the stage that night and was frequently published in the pages of *Partisan Review.*

14. On this understanding of rhetoric as both demonstrative argument and concealing facade, see the opening pages of James Andrews, "Oaths Registered in Heaven: Rhetorical and Historical Legitimacy in the Inaugural Addresses of Jefferson Davis and Abraham Lincoln," in *Doing Rhetorical History: Concepts and Cases,* ed. Kathleen Turner (Birmingham: University of Alabama Press, 1998), 95–117.

15. Thomas Benson, preface to *American Rhetoric: Context and Criticism,* ed. Benson (Carbondale: Southern Illinois University Press, 1989), ix. For a literary historian's version of these convictions, see Roy Harvey Pearce, *Historicism Once More: Problems and Occasions for the American Scholar* (Princeton, N.J.: Princeton University Press, 1969).

Chapter 1: The Dialectics of Assent and Dissent, Yankee Ingenuity, and the Rhetorical Politics of Abolitionism

1. Robert Rantoul Jr.'s speech before the Grand Massachusetts Convention, in Lynn, Mass., 3 April 1851, appears in *Memoirs, Speeches, and Writings of Robert Rantoul, Jr.,* ed. Luther Hamilton (Boston: John Jewett, 1854), 729–51 (epigraph, 731–32); "free trade, no bank," etc. is from Rantoul's speech in Scituate, Mass., 4 July 1836 (ibid., 282). For an analysis of Rantoul's politics, see Marvin Meyers, *The Jacksonian Persuasion: Politics and Beliefs* (New York: Vintage, 1960), 206–33.

2. Gustave de Beaumont, *Marie; or, Slavery in the United States,* trans. Barbara Chapman (Baltimore, Md.: Johns Hopkins University Press, 1999 [1835]), 106. Regarding America's celebration of Washington in song, verse, and image, see Robert Branham and Stephen Hartnett, *Sweet Freedom's Song: "My Country 'Tis of Thee" and Democracy in America* (Oxford: Oxford University Press, 2002), chap. 1.

3. *Declaration of Sentiments of the American Anti-Slavery Society, Adopted at the Formation of said Society, in Philadelphia, on the 14th day of December, 1833* (New York: American Anti-Slavery Society/William S. Dorr, 1844); historians generally agree that this statement was written by William Lloyd Garrison. The declaration covers pages 1–3; the rest of the pamphlet contains a report of the society's tenth anniversary, held in New York, 7 May 1844.

4. John Greenleaf Whittier, "Anti-Slavery Anniversary" (speech read in Philadelphia as part of the fifty-year anniversary celebration of the founding of the AASS, 3 December 1883), in *The Writings of John Greenleaf Whittier,* vol. 7: *Poltics and Reform* (Boston: Houghton Mifflin, 1888), 193–94. On the meetings surrounding the founding of the AASS, see his 1874 essay "The Anti-Slavery Convention of 1833," in ibid., vol. 3, pp. 171–86.

5. Defensor [William Thomas], *The Enemies of the Constitution Discovered, or, An Inquiry into The Origin and Tendency of Popular Violence. Containing A Complete and Circumstantial Account of the Unlawful Proceedings at the City of Utica, October 21st, 1835; the Dispersion of the State Anti-Slavery Convention by the Agitators, The Destruction of a Democratic Press, and of The Causes which Led Thereto. Together with a Concise Treatise on the Practice of the Court of His Honor Judge Lynch* (New York: Leavitt, Lord, 1835 [copyright page has 1836]).

6. Rantoul, speech to Congress against the Fugitive Slave Act, 11 June 1852, in *Memoirs, Speeches, Writings,* ed. Hamilton, 753.

7. For a case study showing how hyperbole and *argumentum ad absurdum* lead to a rhetoric of escalation, see Stephen Hartnett and Ramsey Eric Ramsey, "'A Plain Public Road': Evaluating Arguments for Democracy in a Post-Metaphysical World," *Argumentation and Advocacy* 35, no. 3 (Winter 1999): 95–114.

8. The bounty figure and this quotation are from William Lee Miller, *Arguing about Slavery: The Great Battle in the United States Congress* (New York: Knopf, 1996), 76.

9. It is important to note that the term *lynching* had a wider sense in antebellum America, where, as the following stories indicate, it meant the use of any form of mob-based physical violence to break up political meetings, intimidate activists, or eliminate troublemakers. Hangings sometimes resulted from such actions but in general were not prevalent. Here is a sample of stories, all from *The Liberator* in 1842, detailing the antiabolitionist fury of "Judge Lynch": "Datee J. Pierce and the Mobs in Newport," *The Liberator* 12, no. 1 (7 Jan.): 3; "Mobs, from the Lynn Record," *The Liberator* 12, no. 4 (28 Jan.): 16; "Mob Doings in Arkansas," *The Liberator* 12, no. 12 (25 Mar.): 48; "The Philadelphia Riots," *The Liberator* 12, no. 32 (12 Aug.): 126; "The Late Riots," *The Liberator* 12, no. 33 (19 Aug.): 130; "Judicial Mob Law," *The Liberator* 12, no. 34 (26 Aug.): 133; "Riots in Philadelphia," "Philadelphia Riot," "Another Riot" [Cincinnati], and "Mob Law—Freedom of Speech Destroyed" [Nantucket], *The Liberator* 12, no. 34 (26 Aug.): 134; "Mobocracy in Tazewell County," *The Liberator* 12, no. 37 (16 Sept.): 145; "Infamous Riot at the City Hall," *The Liberator* 12, no. 39 (30 Sept.): 154; "A Lynching Scene, from the New Orleans *Picayune,*" *The Liberator* 12, no. 41 (14 Oct.): 164; "Interesting Report of the Anti-Slavery Convention at Syracuse, N.Y., on the 22nd, 23rd, and 24th, Nov. 1842," *The Liberator* 12, no. 52 (30 Dec.): 205.

10. Aileen Kraditor, *Means and Ends in American Abolitionism: Garrison and His Critics on Strategy and Tactics, 1834–1850* (New York: Pantheon, 1969 [1967]),

6–7 (AASS membership numbers from 6 and from the *Almanac,* cited in note 11). On the "Gag Rule," see Gilbert Hobbs Barns, *The Anti-Slavery Impulse, 1830–1844* (New York: Appleton-Century, 1933), 109–20; and Miller, *Arguing about Slavery.*

11. American Anti-Slavery Society, *The American Anti-Slavery Almanac, for 1839, Being the Third After Leap-Year, and the 63rd of American Independence. Calculated for New York; Adapted to the Northern and Middle States* (New York: S. W. Benedict, 1839), 11. For two remarkable examples of abolitionists' turning violence against them into rhetorical opportunities for persuasion, see Elijah Lovejoy's speech, delivered a few days before his murder, and Wendell Phillips's response to Lovejoy's murder, both in *The Abolitionists: A Collection of Their Writings,* ed. Louis Ruchames (New York: Putnam's, 1963), 139–41 and 141–48, respectively.

12. Stephen Browne, *Angelina Grimké: Rhetoric, Identity, and the Radical Imagination* (East Lansing: Michigan State University Press, 1999), 35, 156. See also James Brewer Stewart, *Holy Warriors: The Abolitionists and American Society* (New York: Hill and Wang, 1976), 50–73.

13. In "Narrative versus Descriptive Historiography" (*New Literary History* 21, no. 3 [1990]: 566) Laurent Stern cautions that the presentist bias leads to work "more about historians than about the events narrated."

14. Theodor Adorno, *Negative Dialectics,* trans. E. B. Ashton (New York: Continuum, 1973 [German original, 1966]), 348–49. On Adorno, see Martin Jay, *Adorno* (Cambridge, Mass.: Harvard University Press, 1984); Fredric Jameson, *Marxism and Form: Twentieth-Century Dialectical Theories of Literature* (Princeton, N.J.: Princeton University Press, 1971), 3–59; Gillian Rose, *The Melancholy Science: An Introduction to the Thought of Theodor Adorno* (London: Macmillan, 1978); Eugene Lunn, *Marxism and Modernism: An Historical Study of Lukacs, Brecht, Benjamin, and Adorno* (Berkeley: University of California Press, 1982), 149–288; and Rainer Nagele, "The Scene of the Other: Theodor Adorno's Negative Dialectics in the Context of Poststructuralism," in *Postmodernism and Politics,* ed. Jonathan Arac (Minneapolis: University of Minnesota Press, 1986), 91–111.

15. On the ironic tension between Adorno's historical sense of permanent catastrophe and his aesthetic sense of the redemptive power of art, see Jean-François Lyotard, "Adorno as the Devil," *Telos* 19 (1974): 127–37.

16. Solomon Northup, *Twelve Years a Slave: Narrative of Solomon Northup, a Citizen of New York, Kidnapped in Washington City in 1841, and Rescued in 1853, from a Cotton Plantation near the Red River, in Louisiana,* ed. Sue Eakin and Joseph Logsdon (Baton Rouge: Louisiana State University Press, 1968 [1853]), 62. Northup worked with an amanuensis, David Wilson. For a nice visual representation of the work of white amanuensis and black narrator, see the cover of William Andrews, *To Tell A Free Story: The First Century of Afro-American Autobiography, 1760–1865* (Urbana: University of Illinois Press, 1986).

17. The reference here is to Harriet Beecher Stowe's Simon Legree, the brutal slavemaster from *Uncle Tom's Cabin* (New York: Bantam, 1981 [1851–52]) who brags, "I tell ye this yer fist has got as hard as iron *knocking down niggers*" (337).

18. This is why *Minima Moralia: Reflections from Damaged Life,* trans. E. F. N. Jephcott (London: Verso, 1984 [German original, [1951]) is such an important work within Adorno's oeuvre: it supplements the synthesizing and academic rigor of

Negative Dialectics with personal memories and observational fragments, thus demonstrating how philosophy and memoir may merge in a powerful new genre. On the best practitioners of this new genre, including Adorno, Peter Dale Scott, and Ann Carson, see Stephen Hartnett, "Four Meditations on the Search for Grace amidst Terror," *Text and Performance Quarterly* 19, no. 3 (Summer 1999): 196–216.

19. Sam Worley, "Solomon Northup and the Sly Philosophy of the Slave Pen," *Callaloo* 20, no. 1 (Winter 1997): 243–59 (quotation, 256).

20. Karl Marx, *The Communist Manifesto,* ed. Frederic Bender (New York: W. W. Norton, 1988 [1848]), 71.

21. The obvious example here is Herbert Marcuse's *One-Dimensional Man: Studies in the Ideology of Advanced Industrial Society* (Boston: Beacon, 1964), whose very title suggests the reductionist perspective I am describing here. See also David Held, *Introduction to Critical Theory: Horkheimer to Habermas* (Berkeley: University of California Press, 1980); Jameson, *Marxism and Form;* Martin Jay, *The Dialectical Imagination: A History of the Frankfurt School and the Institute of Social Research, 1923–1950* (Boston: Little, Brown, 1973); and Lunn, *Marxism and Modernism.*

22. Along these lines, see Clifford Geertz's "Ideology as a Cultural System," *The Interpretation of Cultures* (New York: Basic Books, 1973), chap. 8.

23. Terry Eagleton, *Ideology: An Introduction* (London: Verso, 1991), 2; Fredric Jameson, *Postmodernism: or, The Cultural Logic of Late Capitalism* (Durham, N.C.: Duke University Press, 1991), 46. For a forceful—and disturbing—examination of this thesis, see Peter Sloterdijk, *Critique of Cynical Reason,* trans. Michael Eldred (Minneapolis: University of Minnesota Press, 1987 [German original, 1983]), chap. 2.

24. For a final attempt to salvage ideology as a useful critical tool, see Dominick LaCapra, "Culture and Ideology: From Geertz to Marx," in *The Rhetoric of Interpretation and the Interpretation of Rhetoric,* ed. Paul Hernadi (Durham, N.C.: Duke University Press, 1989), 125–42.

25. William Freehling, *The Road to Disunion: Secessionists at Bay, 1776–1854* (Oxford: Oxford University Press, 1990), 71.

26. Richard Lanham, *A Handlist of Rhetorical Terms,* 2d ed. (Berkeley: University of California Press, 1991), 102; Kenneth Burke, *A Grammar of Motives* (Berkeley: University of California Press, 1969 [1945]), 503, 506; Hayden White, *Metahistory: The Historical Imagination in Nineteenth-Century Europe* (Baltimore, Md.: John Hopkins University Press, 1973), 16–17, 35. Regarding prosopopoeia, Richard Lanigan notes that it "is a special case of metonymy in which there is a comparison by degree of the real (substance) and the imaginary (attribute)." Hence it is "a discourse that creates within the narrative per se a new narrative voice that unexpectedly judges the person by replacing the narrative function with his or her own voice as lived" ("The Algebra of History: Merleau-Ponty and Foucault on the Rhetoric of the Person," in *The Critical Turn: Rhetoric and Philosophy in Postmodern Discourse,* ed. Ian Angus and Lenore Langsdorf [Carbondale: Southern Illinois University Press, 1993], 169*n*2, 141).

27. Pierre Fontanier, *Les Figures du discours* (1821), 404, quoted in Michael Riffaterre, "Prosopopoeia," in *The Lesson of Paul de Man,* ed. Peter Brooks, Shoshana Felman, and J. Hillis Miller (New Haven, Conn.: Yale University Press, 1985), 107.

28. Thomas Jefferson, "A Draft of Instructions to the Virginia Delegates in the Continental Congress" (July 1774), in *The Papers of Thomas Jefferson*, vol. 1: *1760–1776*, ed. Julian P. Boyd (Princeton, N.J.: Princeton University Press, 1950), 130. For a reappraisal of Jefferson's writings on slavery, see Stephen Hartnett and Michael Pfau, "The Confounded Rhetorics of Race in Revolutionary America," in *The Rhetorical History of the United States*, vol. 1: *Rhetoric, Independence, and Nationhood*, ed. Stephen Lucas (East Lansing: Michigan State University Press, forthcoming).

29. For example, Thomas Ritchie argues in "Scriptural Researches" (*The Richmond Enquirer*, 10 February 1820): "We do not vindicate servitude; we wish no slave had touched our soil; we wish it could be terminated. As republicans, we frankly declare before our God and our country, that we abhor its institution. . . . [But] does not every man, unless he be a fanatic, conceive how difficult it is for us to be rid of it, in a manner consistent with our future peace and tranquility?" (quoted in Charles Sydnor, *The Development of Southern Sectionalism, 1819–1848* [Baton Rouge: Louisiana State University Press, 1948], 122).

30. David Walker, *Appeal to the Coloured Citizens of the World, but in Particular, and Very Expressly, to Those of the United States of America* (New York: Hill and Wang, 1992 [1829]). On the progress of abolitionism prior to the transformations elucidated here, see David Brion Davis, *The Problem of Slavery in the Age of Revolution, 1770–1823* (Oxford: Oxford University Press, 1999 [1975]). For a concise review of the fate of abolitionism from roughly 1832 to the start of the Civil War, see Dwight Lowell Dumond, *Antislavery Origins of the Civil War in the United States* (Ann Arbor: University of Michigan Press, 1959 [1939]).

31. Lydia Maria Child, *An Appeal in Favor of That Class of Americans Called Africans*, ed. Carolyn Karcher (Amherst: University of Massachusetts Press, 1996 [1833]), 79.

32. Robert Hariman, *Political Style: The Artistry of Power* (Chicago: University of Chicago Press, 1995), 4; this phrase is italicized in the original.

33. Child's courageous stance cost her dearly, for her abolitionist writings prompted "tolerators" to boycott her other works. Hence her popular magazine, *The Juvenile Miscellany*, was forced to fold, while her previously best-selling books, *The Frugal Housewife* and *The Mother's Book*, both stopped selling, leaving Child in dire economic straits. See Carolyn Karcher's wonderful introduction to Child's *Appeal* (xix–lxii), as well as Karcher, *The First Woman of the Republic: A Cultural Biography of Lydia Maria Child* (Durham, N.C.: Duke University Press, 1994).

34. There is little historical scholarship on Northup's work. For traditional literary analyses, see the passing references to Northup in James Olney, "'I Was Born': Slave Narratives, Their Status as Autobiography and as Literature," in *The Slave's Narrative*, ed. Charles Davis and Henry Louis Gates Jr. (Oxford: Oxford University Press, 1985), 148–74; and Robert Burns Stepto, "I Rose and Found My Voice: Narration, Authentication, and Authorial Control in Four Slave Narratives," in ibid., 225–41.

35. The seminal text on antebellum Rochester is Paul Johnson, *A Shopkeeper's Millennium: Society and Revivals in Rochester, New York, 1815–1837* (New York: Hill and Wang, 1978); regarding Rochester's status as "the fastest growing city in the United States" and its various experiments with mass-produced housing, see ibid., 37–61 ("boom town," 18). Like the rest of the Genesee Valley, Roch-

ester enjoyed its boom because the "Grand Canal" opened new markets and resources to Yankee capitalism. For example, with the advent of the canal, the charge to ship certain commodities from Lake Erie to New York City soon fell from one hundred to three dollars a ton, turning the hinterland into a player in the expanding capitalist marketplace (crop prices from Charles Sellers, *The Market Revolution: Jacksonian America, 1815–1846* [Oxford: Oxford University Press, 1991], 43).

36. For another story that illustrates Northern responses to the Fugitive Slave Act, see James Ford Rhodes's account of the 1854 Anthony Burns case in Boston in *History of the United States from the Compromise of 1850* (Chicago: Chicago University Press, 1966 [1892]), 141–47.

37. The runaway slave story appears in Arna Bontemps, *Free at Last: The Life of Frederick Douglass* (New York: Dodd, Mead, 1971), 194–96; for the controversy regarding the purchase of Douglass's freedom, see Kraditor, *Means and Ends,* 220–24.

38. Frederick Douglass, "What, to the Slave, is the Fourth of July?" (speech at Rochester, N.Y., 5 July 1852), in *Lift Every Voice: African American Oratory, 1787–1900,* ed. Philip S. Foner and Robert James Branham (Tuscaloosa: University of Alabama Press, 1998), 249–68 (quotation, 265).

39. Turning the Declaration's radical promises against the Constitution's compromises was one of Lincoln's great strategies, as Garry Wills eloquently explains in *Lincoln at Gettysburg: The Words That Remade America* (New York: Simon and Schuster, 1992). Americans employed this strategy well before Lincoln, however, as Martha Solomon Watson demonstrates in "The Dynamics of Intertextuality: Re-Reading the Declaration of Independence," in *Rhetoric and Political Culture in Nineteenth-Century America,* ed. Thomas Benson (East Lansing: Michigan State University Press, 1997), 91–112. Charles Mills, "Whose Fourth of July? Frederick Douglass and 'Original Intent,'" in *Frederick Douglass: A Critical Reader,* ed. Bill Lawson and Frank Kirkland (London: Blackwell, 1999), 109 ("thunderbolts").

40. Mills, "Whose Fourth of July?"107.

41. In calling on the self-evident Douglass appropriates a long-standing rhetorical tradition; see Garry Wills, *Inventing America: Jefferson's Declaration of Independence* (New York: Vintage, 1978), 181–92.

42. William Harper, *Memoir on Slavery* (first delivered as a speech before the South Carolina Society for the Advancement of Learning in 1837, published as a pamphlet in 1838, and then reproduced in anthologies in 1852 and 1860), in *The Ideology of Slavery: Proslavery Thought in the Antebellum South, 1830–1860,* ed. Drew Gilpin Faust (Baton Rouge: Louisiana State University Press, 1981), 80.

43. I return to the implications of this print revolution in more detail in chapters 2–4. For an example of its workings, see any of the publications lists printed in various issues of the AASS's *Almanac.* Important secondary texts here include Leonard Richards, *"Gentlemen of Property and Standing": Anti-Abolition Mobs in Jacksonian America* (Oxford: Oxford University Press, 1970); Alexander Saxton, *The Rise and Fall of the White Republic: Class Politics and Mass Culture in Nineteenth-Century America* (London: Verso, 1990); and Ronald Zboray, *A Fictive People: Antebellum Economic Development and the American Reading Public* (Oxford: Oxford University Press, 1993).

44. Douglass had previously argued the opposite of this position. See "No Union with Slaveholders" (an address delivered to the New England Anti-Slavery Society in Boston, 28 May 1844), reproduced in Gregory Lampe, *Frederick Douglass:*

Freedom's Voice, 1818–1845 (East Lansing: Michigan State University Press, 1999), 315–20. Although Lampe's discussion (227–53) of Douglass's thought during this period does not mention it, I suspect Douglass's change of heart was influenced by Lysander Spooner, *The Unconstitutionality of Slavery* (Boston: Marsh, 1853 [1845]). Regarding the Constitution's status as an unquestionably proslavery document, see Paul Finkelman, *Slavery and the Founders: Race and Liberty in the Age of Jefferson* (New York: Sharpe, 1996), 1–33.

45. On Douglass's use of irony, see John Louis Lucaites, "The Irony of 'Equality' in Black Abolitionist Discourse: The Case of Frederick Douglass's 'What to the Slave is the Fourth of July?'" in *Rhetoric and Political Culture*, ed. Benson, 47–70; and James Jasinski, "Rearticulating History in Epideictic Discourse: Frederick Douglass's 'The Meaning of the Fourth of July to the Negro,'" in ibid., 71–90. Curiously enough, neither piece mentions the "scorching irony" passage cited here.

46. See Stowe, *Uncle Tom's Cabin*, 108–9.

47. For example, when Garrison delivered his infamous 1854 Fourth of July speech in Framingham, Mass., he burned a host of such documents, each of which he characterized as sealing "a covenant with death and agreement with Hell." For a discussion of Garrison's fiery performance and the rhetorical genre of turning the Fourth of July on its head, see Branham and Hartnett, *Sweet Freedom's Song*, chap. 3. The best anthology on the subject remains Paul Goetsch and Gerd Hurm, eds., *The Fourth of July: Political Oratory and Literary Reactions, 1776–1876* (Tübingen: Gunter Narr Verlag, 1992). See the calls for uprisings reprinted in *Lift Every Voice*, ed. Foner and Branham, including those by Henry Highland Garnet (198–205), Charles Lenox Remond (205–8), William Wells Brown (213–17), Samuel Ringgold Ward (217–20), and Rev. Jermain Wesley Loguen (223–26). Regarding abolitionists' bearing "side arms," see Stewart, *Holy Warriors*, 139.

48. Ernestine Potowski Rose, "Speech at the National Woman's Rights Convention" (Worcester, Mass., 1851), in *Man Cannot Speak for Her*, vol. 2: *Key Texts of the Early Feminists*, ed. Karlyn Kohrs Campbell (New York: Greenwood, 1989), 108–9.

49. Although I disagree with it in conclusions and methodology, I learned much for this section from Ronald Walters's *Antislavery Appeal: American Abolitionism after 1830* (Baltimore, Md.: Johns Hopkins University Press, 1976), 111–28. See also Daniel McInerney, "'A State of Commerce': Market Power and Slave Power in Abolitionist Political-Economy," *Civil War History* 37, no. 2 (1991): 101–19.

50. For a fascinating debate regarding the relationships among the liberal intellectual promises of the Enlightenment, the procapitalist tendencies of modernity, and the push for abolitionism, see Thomas Haskell, "Capitalism and the Origins of the Humanitarian Sensibility, Part One," *American Historical Review* 90, no. 2 (Apr. 1985): 339–61; and idem, "Capitalism and the Origins of the Humanitarian Sensibility, Part Two" *American Historical Review* 90, no. 3 (June 1985): 547–66. For responses to Haskell, see David Brion Davis, "Reflections on Abolitionism and Ideological Hegemony," *American Historical Review* 92, no. 4 (Oct. 1987): 797–812; and John Ashworth, "The Relationship between Capitalism and Humanitarianism," *American Historical Review* 92, no. 4 (Oct. 1987): 813–28. These essays appear in Thomas Bender, ed., *The Antislavery Debate: Capitalism and Abolitionism as a Problem in Historical Interpretation* (Berkeley: University of California Press, 1992).

51. Although Child provides no formal citation, I am certain that she is quoting from Charles James Faulkner, *Speech in the House of Delegates of Virginia, on the Policy of the State with Respect to Her Slave Population, 20 January 1832* (Richmond, Va.: Thomas White, 1832).

52. See Robert Sutcliff, *Travels in Some Parts of North America, in the Years 1804, 1805 & 1806,* 2d ed. (London: Longman, Hurst, 1815) ("mercantile," v). Sutcliff was a Quaker merchant from Sheffield. His testimony is thus less objective than it may seem, for by 1815 the Quakers in both England and America were at the forefront of abolitionist activism; see Thomas Drake, *Quakers and Slavery in America* (Gloucester, Mass.: Peter Smith, 1965).

53. For examples of Leavitt's and Phillips's high praise for Yankee ingenuity and the general rhetorical strategy of abolitionists subscribing to the "gospel of progress," see John Ashworth, *Slavery, Capitalism, and Politics in the Antebellum Republic,* vol. 1: *Commerce and Compromise* (Cambridge: Cambridge University Press, 1995), 125–91.

54. "72-hour work week" from Jonathan Prude, "Town-Factory Conflicts in Antebellum Rural Massachusetts," in *The Countryside in the Age of Capitalist Transformation,* ed. Steven Hahn and Jonathan Prude (Chapel Hill: University of North Carolina Press, 1985), 89; also see Prude's outstanding work *The Coming of Industrial Order: Town and Factory Life in Rural Massachusetts, 1810–1860* (Cambridge: Cambridge University Press, 1983).

55. Edward Pessen, "The Egalitarian Myth and the American Social Reality: Wealth, Mobility, and Equality in 'The Era of the Common Man,'" *American Historical Review* 76, no. 4 (Oct. 1971): 1021–25 (figures from 989–1034); Prude, *Industrial Order,* 186; Jonathan Turner and Charles Starnes, *Inequality: Privilege and Poverty in America* (Pacific Palisades, Calif.: Goodyear, 1976), 18–19; Bruce Laurie, *Artisans into Workers: Labor in Nineteenth-Century America* (New York: Noonday, 1989), 58, 59.

56. See Pessen, "The Egalitarian Myth," 1021–25, tables 1–6; Sellers, *The Market Revolution,* 238–39; and, for an overview of the period, Douglass North, *The Economic Growth of the United States, 1790–1860* (New York: W. W. Norton, 1966 [1961]).

Chapter 2: Proslavery Cultural Fictions, White Fear, and the Rhetoric of Serious Evils

1. Thomas Paine, "African Slavery in America" (originally published under the nom de guerre "Justice and Humanity" in *The Pennsylvania Journal,* 8 March 1775), in *The Thomas Paine Reader,* ed. Michael Foot and Isaac Kramnick (New York: Penguin Books, 1987), 52–56 (quotation, 53; epigraph, 53–54); subsequent citations appear parenthetically in the text. I have altered Paine's prose slightly for readability.

2. On the early phases of abolitionist movements in both Britain and the colonies, see David Brion Davis, *The Problem of Slavery in the Age of Revolution, 1770–1823* (Oxford: Oxford University Press, 1999 [1975]); Winthrop Jordan, *White over Black: American Attitudes toward the Negro, 1550–1812* (New York: W. W. Norton, 1968), 342–74; and William Sumner Jenkins, *Pro-Slavery Thought in the Old South* (Gloucester, Mass.: Peter Smith, 1960), 3–47.

3. Benjamin Franklin, "An Address to the Public, from the Pennsylvania Society for Promoting the Abolition of Slavery" (9 November 1789), in *The Complete Works in Philosophy, Politics, and Morals, of the Late Dr. Benjamin Franklin,* vol. 3 (London: Longman, Hurst, Rees and Orme, 1806), 517.

4. Regarding Franklin's chilling call for police attention to blacks and the contemporary manifestation of this legacy of white fear, see Stephen Hartnett, "A Rhetorical Critique of the Drug War, Slavery, and 'The Nauseous Pendulum' of Reason and Violence," *Journal of Contemporary Criminal Justice* 16, no. 3 (Aug. 2000): 247–71; idem, "Prisons, Profit, Crime, and Social Control: A Hermeneutic of the Production of Violence," in *Race, Class, and Community Identity,* ed. Andrew Light and Mechthild Nagel (New York: Humanities, 2000), 199–221; idem, "Lincoln and Douglas Meet Abolitionist Walker in Prison Debate on Slavery: Empowering Education, Applied Communication, and Social Justice," *Journal of Applied Communication* 26, no. 2 (May 1998): 232–53; and idem, "Prisons, Labor, Slavery, and Capitalism in Historical Perspective," *Dark Night Field Notes* 11 (1988): 25–29, 36–37.

5. The "Plan for Improving the Condition of Free Blacks" was initially published 26 October 1789 by the Pennsylvania Society for Promoting the Abolition of Slavery. It is assumed that Franklin authored this text; it may be found in his *Complete Works,* vol. 3, pp. 519–21; subsequent citations appear parenthetically in the text.

6. Thomas Roderick Dew's "Abolition of Negro Slavery" originally appeared in *American Quarterly Review* 12 (1832) and subsequently evolved into his major work, *Review of the Debate in the Virginia Legislature of 1831 and 1832* (Richmond, 1832). The quotation here is from the version of the former that appears in *The Ideology of Slavery: Proslavery Thought in the Antebellum South, 1830–1860,* ed. Drew Gilpin Faust (Baton Rouge: Louisiana State University Press, 1981), 47. For an overview of Dew's work, see Allen Kaufman, *Capitalism, Slavery, and Republican Values: American Political Economists, 1819–1848* (Austin: University of Texas Press, 1982), 82–103, 104–20.

7. This paradox still haunts us; see Michael Rogin, "The Two Declarations of American Independence," *Representations* 55 (Summer 1996): 13–30. For two alternative readings, see Stephen Hartnett and Michael Pfau, "The Confounded Rhetorics of Race in Revolutionary America," in *The Rhetorical History of the United States,* vol. 1: *Rhetoric, Independence, and Nationhood,* ed. Stephen Lucas (East Lansing: Michigan State University Press, forthcoming); and Celeste Michelle Condit and John Louis Lucaites, *Crafting Equality: America's Anglo-African World* (Chicago: University of Chicago Press, 1993).

8. Peter Dorsey, "Becoming the Other: The Mimesis of Metaphor in Douglass's My Bondage and My Freedom," *Publications of the Modern Language Association* 111, no. 3 (May 1996): 446–47. Also see T. Gregory Garvey, "Frederick Douglass's Change of Opinion on the U.S. Constitution: Abolitionism and the 'Elements of Moral Power,'" *ATQ* 9, no. 3 (1995): 229–43, as well as comments in chapter 1 of this book.

9. Chief Justice Roger B. Taney, 6 March 1857 majority opinion in *Dred Scott v. John F. A. Sanford,* in *The Civil Rights Record: Black Americans and the Law, 1849–1970,* ed. Richard Bardolph (New York: Thomas Y. Crowell, 1970), 17–19. Taney's verdict was perceived as doubly damaging to the North, for it not only supported Southern interests in enforcing the Fugitive Slave Act but also ruled

that the 1820 Missouri Compromise was unconstitutional. In doing so, however, it suggested that Steven Douglas's "popular sovereignty" platform—which held out the possibility that local constituents could vote against slavery and hence for extending democratic rights to all citizens—was but a ruse employed by proslavery advocates. Thus Rush Welter concludes in *The Mind of America, 1820–1860* (New York: Columbia University Press, 1975) that "the action of the Court in outlawing Douglas's panacea clearly doomed his hopes for the presidency and guaranteed the failure of the Democratic Union" (378). Also see David M. Potter, *The Impending Crisis: 1848–1861* (New York: Harper, 1963), 267–96; Priscilla Wald, "Terms of Assimilation: Legislating Subjectivity in the Emerging Nation," in *Cultures of United States Imperialism,* ed. Amy Kaplan and Donald Pease (Durham, N.C.: Duke University Press, 1993), 59–84; and Todd McDorman, "Challenging Constitutional Authority: African American Responses to *Scott v. Sandford,*" *Quarterly Journal of Speech* 83, no. 2 (May 1997): 192–209.

10. John Quincy Adams, "Address of the Honorable J. Q. Adams, to his Constituents of the Eighth Congressional District, in Dedham, October 21, 1843" (first published in the *Boston Atlas,* 26 October 1843), reproduced in Frederick Merk, *Slavery and the Annexation of Texas* (New York: Knopf, 1972), 237–44 (quotations, 240, 239). For additional discussion of Adams's complicated battles with slavery, see William Lee Miller, *Arguing about Slavery: The Great Battle in the United States Congress* (New York: Knopf, 1996).

11. The crucial passages on Marx's theory of reification are found in *Capital: A Critique of Political Economy,* vol. 1, trans. Ben Fowkes (New York: Vintage Books, 1977 [German original, 1867]), 125–244. Regarding the three-fifths clause, see Harold Ohline, "Republicanism and Slavery: Origins of the Three-Fifths Clause in the United States Constitution," *William and Mary Quarterly* 28 (October 1971): 563–84.

12. Robert Rantoul Jr., speech before the Grand Massachusetts Convention in Lynn, Mass., 3 April 1851, in *Memoirs, Speeches, and Writings of Robert Rantoul, Jr.,* ed. Luther Hamilton (Boston: John Jewett, 1854), 733; see also comments on Rantoul in chapter 1 of this book. Although Adams—much like Rantoul—strives here to distance himself from radical abolitionism, his critics mercilessly portrayed him as a raving agent of destruction. For example, in a long letter published in the *Boston Post* (10 Oct. 1843), the *New York Herald* (12 Oct. 1843), and *Niles' Register* (21 Oct. 1843), Duff Green refers to Adams as a "venerable but deluded man" whom Green says is conspiring with the British in a plot to abolish slavery and steal Texas (the letter is reproduced in Merk, *Slavery and Annexation,* 231–34). In an editorial written explicitly as a response to Adams's Dedham speech of 21 October, *The Madisonian* (31 Oct. 1843) attacked Adams as an "abolitionist fanatic" and as "the acknowledged leader in this work of contemplated destruction" (in Merk, *Slavery and Annexation,* 247). And see Miller, *Arguing about Slavery.*

13. See Larry Gara, "Slavery and the Slave Power: A Crucial Distinction," *Civil War History* 15, no. 1 (Mar. 1969): 5–18.

14. Abraham Lincoln, in his first rejoinder to Douglas's opening remarks at the 21 August 1858 debate in Ottawa, Illinois, in *The Lincoln-Douglas Debates: The First Complete, Unexpurgated Text,* ed. Harold Holzer (New York: HarperPerennial, 1993), 63. For a concise introduction to Lincoln's thoughts on slavery, see Robert Johannsen, *Lincoln, the South, and Slavery: The Political Dimension* (Ba-

ton Rouge: Louisiana State University Press, 1991). The best rhetorical analysis of the debates remains David Zarefsky, *Lincoln, Douglas, and Slavery: In the Crucible of Public Debate* (Chicago: University of Chicago Press, 1990).

15. George Fitzhugh, "To the People of the South," author's preface to *Sociology for the South; or The Failure of Free Society* (Richmond: A. Morris, 1854), iii.

16. I am thinking here of Bernard Bailyn's eloquent argument for studying the pamphlets popular during the War of Independence: "For all their variety they have in common one distinctive characteristic: they are, to an unusual degree, *explanatory.* They reveal not merely positions taken but the reasons why positions were taken; they reveal motive and understanding: the assumptions, beliefs, and ideas—the articulated world view—that lay behind the manifest events of the time" (*The Ideological Origins of the American Revolution* [Cambridge, Mass.: Harvard University Press, 1967], vi).

17. Eric McKitrick, "A Hero of Antislavery" (review of Miller, *Arguing about Slavery*), *New York Review of Books,* 14 Nov. 1996, p. 46; Louis Hartz, *The Liberal Tradition in America: An Interpretation of American Political Thought Since the Revolution* (New York: Harcourt, Brace, 1955), 147. In this same chapter Hartz, like McKitrick, relies on the charge of madness to describe proslavery advocates; see his discussion of Calhoun and Fitzhugh, 158–67.

18. Justin Smith, *The Annexation of Texas* (New York: AMS, 1971 [1911]), 120. Upshur was Tyler's secretary of the navy from 1841 to 1843 and was appointed secretary of state in 1843.

19. The *Vicksburg Daily Whig,* 1860, quoted in Philip Foner, *Business and Slavery: The New York Merchants and the Irrepressible Conflict* (New York: Russell and Russell, 1968 [1941]), 10, 7.

20. First published in Charleston in 1838 as *Memoir on Slavery, Read Before the Society for the Advancement of Learning of South Carolina at Its Annual Meeting at Columbia, 1837,* and then as *Slavery in the Light of Social Ethics* in the massive proslavery anthology *Cotton Is King, and Pro-Slavery Arguments: Comprising the Writings of Hammond, Harper, Christy, Stringfellow, Hodge, Bledsoe, and Cartwright, on this Important Subject,* ed. E. N. Elliott (Augusta, Ga.: Pritchard, Abbott and Loomis, 1860), 547–626; I quote from the version in *Ideology of Slavery,* ed. Faust, 92.

21. J. D. B. De Bow, "The Cause of the South," *De Bow's Review* 9 (July 1850), in *The Cause of the South: Selections from De Bow's Review, 1846–1867,* ed. Paul Paskoff and Daniel Wilson (Baton Rouge: Louisiana State University Press, 1982), 185.

22. Lydia Maria Child, *An Appeal in Favor of That Class of Americans Called Africans,* ed. Carolyn Karcher (Amherst: University of Massachusetts Press, 1996 [1833]), 186–87.

23. See Eric Hobsbawm, *The Age of Revolution, 1789–1848* (New York: Vintage, 1996 [1962]), 27–52; Fernand Braudel, *The Wheels of Commerce: Civilization and Capitalism, 15th–18th Century,* vol. 2 (New York: Harper and Row, 1982 [1979]), 264–81; Raimondo Luraghi, "The Civil War and the Modernization of American Society: Social Structure and Industrial Revolution in the Old South before and during the War," *Civil War History* 18, no. 3 (1972): 230–50; and Immanuel Wallerstein, "American Slavery and the Capitalist World Economy," *American Journal of Sociology* 81, no. 5 (Mar. 1976): 1199–1213.

24. Gavin Wright, *The Political Economy of the Cotton South: Households,*

Markets, and Wealth in the Nineteenth Century (New York: W. W. Norton, 1978), 108, table 4.1. For more along these same lines, see Eugene Genovese, *The Political Economy of Slavery: Studies in the Economy and Society of the Slave South* (New York: Vintage Books, 1967 [1961]), where Genovese argues that "negro slavery retarded technological progress" (50).

25. Cited in Leonard Richards, *"Gentlemen of Property and Standing": Anti-Abolition Mobs in Jacksonian America* (Oxford: Oxford University Press, 1970), 123–24.

26. Hinton Rowan Helper, *Compendium of the Impending Crisis of the South* (New York: A. B. Burdick, 1860), 12–14 (originally issued in 1857 as *The Impending Crisis of the South: How to Meet It*).

27. Robert William Fogel and Stanley Engerman, *Time on the Cross: The Economics of American Negro Slavery,* vol. 1 (Boston: Little, Brown, 1974), 41. Fogel and Engerman's book prompted a firestorm of criticism; see Herbert Gutman, *Slavery and the Numbers Game: A Critique of Time on the Cross* (Urbana: University of Illinois Press, 1975); and Paul David and Peter Temin, "Capitalist Masters, Bourgeois Slaves," *Journal of Interdisciplinary History* 5, no. 3 (Winter 1975): 445–57.

28. Robert William Fogel, *Without Consent or Contract: The Rise and Fall of American Slavery* (New York: W. W. Norton, 1989), 44–45.

29. See Fred Bateman and Thomas Weiss, "Comparative Regional Development in Ante-Bellum Manufacturing," *Journal of Economic History* 35, no. 1 (Mar. 1975): 184, table 1; Wright, *Political Economy of the South,* 110, table 4.2; and Fred Bateman and Thomas Weiss, *A Deplorable Scarcity: The Failure of Industrialization in the Slave Economy* (Chapel Hill: University of North Carolina Press, 1981).

30. Regarding the question of monopoly, Howard Temperley has estimated in "Capitalism, Slavery and Ideology" (*Past and Present* 75 [May 1977]: 102) that the antebellum United States controlled 80 percent of world cotton production.

31. Solomon Northup, *Twelve Years a Slave: Narrative of Solomon Northup, a Citizen of New York, Kidnapped in Washington City in 1841, and Rescued in 1853, from a Cotton Plantation near the Red River, in Louisiana,* ed. Sue Eakin and Joseph Logsdon (Baton Rouge: Louisiana State University Press, 1968 [1853]), 240.

32. The debate over plantation self-sufficiency is long-standing and typically heated. See Robert Gallman, "Self Sufficiency in the Cotton Economy of the Ante-Bellum South," in *The Structure of the Cotton Economy of the Ante-Bellum South,* ed. William Parker (Washington, D.C.: Agricultural Historical Society, 1970), 5–23; Lacy Ford, "Self-Sufficiency, Cotton, and Economic Development in the South Carolina Upcountry, 1800–1860," *Journal of Economic History* 45, no. 2 (June 1985): 261–67; and Gavin Wright, "The Efficiency of Slavery: Another Interpretation," *American Economic Review* 69, no. 1 (Mar. 1979): 219–26.

33. Stephen Colwell, *The Five Cotton States and New York; or, Remarks Upon the Social and Economical Aspects of the Southern Political Crisis* (N.p.: n.p., 1861), 22–26. Foner suggests that Colwell's figures are too low and that the trade deficit with New York was actually much higher; see Foner, *Business and Slavery,* 7–8.

34. Thomas Prentice Kettell, *Southern Wealth and Northern Profits: As Exhibited in Statistical Facts and Official Figures; Showing the Necessity of Union to*

the Future Prosperity and Welfare of the Republic (Birmingham: University of Alabama Press, 1965 [1860]), 98. Kettell drew a much different conclusion from this fact than did either Colwell or Foner, for Kettell argues that these figures suggest the North to be economically dependent on the South, not the reverse.

35. Quoted in James Oakes, "From Republicanism to Liberalism: Ideological Change and the Crisis of the Old South" (1985), in *Articles on American Slavery*, vol. 12: *Proslavery Thought, Ideology, and Politics*, ed. Paul Finkelman (New York: Garland, 1989), 351.

36. One obvious result of this lack of investment in infrastructural developments is the South's marked lack of institutions of higher education. Thus the 1850 census reports that whereas illiteracy was less than 1 percent in New England, it was a shocking 20.3 percent in the South. See Drew Gilpin Faust, *A Sacred Circle: The Dilemma of the Intellectual in the Old South, 1840–1860* (Baltimore, Md.: Johns Hopkins University Press, 1977), 7–11 (census figures, 8).

37. "Super-exploitation" is clearly the key to the productivity of slavery. As Kenneth Stampp observes in *The Peculiar Institution: Slavery in the Ante-Bellum South* (New York: Vintage Books, 1956), "Slave labor had several competitive advantages over free white labor . . . It was paid less. . . . masters exploited women and children more fully than did the employers of free labor. . . . [Compared to free white labor,] the bondsman worked longer hours and was subjected to a more rigid discipline" (400).

38. Quotations from Paul David and Peter Temin, "Explaining the Relative Efficiency of Slave Agriculture in the Antebellum South: Comment," *American Economic Review* 69, no. 1 (Mar. 1979): 213–18.

39. Fogel and Engerman, *Time on the Cross*, 248, 249.

40. Fogel, *Without Consent or Contract*, 84.

41. The figure of 3.1 white males per family is from Lee Soltow, "Economic Inequality in the United States in the Period from 1790 to 1860," *Journal of Economic History* 21, no. 4 (Dec. 1971): 835. Regarding the figures in this paragraph on slave ownership, see James Foust, *The Yeoman Farmer and Westward Expansion of U.S. Cotton Production* (New York: Arno, 1975), esp. 71, table 14.

42. Otto Olsen, "Historians and the Extent of Slave Ownership in the Southern United States," *Civil War History* 18, no. 2 (1972): 112, 113.

43. I have been influenced here by Morton Rothstein's argument in "The Antebellum South as a Dual Economy: A Tentative Hypothesis" (*Agricultural History* 41, no. 4 [Oct. 1967]: 375) that "self-sufficiency," when used to describe small-scale Southern farmers, amounts to "a delightful euphemism for rural poverty."

44. Wright, *Political Economy*, 34, 35.

45. Ralph Anderson and Robert Gallman, "Slaves as Fixed Capital: Slave Labor and Southern Economic Development," *Journal of American History* 64, no. 1 (June 1977): 38–39. For the economic rationality of slavery, see Heywood Fleisig, "Slavery, the Supply of Agricultural Labor, and the Industrialization of the South," *Journal of Economic History* 36, no. 3 (Sept. 1976): 572–97.

46. *The Annual Report of the American Anti-Slavery Society for 1855*, 80–81, quoted in Foner, *Business and Slavery*, 53; response quoted in ibid., 14.

47. George Foster, "Butter Cake Dick's" (originally printed in 1850 in Foster's tour guide, *New York by Gas-Light, with Here and There a Streak of Sunshine*), in *New York by Gas-Light and Other Urban Sketches by George Foster*, ed. Stuart Blumin (Berkeley: University of California Press, 1990), 119.

48. For important antebellum examples of proslavery arguments based on religion, see the following, all reproduced in *Cotton Is King,* ed. Elliot: Albert Taylor Bledsoe, *Liberty and Slavery: or, Slavery in the Light of Moral and Political Philosophy* (337–80); Thornton Stringfellow, *The Bible Argument: or, Slavery in the Light of Divine Revelation* (459–521); and Charles Hodge, *The Bible Argument on Slavery* (841–77). For a colorful account of the use of "Scripter" to intimidate slaves, see Northup, *Twelve Years a Slave,* 94.

49. For the historical roots of the "positive good" thesis, see Larry Tise, *Proslavery: A History of the Defense of Slavery in America, 1701–1840* (Athens: University of Georgia Press, 1987), 97–124; Jenkins, *Pro-Slavery Thought,* 65–81; and W. B. Hesseltine, "Some Aspects of the Pro-Slavery Argument," *Journal of Negro History* 21, no. 1 (Jan. 1936): 1–14. Similar positive good arguments may be found in G. W. F. Hegel, *The Philosophy of History,* trans. J. Sibree (New York: Prometheus, 1991 [German original, 1822]), 98–99.

50. Laurence Shore, *Southern Capitalists: The Ideological Leadership of an Elite, 1832–1885* (Chapel Hill: University of North Carolina Press, 1986), 22. See also Kenneth Stampp, "An Analysis of T. R. Dew's *Review of the Debates in the Virginia Legislature,*" *Journal of Negro History* 27 (1942): 380–87.

51. Faust notes that between 1817 and 1829, land values fell by "more than half," and "exports slumped by two-thirds" (*Sacred Circle,* 11). Hesseltine reports that by 1827 over one hundred abolitionist societies existed in the South ("Some New Aspects," 8). For an example of the tone of the debates, see Charles James Faulkner, *Speech in the House of Delegates of Virginia, on the Policy of the State with Respect to Her Slave Population, 20 January 1832* (Richmond, Va.: Thomas White, 1832).

52. Quoted in Harvey Wish's introduction to *Ante-Bellum: Three Classic Works on Slavery in the Old South by Hinton Rowan Helper and George Fitzhugh,* ed. Wish (New York: Capricorn, 1960), 6.

53. David Christy, *Cotton Is King: or, The Culture of Cotton, and Its Relation to Agriculture, Manufactures, and Commerce* (Cincinnati, Ohio: Moore, Wilstach, Keys, 1855), 43.

54. Edmund Ruffin, *The Political Economy of Slavery; or, The Institution Considered in Regard to Its Influence on Public Wealth and the General Welfare* (N.p.: n.p., n.d.; the text has been cited elsewhere as having been published in Washington, D.C., 1853), 5. See William Mathew, *Edmund Ruffin and the Crisis of Slavery in the Old South* (Athens: Georgia University Press, 1988), 56–66.

55. The sentence immediately preceding the one quoted here observes that "those who have praised savage life are those who know nothing of it, or who have become savages themselves" (91). Perhaps later research on Harper will be able to determine convincingly whether, as I suspect, this barb is directed at Rousseau's *Discourse on Inequality* (New York: Penguin Books, 1984 [1754]), where, amid a celebration of "savage man," Rousseau attacks slavery as "violence to nature" (128).

56. Eugene Genovese, "Yeoman Farmers in a Slaveholders' Democracy," *Agricultural History* 49 (1975): 338, 340; reprinted in Elizabeth Fox-Genovese and Eugene Genovese, *Fruits of Merchant Capital: Slavery and Bourgeois Property in the Rise and Expansion of Capitalism* (Oxford: Oxford University Press, 1983): 249–64. See also William Freehling, *The Road to Disunion: Secessionists at Bay, 1776–1854* (Oxford: Oxford University Press, 1990), 39–58.

57. For an example of this class longing, see "A Small Farmer," "Management of Negroes," *De Bow's Review* 11 (1851), where the author imagines himself as a future plantation master (reproduced in Paskoff and Wilson, eds., *Cause of the South,* 44–47).

58. "J," "The National Anniversary," *Southern Quarterly Review,* n.s., 2, no. 3 (Sept. 1850): 170–91 (quotation, 182).

59. Regarding the rhetorical precedents established in Britain's earlier debates on slavery, the earl of Abingdon, in a classic example of the impending doom thesis spun on as wide a scale as possible, argued in Parliament in 1793 that by considering abolition, "the Order, and Subordination, *the Happiness of the whole habitable Globe* is threatened" (quoted in Davis, *The Problem of Slavery,* 345).

60. Again, this apparently hyperbolic claim is based at least in part in a sound understanding of the laws of capitalism. Indeed, Foner (*Business and Slavery,* 217–18) reports that with the outbreak of war, New York merchants found themselves stiffed for loans and services to Southern plantations totaling as much as $150,000,000.

61. "White Slavery," *The Madisonian,* 30 October 1843, pp. 245–47 (quotation, 246–47), reproduced in Merk, *Slavery and Annexation,* 246–47. The threat of impending civil war is repeated again in "The Extension of Slavery," *The Madisonian,* 27 November 1843, also in Merk, *Slavery and Annexation,* 255–57.

62. Thomas Slaughter, *Bloody Dawn: The Christiana Riot and Racial Violence in the Antebellum North* (Oxford: Oxford University Press, 1991), xi. On the impact of the Haitian revolution on American thought regarding race and slavery, see Jordan, *White over Black,* 375–426.

63. John Greenleaf Whittier, verse 12 from "Our Countrymen in Chains!" reproduced in Lydia Maria Child, *The Evils of Slavery, and the Cure of Slavery. The First Proved by the Opinion of Southerners Themselves, the Last Shown by Historical Evidence,* 2d ed. (Newburyport, Mass.: Charles Whipple, 1839), 22. Whittier, a passionate opponent of slavery, was frequently called the "muse of the movement"; see the poems collected under the subheading "Voices of Freedom" in *The Poetical Works of John Greenleaf Whittier* (Boston: Ticknor and Fields, 1857), 41–80.

64. David Walker, *Appeal to the Coloured Citizens of the World, but in Particular, and Very Expressly, to Those of the United States of America* (New York: Hill and Wang, 1992 [1829]), 39. See also Jacqueline Bacon, "'Do You Understand Your Own Language?' Revolutionary *Topoi* in the Rhetoric of African-American Abolitionists," *Rhetoric Society Quarterly* 28, no. 2 (Spring 1988): 55–75.

65. Alexis de Tocqueville, *Democracy in America,* vol. 1 (New York: Vintage, 1990 [1835]), 379, 376, 379.

66. Robert Hariman, "Prudence/Performance," *Rhetoric Society Quarterly* 21, no. 2 (Spring 1991): 26, 27, 29; also see James Jasinski, "The Forms and Limits of Prudence in Henry Clay's Defense of the Compromise Measures," *Quarterly Journal of Speech* 81 (1995): 454–78.

67. Thomas Walker Gilmer, "Texas and the United States," *Baltimore Republican and Argus,* 10 January 1843, reproduced in Merk, *Slavery and Annexation,* 200–204 (quotation, 202).

68. "White Slavery," *The Madisonian,* 30 October 1843, p. 246.

69. Anonymous, "Modern Philanthropy and Negro Slavery," *De Bow's Review* 16, no. 3 (Mar. 1854): 263.

70. Catharine Beecher, *An Essay on Slavery and Abolitionism, with Reference to the Duty of American Females* (Philadelphia: Henry Perkins, 1837), 13–14.

71. "Do Nothingism" from Freehling, *Road to Disunion,* 427.

72. For reviews of these debates, see William Freehling, *The Reintegration of American History* (Oxford: Oxford University Press, 1994), 12–33; Paul Finkelman, "Slavery and the Constitutional Convention: Making a Covenant with Death," in *Beyond Confederation: Origins of the Constitution and American National Identity,* ed. Richard Beeman, Stephen Botein, and Edward C. Carter II (Williamsburg, Va.: Institute of Early American History and Culture, 1987), 188–225; Herbert Storing, "Slavery and the Moral Foundations of the American Republic," in *The Moral Foundations of the American Republic,* ed. Robert Horwitz (Charlottesville: University of Virginia Press, 1979), 214–33; Earl Maltz, "The Idea of the Proslavery Constitution," *Journal of the Early Republic* 17, no. 1 (Spring 1997): 37–59; Davis, *The Problem of Slavery,* 164–212; and Jenkins, *Pro-Slavery Thought,* 121–73.

73. The term *miscegenation* was first used in public by David Croly in an 1864 essay in the *New York Daily Graphic.* Regarding the first slew of amalgamation laws (Virginia in 1662; six other colonies by 1725), see James Kinney, *Amalgamation! Race, Sex, and Rhetoric in the Nineteenth-Century Novel* (Westport, Conn.: Greenwood, 1985), 1–34; and Jordan, *White over Black,* 136–78.

74. Gustave de Beaumont, *Marie; or, Slavery in the United States,* trans. Barbara Chapman (Baltimore, Md.: Johns Hopkins University Press, 1999 [1835]), 5.

75. Quoted in Richards, *"Gentlemen of Property,"* 109. Lovejoy was killed in the attack. Also see Dwight Lowell Dumond, *Antislavery Origins of the Civil War in the United States* (Ann Arbor: University of Michigan Press, 1959 [1939]), 51–66.

76. See Linda Kerber, "Abolitionists and Amalgamators: The New York City Race Riots of 1834," *New York History* 48, no. 1 (Jan. 1967): 28–39; Richards, *"Gentlemen of Property,"* 111–21; and Beaumont, *Marie,* 243–52.

77. Quoted in Richards, *"Gentlemen of Property,"* 122.

78. Quoted in Eric Foner, *Free Soil, Free Labor, Free Men: The Ideology of the Republican Party before the Civil War* (Oxford: Oxford University Press, 1970), 263.

79. Kenneth Burke, "Four Master Tropes," *A Grammar of Motives* (Berkeley: University of California Press, 1969 [1945]), 503, 506.

80. Dr. Josiah C. Nott, *Two Lectures on the Natural History of the Caucasian and Negro Races* (originally published in Mobile, Ala., in 1844), reproduced in Faust, *Ideology of Slavery,* 208–38 (quotations, 228 and 219).

81. *Ruthey Ann Hansley v. Samuel G. Hansley,* argued before the North Carolina Supreme Court, 1849, in *A Documentary History of Slavery in North America,* ed. Willie Lee Rose (Oxford: Oxford University Press, 1976), 427–34 (quotations, 428–29).

82. For the abolitionist version of this thesis, in which amalgamation is understood as the result of the institutionally sanctioned rape of slaves, see Theodor Weld et al., *American Slavery as It Is: Testimony of a Thousand Witnesses* (New York: American Anti-Slavery Society, 1839), 15.

83. See Thomas Brown, "The Miscegenation of Richard Mentor Johnson as an Issue in the National Election Campaign of 1835–1836," *Civil War History* 39, no. 1 (1993): 5–30. Amalgamation was so common in the Deep South that, according to Joel Williamson in *New People: Miscegenation and Mulattoes in the United*

States (New York: Free Press, 1980), "on the eve of the Revolution, Charleston was half white and half Negro, and its Negro half was more white than black" (41). According to estimates drawn from the 1850 census, as much as 75 percent of the "Negro" population had some "white blood" (this figure appears in both Williamson, *Miscegenation,* 63, and Eugene Genovese, *Roll, Jordan, Roll: The World the Slaves Made* [New York: Vintage, 1972], 414).

84. Regarding Lincoln's conspiracy charges, see Zarefsky, *Lincoln, Douglas, and Slavery,* 68–110; and Fred Kauffeld, "Veracity, Accusation and Conspiracy in Lincoln's Campaign for the Senate," *Rhetoric Society Quarterly* 24, nos. 1–2 (1994): 5–26.

85. See James Bilotta, *Race and the Rise of the Republican Party, 1848–1865* (New York: Peter Lang, 1992), 227–301; Foner, *Free Soil;* and William Gienapp, "Nativism and the Creation of a Republican Majority in the North before the Civil War," *Journal of American History* 72, no. 3 (Dec. 1985): 529–59.

86. Regarding women as objects, Genovese reports that "fancy girl markets" were common in New Orleans and "a few other cities" and that in these markets, whereas "first-class blacksmiths were being sold for $2,500 and prime field hands for about $1,800, a particularly beautiful girl or young woman might bring $5,000" (*Roll, Jordan, Roll,* 416). This price is corroborated in Northup, *Twelve Years a Slave,* 58.

87. Eva Saks, "Representing Miscegenation Law," *Raritan* 8, no. 2 (Fall 1988): 41, 50, 58.

88. See James Hugo Johnston, *Miscegenation in the Ante-Bellum South* (Chicago: University of Chicago Libraries, 1939).

89. Regarding the tortured question of slavery and science, see William Stanton, *The Leopard's Spots: Scientific Attitudes toward Race in America, 1815–1859* (Chicago: University of Chicago Press, 1960); and Jenkins, *Pro-Slavery Thought,* 242–84.

90. Benjamin Bowman to his brother, 24 July 1860, quoted in Randolph Campbell, *An Empire for Slavery: The Peculiar Institution in Texas* (Baton Rouge: Louisiana State University Press, 1989), 225–26 (match information, 224).

91. George Fitzhugh, "The Conservative Principle; or, Social Evils and Their Remedies," *De Bow's Review* 22 (Apr. 1857): 419–30 (quotation, 420).

92. See Sigmund Freud, *Group Psychology and the Analysis of the Ego,* trans. and ed. James Strachey (New York: W. W. Norton, 1989 [1921]); and Herbert Marcuse, *Eros and Civilization: A Philosophical Inquiry into Freud* (Boston: Beacon, 1966 [1955]).

93. Letter to Edward Everett, 27 April 1843, reproduced in Merk, *Slavery and Annexation,* 211–12 (quotation, 211).

94. Conservative forces in Germany used this metonymic critique of British imperial interests when they referred to British market encroachments as the onslaught of "Manchesterism." See Eric Hobsbawm, *The Age of Capital, 1848–1875* (New York: Random House, 1996 [1975]), 104.

95. See Wilfred Carsel, "The Slaveholders' Indictment of Northern Wage Slavery," *Journal of Southern History* 6, no. 4 (Nov. 1940): 504–20.

96. Walter Whitman, "Black and White Slaves," *New York Aurora,* 2 April 1842, in *Walt Whitman of the New York Aurora; Editor at Twenty-Two,* ed. Joseph Rubin and Charles Brown (State College, Pa.: Bald Eagle, 1950), 126.

97. George Holmes, "The Failure of Free Societies," *Southern Literary Messenger* 21, no. 3 (Mar. 1855): 136. For the permutations of this argument within abolitionist discourse, see Aileen Kraditor, *Means and Ends in American Abolitionism: Garrison and His Critics on Strategy and Tactics, 1834–1850* (New York: Pantheon, 1969 [1967]), 247–60.

98. George Fitzhugh, *Cannibals All! or Slaves Without Masters,* ed. C. Vann Woodward (Cambridge, Mass.: Harvard University Press, 1960 [1857]), 59.

99. Fitzhugh's use of the word *socialism* has caused much controversy. Relevant responses from his peers include that of Holmes in "Failure of Free Societies." In the only extended biography of Fitzhugh (*George Fitzhugh: Propagandist of the Old South* [Baton Rouge: Louisiana State University, 1943]), Harvey Wish uses the reference to socialism as a pretext for associating both Marx and Marxism with slavery (182–83). For a blistering, almost comically vindictive response to Wish, see Eugene Genovese, *The World the Slaveholders Made: Two Essays in Interpretation* (New York: Vintage Books, 1969), 181–84.

100. The first quotation is from David Donald, "The Proslavery Argument Reconsidered," *Journal of Southern History* 37, no. 1 (Feb. 1971), 10; the second and third quotations are from Faust, *Sacred Circle,* 129 and 128. For a contrasting view to Donald's and Faust's, see Robert Garson, "Proslavery as Political Theory: The Examples of John C. Calhoun and George Fitzhugh," *South Atlantic Quarterly* 84 (1985): 197–212.

101. Genovese, "Yeoman Farmers," 336, 335. See also Arthur Bestor, "State Sovereignty and Slavery: A Reinterpretation of Proslavery Constitutional Doctrine, 1846–1860," *Journal of the Illinois State Historical Society* 54 (1961): 117–80.

102. See Charles Sellers, *The Market Revolution: Jacksonian America, 1815–1846* (Oxford: Oxford University Press, 1991), 103–36.

103. See B. F. Wright Jr., "George Fitzhugh on the Failure of Liberty," *Southwestern Political and Social Science Quarterly* 6, no. 3 (1926): 219–41.

104. Hammond, then serving as a South Carolina representative, delivered his famous "mud-sill" speech in the Senate on 4 March 1858. Regarding this organic, "mud-sill" thesis, see Jenkins, *Pro-Slavery Thought,* 286; and Ruffin, *Political Economy of Slavery,* 3.

105. For more along these lines, see Freehling, *Reintegration of American History,* 82–104; and Garson, "Proslavery as Political Theory."

106. Marvin Meyer, *The Jacksonian Persuasion: Politics and Belief* (New York: Vintage, 1960), 161, 164.

107. For additional examples of this claim, see L.C.B., "The Country in 1950, or The Conservatism of Slavery," *Southern Literary Messenger* 22 (June 1856): 426–39; and J. D. B. De Bow's review of Fitzhugh in "Cannibals All; or, Slaves Without Masters," *De Bow's Review* 22 (May 1857): 543–49. For reviews of this claim, see Carsel, "The Slaveholders' Indictment"; and Hartz, *Liberal Tradition in America,* 145–77.

108. *Federalist* no. 10, in James Madison, Alexander Hamilton, and John Jay, *The Federalist: A Collection of Essays Written in Favour of the New Constitution, as Agreed Upon by the Federal Convention, September 17, 1787,* ed. Isaac Kramnick (New York: Penguin Books, 1987 [1788]), 122–28 (quotation, 128).

109. L.C.B., "The Country in 1950," 433, 428.

110. Even Fitzhugh's contemporaries considered his rhetoric troublesome. For example, although his review of *Sociology for the South* is overwhelmingly pos-

itive, Holmes describes Fitzhugh's rhetoric as suffering from "a want of fullness, of precision, and of moderation," and as engaging in a "profusion of wild fantasies" that "render it unsuitable for a text-book" (for college students) and that "might perhaps prove hazardous to youthful students" ("Failure of Free Societies," 129, 130). In a similar vein, although J. D. B. De Bow suggests in "Cannibals All" that Fitzhugh should be celebrated as "one of the boldest and most daring thinkers of the age" (543), he also cautions, "We doubt not that there are points which the author strains too far" (545).

111. See Bruce Laurie, *Artisans into Workers: Labor in Nineteenth-Century America* (New York: Noonday, 1989), 74–112 (quotations, 97–98). Readers may follow the riots in great detail in the pages of *The Liberator,* beginning with the multiple stories in 12, no. 32 (12 Aug. 1842), and continuing for several issues.

112. See Michael Holt, "The Politics of Impatience: The Origins of Know Nothingism," *Journal of American History* 60, no. 2 (Sept. 1973): 309–31; Leon Cyprian Soule, *The Know Nothing Party in New Orleans: A Reappraisal* (Baton Rouge: Louisiana Historical Association, 1961); Anthony Gene Carey, "Too Southern to Be Americans: Proslavery Politics and the Failure of the Know-Nothing Party in Georgia, 1854–1856," *Civil War History* 61, no. 1 (Mar. 1995): 22–40; and Tyler Anbinder, *Nativism and Slavery: The Northern Know Nothings and the Politics of the 1850s* (Oxford: Oxford University Press, 1992).

113. Laurie, *Artisans into Workers,* 105, 106; Foner, *Free Soil,* 250. For an analysis of the anti-Catholic sentiments behind the nativist movement, see John Higham, *Strangers in the Land: Patterns of American Nativism, 1860–1925* (New York: Athenaeum, 1965), 3–34; and Gienapp, "Nativism."

114. Quoted in Gienapp, "Nativism," 531.

115. "Beware of Foreign Influence," 22" × 28½" broadside from Kingston, New York, printed by the American Republican Town Nominations Committee. No date is given on the broadside, yet one may safely situate it as part of the November 1843 elections; see Anbinder, *Nativism and Slavery,* 11–12.

116. Michael Holt, *The Political Crisis of the 1850s* (New York: Wiley, 1978), 174.

117. The crash of 1837 was devastating; see Samuel Reznick, "The Social History of an American Depression, 1837–1843," *American Historical Review* 40, no. 4 (July 1935): 662–87. On the drought of 1854 and its damaging effects on river and canal transportation, see Holt, *Political Crisis of the 1850s,* 159–61.

118. Sean Wilentz, *Chants Democratic: New York City and the Rise of the American Working Class, 1788–1850* (Oxford: Oxford University Press, 1984), 323.

119. Child, *Evils of Slavery,* back page (unnumbered); Lydia Maria Child, *Anti-Slavery Catechism,* 2d ed. (Newburyport, Mass.: Charles Whipple, 1839), back page (unnumbered).

120. Tyler's speech quoted in Richards, *"Gentlemen of Property,"* 55–58.

121. Richards, *"Gentlemen of Property,"* 168.

122. Dumond, *Antislavery Origins,* 19.

123. See Douglas Egerton, "'Its Origin is not a Little Curious': A New Look at the American Colonization Society," in *Proslavery Thought,* ed. Finkelman, 111–28; Thomas Hietala, *Manifest Design: Anxious Aggrandizement in Late Jacksonian America* (Ithaca, N.Y.: Cornell University Press, 1985), 13; and Dale Knobel, "'Native Soil': Nativists, Colonizationists, and the Rhetoric of Nationality," *Civil War History* 27, no. 4 (Dec. 1981): 314–37.

124. Foner, *Free Soil,* 276; anonymous author quoted in Richard Wade, "The Negro in Cincinnati, 1800–1830," *Journal of Negro History* 39, no. 1 (Jan. 1954): 54. For a particularly vitriolic version of such rhetoric, see *Proceedings of the Colonization Society of the City of New York, at Their Third Annual Meeting, Held on the 13th and 14th of May, 1835, Including the Annual Report of the Board of Managers to the Society* (New York: Wm. A. Mercein and Son, 1835).

125. Dumond, *Antislavery Origins,* 106. Foner summarizes this thinking as follows: "In the eyes of Republican colonizationists, the Negroes were to be emissaries of a different kind; as black agents of an American Empire, they would help establish the commercial and political hegemony of the United States in Latin America" (*Free Soil,* 272).

Chapter 3: Senator Robert Walker's Letter on Texas Annexation, The South in Danger, *and the Rhetoric of Manifest Destiny*

1. James Buchanan, speech in the Senate, 12 March 1844, in *The Appendix to the Congressional Globe, for the First Session, Twenty-Eighth Congress: Containing Speeches and Important State Papers* (Washington, D.C.: Blair and Rives, 1844), 350.

2. Alexis de Tocqueville, *Democracy in America,* vol. 1 (New York: Vintage Books, 1990 [1835]), 332, 398. On Jacksonian Democracy, see Marvin Meyers, *The Jacksonian Persuasion: Politics and Belief* (New York: Vintage Books, 1960); Lee Benson, *The Concept of Jacksonian Democracy: New York as a Test Case* (Princeton, N.J.: Princeton University Press, 1961); Edward Pessen, *Jacksonian America: Society, Personality, Politics* (Homewood, Ill.: Dorsey, 1969); and Michael Paul Rogin, *Fathers and Children: Andrew Jackson and the Subjugation of the American Indian* (New York: Knopf, 1975).

3. Carroll Smith Rosenberg, "Dis-Covering the Subject of the 'Great Constitutional Discussion,' 1786–1789," *Journal of American History* 79, no. 3 (Dec. 1992): 841. Washington's letter was published in the first issue of *The American Museum* in Philadelphia, May 1787.

4. James Madison, Alexander Hamilton, and John Jay, *The Federalist: A Collection of Essays Written in Favour of the New Constitution, as Agreed Upon by the Federal Convention, September 17, 1787,* ed. Isaac Kramnick (New York: Penguin Books, 1987 [1788]), 120, 129, 130, 133–34, 139. Hamilton first used the term *empire* in *Federalist* no. 1 (87, 88).

5. Congressman John W. Tibbatts, speech in the House of Representatives, 7 May 1844, in *Appendix to the Congressional Globe, First Session, Twenty-Eighth Congress,* 448–49.

6. See Sebastiano Timpanaro, *The Freudian Slip: Psychoanalysis and Textual Criticism,* trans. Kate Super (London: Verso, 1985 [Italian original, 1974]).

7. John L. O'Sullivan, "The Great Nation of Futurity," *United States Magazine and Democratic Review* 6, no. 23 (Nov. 1839): 427.

8. John L. O'Sullivan, "Annexation," *United States Magazine and Democratic Review* 17, no. 85 (July–Aug. 1845): 5, 7. Regarding his thesis that war with Britain over Oregon is imminent, O'Sullivan writes in "Edinburgh and Foreign Quarterly on the Oregon" (*United States Magazine and Democratic Review* 17, no. 89 [Nov. 1845]): "You are profoundly ignorant of America; you are blind to

her history, her progress, her condition, and her destiny. You exaggerate your own importance, and you depreciate your adversaries; two errors, of which you will reap the fruits in your next wars" (330). In a similar vein, even though James Buchanan claims, "There is nothing like blustering in my nature," he barks at the Senate on 12 March 1844 that Britain's ceaseless colonizing conquests and America's intentions in Oregon will surely collide. "Yes Sir," Buchanan boasts, "War is inevitable!" Senator George McDuffie, a Democrat from South Carolina, goes so far in May of 1844 as to welcome this supposedly inevitable conflict as "a third war for independence" (*Appendix to the Congressional Globe, First Session, Twenty-Eighth Congress,* 350, 349, 529).

9. Robert C. Winthrop, speech in the House of Representatives, 3 January 1846, in *The Appendix to the Congressional Globe, for the First Session, Twenty-Ninth Congress: Containing Speeches and Important State Papers* (Washington, D.C.: Blair and Rives, 1846), 98–99.

10. See Julius Pratt, "John L. O'Sullivan and Manifest Destiny," *New York History* 14, no. 3 (July 1933): 213–34; and idem, "The Origin of 'Manifest Destiny,'" *American Historical Review* 32, no. 4 (July 1927): 795–98.

11. John L. O'Sullivan's father, John T. O'Sullivan, was a notorious rogue of the high seas. In fact, according to Pratt ("John L. O'Sullivan"), John L. launched the *Democratic Review* with funds that Congress granted his mother as damages for the controversial imprisonment of *The Dick,* a ship captained by John T. After participating in an illegal military raid against Venezuela in 1806 and engaging in dubious shipping practices that "hung on the ragged edges of legality" (216) throughout the Mediterranean and South America (including Tangier, Gibraltar, Peru, and the Canary Islands), *The Dick* sailed from Buenos Aires in 1823. The ship was seized under "suspicion of piracy" (217). The 1836 settlement in favor of John T., who had since died, awarded his wife, Mary O'Sullivan, the then gigantic sum of $19,968.

12. Benedict Anderson, *Imagined Communities: Reflections on the Origin and Spread of Nationalism* (London: Verso, 1991), 7–11.

13. The figures on slave ownership and property percentiles are from Randolph Campbell and Richard Lowe, *Wealth and Power in Antebellum Texas* (College Station: Texas A&M Press, 1977), 38 (table 8), 41 (figure 2), and 44 (table 9). The figures on the control of cotton production are from Randolph Campbell, *An Empire For Slavery: The Peculiar Institution in Texas, 1821–1865* (Baton Rouge: Louisiana State University Press, 1989), 210. The argument that owning twenty or more slaves was the approximate dividing line between those slaveholders who were little more than local, small-scale farmers and those plantation-based capitalists who constituted the dominant "planter class" was first put forth by Kenneth Stamp in *The Peculiar Institution: Slavery in the Antebellum South* (New York: Knopf, 1956), 30. According to Campbell's *Empire for Slavery,* roughly 78 percent of all slave owners in Texas held fewer than ten slaves, whereas 14 percent of all slave owners held between ten and nineteen slaves; thus, only 8 percent of all slave owners (approximately 2 percent of the total white population) constituted the dominant planter class, those who owned twenty or more slaves.

14. Regarding the diplomatic and political intrigue surrounding Texas annexation, see David Pletcher, *The Diplomacy of Annexation: Texas, Oregon, and the Mexican War* (Columbia: University of Missouri Press, 1973), 113–226; Justin Smith, *The Annexation of Texas* (New York: AMS, 1971 [1911]); and Frederick Merk, *Slavery and the Annexation of Texas* (New York: Knopf, 1972). Thomas

Streeter's three-volume *Bibliography of Texas, 1795–1845* (Cambridge, Mass.: Harvard University Press, 1960) is an indispensable source, as is *The Annual Report of the American Historical Association for the Year 1908,* vol. 2, part 1: *Diplomatic Correspondence of the Republic of Texas.* The best two contemporary sources are Thomas Hietala, *Manifest Design: Anxious Aggrandizement in Late Jacksonian America* (Ithaca, N.Y.: Cornell University Press, 1985), 10–54; and William Freehling, *The Road to Disunion: Secessionists at Bay, 1776–1854* (Oxford: Oxford University Press, 1990), 353–452.

15. Robert William Fogel, *Without Consent or Contract: The Rise and Fall of American Slavery* (New York: W. W. Norton, 1989), 65.

16. These figures are from *The United States 8th Census* (1860); also see James Foust, *The Yeoman Farmer and Westward Expansion of U.S. Cotton Production* (New York: Arno, 1975), 208–18.

17. The downward pressure on wages resulting from massive immigration, coupled with the growth of America's first substantial urban centers, deeply affected labor relations in the South. For example, between 1850 and 1860 Richmond grew by 38 percent; Mobile, by 43 percent; Nashville, by 67 percent; and Baton Rouge, by 27 percent. The percentage of immigrants (including both American-born North-to-South immigrants and European-born immigrants) among free adult workingmen likewise expanded rapidly, reaching 58 percent in Charleston in 1860, 78 percent in Mobile, 53 percent in Nashville, and 58 percent in Baton Rouge (see Ira Berlin and Irving Gutman, "Native and Immigrants, Free Men and Slaves: Urban Workingmen in the Antebellum American South," *American Historical Review* 88, no. 5 [Dec. 1983]: 1177 [table 1] and 1179 [table 5]). Clearly, these two factors influenced the South's emerging capitalist elite to reconsider the economic rationale for slavery.

18. Laurence Shore, *Southern Capitalists: The Ideological Leadership of an Elite, 1832–1885* (Chapel Hill: University of North Carolina Press, 1986), 49.

19. Whereas cotton sold for an average price of 16.4 cents per pound in 1835 and 1836, William Freehling observes in "The Complex Career of Slaveholder Expansionism" (*The Reintegration of American History: Slavery and the Civil War* [Oxford: Oxford University Press, 1994], 158–75) that "cotton plunged, after the devastating panic of 1837, to an average of 7.9 cents per pound" (164).

20. Campbell and Lowe, *Wealth and Power,* 54–55; Campbell, *Empire for Slavery,* 56, 4. For less enthusiastic views of Texas's prospects in the early to mid 1840s, see Smith's wry comments on pigs roaming the streets of Galveston in *The Annexation of Texas,* 41; and Paul Lack, "Slavery and the Texas Revolution," *Southwestern Historical Quarterly* 89, no. 2 (Oct. 1985): 181–202.

21. For example, circa 1816–17, the infamous pirate Jean Laffite, in league with secessionist factions of Mexicans, used Galveston as a staging ground for seizing Spanish slave ships and then smuggling the (now twice-) stolen slaves into America. See Campbell, *Empire for Slavery,* 11–12.

22. Slavery was initially abolished in Mexico in 1823 by Emperor Agustín de Iturbide, but his overthrow that same year plunged the fragile new constitution (and its antislavery clause, particularly regarding Texas) into controversy. In 1827 the new constitution for Coahuila and Texas again outlawed the importation of slaves, but Texans outmaneuvered this law by bringing slaves into the territory as indentured servants. The Mexican president Vicente Guerrero then again out-

lawed the importation of slaves from the United States to Texas on 15 September 1829; however, by December of that same year Texas's cotton elite had persuaded him to grant Texas exemption from this law. Then, on 6 April 1830, President Anastasio Bustamante issued a decree calling for "the strict enforcement of rules against the further introduction of slaves" (Campbell, *Empire for Slavery,* 25–27). See Josefina Zoraida Vasquez, "The Texas Question in Mexican Politics, 1836–1845," *Southwestern Historical Quarterly* 89, no. 3 (Jan. 1986): 309–44; and Nettie Lee Benson, "Texas as Viewed from Mexico, 1820–1834," *Southwestern Historical Quarterly* 90, no. 3 (Jan. 1987): 219–91.

23. This is not the place for an extended history of military violence in antebellum America, but mob violence, thuggery, mercenary ventures, lynchings, revolts, border raiding parties, and the everyday violence of whippings and other physical punishments were a constant reality within the political economy of slavery, particularly on the frontier of Texas. Violence in a chilling variety of forms was not the exception but the dominant rule, the culture's modus operandi. See Herbert Aptheker, *American Negro Slave Revolts* (New York: Columbia University Press, 1943); Wendell Addington, "Slave Insurrections in Texas," in *Articles on American Slavery,* vol. 13: *Rebellions, Resistance, and Runaways within the Slave South,* ed. Paul Finkleman (New York: Garland, 1989), 2–28; Paul Lack, "Slavery and Vigilantism in Austin, Texas, 1840–1860," *Southwestern Historical Quarterly* 85, no. 1 (July 1981): 1–20; and Richard Maxwell Brown, *Strains of Violence: Historical Studies of American Violence and Vigilantism* (Oxford: Oxford University Press, 1975), 301–26.

24. Ward Churchill, *Struggle for the Land: Indigenous Resistance to Genocide, Ecocide, and Expropriation in Contemporary North America* (Monroe, Me.: Common Courage, 1993), 71. Churchill notes that the Native American population in Texas plummeted from over 100,000 in 1828 to fewer than 10,000 in 1880 (46).

25. Pierre Henri Laurent, "Belgium's Relations with Texas and the United States, 1839–1844," *Southwestern Historical Quarterly* 68, no. 2 (Oct. 1964): 225.

26. Texas president Sam Houston, speech before the House of Representatives on 9 December 1844, quoted in Hietala, *Manifest Design,* 51. While Houston was publicly talking big in Washington, he was privately begging the United States for military protection from potential Mexican aggression in the event of annexation. For example, in February 1844 William Murphy, the U.S. chargé d'affaires in Texas, wrote to Abel Upshur, Tyler's secretary of state, stating, "The President of Texas begs me to request you, that no time be lost in sending a sufficient fleet into the Gulf, subject to my order, to act in defense of the Texan coast in case of naval descent by Mexico" (quoted in Merk, *Slavery and Annexation,* 41). John Tod describes Houston as follows in a letter to Senator Robert Walker dated 18/23 December 1844: "When sober, Houston was for annexation; but when drunk, or in liquor, he would express himself strongly against the measure!" (quoted in Pletcher, *The Diplomacy of Annexation,* 177).

27. Andrew Jackson, personal letter of 12 April 1844, quoted in Hietala, *Manifest Design,* 24.

28. Ambrose Sevier, speech in the Senate, 7 June 1844, in *Appendix to the Congressional Globe, First Session, Twenty-Eighth Congress,* 557.

29. Lundy's charge appears as the subtitle to his pamphlet *The War in Texas; a Review of Facts and Circumstances* (Philadelphia, 1836).

30. Senator George McDuffie, speech in the Senate, 23 May 1844, in *Appendix to the Congressional Globe, First Session, Twenty-Eighth Congress*, 532.

31. See H. Donaldson Jordan, "A Politician of Expansion: Robert J. Walker," *Mississippi Valley Historical Review* 19, no. 3 (Dec. 1932): 362–81; William Edward Dodd, *Robert J. Walker: Imperialist* (Gloucester, Mass.: Peter Smith, 1967 (this material was originally presented as a lecture at the Chicago Literary Club, 28 October 1912); and idem, "Robert J. Walker," *United States Magazine and Democratic Review* 16, no. 80 (Feb. 1845): 157–64.

32. See Thomas Cockrell, "The Politics of Land in Jacksonian Mississippi," *Journal of Mississippi History* 47, no. 1 (Feb. 1985): 1–14. For earlier examples of shady land dealings in Texas, see the anonymously authored *Address to the Reader of the Documents Relating to the Galveston Bay & Texas Land Company* (New York: G. F. Hopkins, 1831). The charge that Walker's letter of support from Jackson was forged is found in Jordan, "A Politician of Expansion," 367.

33. Elgin Williams, *The Animating Pursuits of Speculation: Land Traffic in the Annexation of Texas* (New York: Columbia University Press, 1949), 18, 25.

34. Regarding Walker's landholdings in Texas, see the confusing 15 October 1845 letter from Henry Smith, of Brazoria, Texas, to Robert Walker, exhibit 38 in the Walker Papers, New York Historical Society. Also see Andreas Reichstein, *The Rise of the Lone Star* (College Station: Texas A&M University Press, 1989), 94–112; and Eugene Barker, "Land Speculation as a Cause of the Texas Revolution," *Texas Historical Quarterly* 10, no. 1 (July 1906): 76–95. Many archives list the much older *Texas Historical Quarterly* under its offspring journal, *The Southwestern Historical Quarterly*.

35. In fact, prior to the Democratic Convention, twenty-four of twenty-six states had already pledged their delegates to Van Buren (Smith, *Annexation of Texas*, 235).

36. For discussion of this postponement, see James C. N. Paul, *Rift in the Democracy* (Philadelphia: University of Pennsylvania Press, 1951), 62–70.

37. On the labyrinthine factionalism of the Democratic party and the backroom maneuvering against Van Buren, see Michael Morrison, "Martin Van Buren, the Democracy, and the Partisan Politics of Texas Annexation," *Journal of Southern History* 61, no. 4 (Nov. 1995): 695–724. For additional accounts of this story, see Pletcher, *The Diplomacy of Annexation*, 139–41; Freehling, *Road to Disunion*, 402–39; Smith, *Annexation of Texas*, 234–57; and Paul, *Rift in the Democracy*, 144–68.

38. Robert J. Walker, *Letter of Mr. Walker, of Mississippi, Relative to the Annexation of Texas; in Reply to the Call of the People of Carroll County, Kentucky, to Communicate His Views on the Subject*, first published 3 February 1844 in the *Washington Globe*. For convenience I subsequently cite the *Letter* by column and page number as reproduced in facsimile in Frederick Merk, *Fruits of Propaganda in the Tyler Administration* (Cambridge: Harvard University Press, 1971), 221–52. I have also examined original copies of the *Letter* at the New York Historical Society and the Newberry Library in Chicago; for a complete listing of locations holding original copies of the *Letter*, see Streeter, *Bibliography of Texas*.

39. Merk, *Fruits of Propaganda*, 123.

40. Later, in 1859, the Republicans attempted a similar ploy, this time using a shortened version of Hinton Rowan Helper's *Impending Crisis*. The Republicans, enjoying the support of Horace Greeley and playing off the topical news of the

fierce debate over electing a new speaker of the House, were, according to Shore's *Southern Capitalists,* "able to launch *Compendium of The Impending Crisis* beyond even Harriet Beecher Stowe's *Uncle Tom's Cabin* in sales and political significance" (67). This view is shared by George Fredrickson, author of the excellent introduction to Helper's *Impending Crisis* (Cambridge, Mass.: Harvard University Press, 1968), who claims that it is "the most important single book, in terms of its political impact, that has ever been published in the United States. Even more perhaps than *Uncle Tom's Cabin*" (ix).

41. Dodd, "Robert J. Walker," 162. For further evidence of the reception of Walker's *Letter,* it is illuminating to read the correspondence contained in the Walker Papers at the New York Historical Society. For example, the venerable R. W. Johnson (a war hero, senator, head of the U.S. Post Office, and vice president under Van Buren) wrote, "I have reread your letter upon the reannexation of Texas to the States. It is a 120-pounder—it does you honor & credit, proving your patriotism, your talents & your industry. It is a master piece of composition and information" (letter dated 24 February 1844, from White Sulphur, Kentucky, exhibit 7 of the Walker Papers).

42. Election figures from Freehling, *Road to Disunion,* 439.

43. Merk, *Slavery and Annexation,* 101.

44. See ibid., 57; Freehling, *Road to Disunion,* 431–33.

45. For a wonderfully colorful description of the Senate debate of 27 February 1845, see J. Y. Bryan, "Texas by a Nose," *Southwest Review* 55, no. 2 (Spring 1970): 165–74.

46. According to Walker, the Adams-Onis Treaty of 1819 "surrendered" Texas to Spain. The boundaries of the 1803 Louisiana Purchase were in fact controversial, so the debate over whether Texas was to be annexed or reannexed could be traced back to the various machinations surrounding this previous land deal with Spain. What Walker does not mention, however, is that the Adams-Onis Treaty—whether it surrendered Texas or not—secured vast new lands for the United States. As Merk summarizes the deal, it "ceded East Florida to the United States, gave recognition to America's seizure of West Florida, and transferred Spanish claims to the Pacific Northwest north of the line at 42 degrees to the United States"—that is, all the lands that now constitute Oregon and Washington (Frederick Merk, *Manifest Destiny and Mission in American History: A Reinterpretation* [New York: Knopf, 1963], 15). Walker's portrayal of Texas as unjustly surrendered to Spain is thus more than a little deceptive, because Texas was used as a bartering chip within a lucrative deal that without doubt favored the United States.

47. Robert Walker, speech in the Senate, 20 May 1844, in *Appendix to the Congressional Globe, First Session, Twenty-Eighth Congress,* 549. After Walker used it, the term *reannexation* quickly became ubiquitous among proannexation forces. For example, in a long (and remarkably erudite) document entitled "Message from the President of the United States to the Senate" and reprinted as a letter to the *Southwestern Quarterly Review* (12 [Oct. 1844]), President Tyler argues that "reannexation" designates "not the acquisition of territory, to which we never had a claim, but the recovery of what was once ours, and was lost, unwisely and improvidently lost" (486). Likewise, Congressman Tibbatts titles his 7 May 1844 speech in Congress "The Reannexation of Texas" (*Appendix to the Congressional Globe, First Session, Twenty-Eighth Congress,* 445). *The Appendix to the Congressional Globe for the First Session, Twenty-Eighth Congress, The Madisonian,*

The United States Magazine and Democratic Review, and other contemporary sources are full of examples of this switch to *reannexation.*

48. "The Texas Question: A Letter from Alexander H. Everett," *United States Magazine and Democratic Review* 15, no. 75 (Sept. 1844): 256. Alexander Everett was a Harvard valedictorian, had been editor of the prestigious *North American Review,* and was appointed by John Quincy Adams to the important post of minister to Spain. He was, then, one of the North's chosen few, one of the great lettered men of the Republic. His move to the Democrats in 1832 was thus considered nothing less than a defection. This essay was therefore doubly powerful as an indictment of traditional Whig politics (see the discussion of Everett in Merk, *Fruits of Propaganda,* 115–16).

49. Thomas Walker Gilmer, "Texas and the United States," *Baltimore Republican and Argus,* 10 January 1843, reproduced in Merk, *Slavery and Annexation,* 200–204 (quotation, 203). Regarding Gilmer's involvement with Texas land speculation via the Galveston Island Land Company, see Williams, *Animating Pursuits of Speculation,* 144–52.

50. O'Sullivan, "Annexation," 9.

51. Sacvan Bercovitch, *The Rites of Assent: Transformations in the Symbolic Construction of America* (New York: Routledge, 1993), 32–33. See also Timothy Brennan, "The National Longing for Form," in *Nation and Narration,* ed. Homi Bhabha (London: Routledge, 1990), 44–70.

52. Thomas Prentice Kettell, *Southern Wealth and Northern Profits: As Exhibited in Statistical Facts and Official Figures; Showing the Necessity of Union to the Future Prosperity and Welfare of the Republic* (Birmingham: University of Alabama Press, 1965 [1860]), 7, 173.

53. The best examination of this thesis remains Edmund Morgan's *Inventing the People: The Rise of Popular Sovereignty in England and America* (New York: W. W. Norton, 1988), 153–306.

54. Michael Warner, *Letters of the Republic: Republicanism and the Public Sphere in Eighteenth-Century America* (Cambridge, Mass.: Harvard University Press, 1990), 101.

55. Smith, *Annexation of Texas,* 133.

56. Gilmer, "Texas and the United States," 203.

57. Bercovitch, *Rites of Assent,* 41.

58. Leonard Richards, *"Gentlemen of Property and Standing": Anti-Abolition Mobs in Jacksonian America* (Oxford: Oxford University Press, 1970), 71.

59. George Bancroft, Boston, to Walker, 19 June 1844, exhibit 15 of the Walker Papers, New York Historical Society. Bancroft was one of America's early philosopher-kings: he received a Ph.D. from the University of Göttingen in 1820 (when he met Goethe), wrote the remarkable ten-volume *History of the United States,* served as Polk's secretary of the navy, founded the Naval Academy at Annapolis, and eventually was appointed minister to Great Britain.

60. Aberdeen's "letter" of 26 December 1843, read into the Congressional Record, in *Appendix to the Congressional Globe, First Session, Twenty-Eighth Congress,* 448. The document was later named "the Pakenham letter" because it was written to the British minister Richard Pakenham, although it was launched into mythic status by Calhoun; the best analysis of it remains Freehling, *Road to Disunion,* 407–15.

61. "The Re-Annexation of Texas," *United States Magazine and Democratic Review* 15, no. 63 (July 1844): 16; given his strong role as editor, it is safe to postulate that many of the *Review*'s unattributed essays (such as this one) were written by O'Sullivan.

62. See Smith, *Annexation of Texas,* 123.

63. See Freehling, *Road to Disunion,* 397; Merk, *Slavery and Annexation,* 23; and Harriet Smither, "English Abolitionism and the Annexation of Texas," *Southwestern Historical Quarterly* 32, no. 3 (July 1988): 193–205. For an extended example of the claim that Britain's abolitionist impulses are but masks for more sinister designs on global capitalist domination, see Tyler's "Message of the President."

64. In Albert Deutsch, "The First U.S. Census of the Insane (1840) and Its Use as Pro-Slavery Propaganda," *Bulletin of the History of Medicine* 15 (1944): 475. Like Jarvis, Deutsch concludes that the 1840 census report was "one of the most amazing tissues of statistical falsehood and error ever woven together under government imprint" (475). For a proslavery editorial supporting Walker's (and the *Sixth Census*'s) thesis, see "Modern Philanthropy and Negro Slavery," *De Bow's Review* 16, no. 3 (Mar. 1854): 263–76.

65. American Anti-Slavery Society, *The American Anti-Slavery Almanac, for 1839, Being the Third After Leap-Year, and the 63rd of American Independence. Calculated for New York; Adapted to the Northern and Middle States* (New York: S. W. Benedict, 1839), 46.

66. William Channing, personal letter to Henry Clay, 1837, quoted in *Manifest Destiny,* ed. Norman Graebner (New York: Bobbs-Merrill, 1968), 50.

67. Theodore Sedgwick, *Thoughts on the Annexation of Texas* (New York: D. Fanshaw, 1844), 38. Sedgwick's pamphlet, published under the name "VETO," is a collection of essays initially published in the *New York Evening Post* as responses to Walker's *Letter.*

68. Charles Francis Adams, *Report of the Massachusetts Committee to Prevent the Admission of Texas as a Slave State* (Boston, 1845), 3.

69. Gilmer, "Texas and the United States," 203.

70. Thomas Walker Gilmer, letter to *Niles' Register* (published in Charlottesville), 15 May 1843, reproduced in Merk, *Slavery and Annexation,* 213–17 (quotation, 214).

71. Charles James Faulkner, *Speech in the House of Delegates of Virginia, on the Policy of the State with Respect to Her Slave Population, 20 January 1832* (Richmond: Thomas White, 1832), 10.

72. O'Sullivan, "The Re-Annexation of Texas," 15.

73. O'Sullivan, "Annexation," 7.

74. Tyler, "Message of the President," 518.

75. For an overview of such promises of imminent U.S. hemispheric dominion, see Robert May, *The Southern Dream of a Caribbean Empire* (Baton Rouge: Louisiana State University Press, 1973).

76. See note 13 to this chapter.

77. Freehling, *Road to Disunion,* 376, 377.

78. Anderson, *Imagined Communities,* 7.

79. Alexander Saxton, *The Rise and Fall of the White Republic: Class Politics and Mass Culture in Nineteenth-Century America* (London: Verso, 1990), 144.

80. For example, Upshur wrote on 13 March 1844, "The radical defect is in the Constitutional body. How can a country be governed except by those who own it?" (in Freehling, *Road to Disunion*, 391).

81. Richard Rush, Lydenham (near Philadelphia), Pa., to Robert Walker, 20 April 1844, exhibit 10 of the Walker Papers, New York Historical Society.

82. "The Texas Question," *United States Magazine and Democratic Review* 14, no. 70 (Apr. 1844): 429.

83. See O'Sullivan, "Annexation," 9; Tyler, "Message of the President," 487; and Senator James Buchanan, speech in the Senate, 12 March 1844, in *Appendix to the Congressional Globe, First Session, Twenty-Eighth Congress*, 350.

84. Michael Warner, "Franklin and the Letters of the Republic," *Representations* 16 (Fall 1986): 111. For more along these lines, see Tocqueville, *Democracy in America*, 181–90.

85. Saxton, *Rise and Fall*, 95–97. See also Stuart Blumin's introduction to *New York by Gas-Light and Other Urban Sketches by George Foster*, ed. Blumin (Berkeley: University of California Press, 1990), 1–61.

86. Ronald Zboray, *A Fictive People: Antebellum Economic Development and the American Reading Public* (Oxford: Oxford University Press, 1993); see 6–16 for an overview of these changes and subsequent chapters for more detailed elaborations. For a similar study of an earlier period, see Rosalind Remer, *Printers and Men of Capital: Philadelphia Book Publishers in the New Republic* (Philadelphia: University of Pennsylvania Press, 1996).

87. Saxton, *Rise and Fall*, 100, 105; Zboray, *Fictive People*, 15.

88. Anderson, *Imagined Communities*, 35.

89. My use of the "legitimacy" and "authority" framework is derived from Hannah Arendt, *On Revolution* (New York: Penguin Books, 1963), 141–78.

90. Tyler, "Message of the President," 498.

91. Robert Walker, *The South in Danger: Read Before You Vote. An Address of the Democratic Association of Washington, D.C.* (Washington, D.C.: 1844), hereafter cited parenthetically in the text. I am working from a photocopy courtesy of the Center for American History, the University of Texas at Austin. For a complete list of archival holdings of this document, see Streeter, *Bibliography of Texas*, 450–52.

92. However one appraises his politics, one must acknowledge that Walker is remarkably adept at finding show-stopping evidence. His familiarity with an incredible number of Northern newspapers, circulars, and pamphlets demonstrates a man deeply committed both to the concept of research and to the possibilities of using print capitalism for sensational ends. Not only do *Letter on Texas Annexation* and *The South in Danger* display impressive research, but Walker's two-day long speech in the Senate (20 and 21 May 1844) is a tour de force of using Whig statements from over two dozen regional sources to implicate National Whig leadership in blatant campaign hypocrisy (see *Appendix to the Congressional Globe, First Session, Twenty-Eighth Congress*, 548–57).

93. Regarding nationalism and modernity, see Ernest Renan, "What Is a Nation?" (a speech presented in Paris, 11 March 1882), in *Nation and Narration*, ed. Homi Bhabha, 8–22; Tom Nairn, "What Nations Are For," *London Review of Books*, 8 Sept. 1994, pp. 7–8; Ernest Gellner, *Nations and Nationalism* (Ithaca, N.Y.: Cornell University Press, 1983); and E. J. Hobsbawm, *Nations and Nation-*

alism since 1780: Programme, Myth, Reality, 2d ed. (Cambridge: Cambridge University Press, 1990).

Chapter 4: Whitman's Pose, the Daguerreotype, and the Dialectics of Commodification, Self-Making, and Democracy

1. Ralph Waldo Emerson, "The American Scholar" (1837), *Selected Essays* (New York: Penguin, 1985), 94 (epigraph, 104). On character, see Nancy Ruttenburg, *Democratic Personality: Popular Voice and the Trial of American Authorship* (Stanford, Calif.: Stanford University Press, 1998), chap. 6.

2. Samuel Rezneck, "The Social History of an American Depression, 1837–1843," *American Historical Review* 40, no. 4 (July 1953): 662–87; Sean Wilentz, *Chants Democratic: New York City and the Rise of the American Working Class, 1788–1850* (Oxford: Oxford University Press, 1984), 286, 288, 292.

3. Charles Sellers, *The Market Revolution: Jacksonian America, 1815–1846* (Oxford: Oxford University Press, 1991), 375; F. O. Matthiessen, *American Renaissance: Art and Expression in the Age of Emerson and Whitman* (Oxford: Oxford University Press, 1968 [1941]), 65.

4. Karl Marx, *The Communist Manifesto* (New York: W. W. Norton, 1988 [1848]), 61, 70. For more detailed explanations of this transformation, see Stuart Blumin, *The Emergence of the Middle Class: Social Experience in the American City, 1760–1900* (Cambridge: Cambridge University Press, 1989); Richard Brown, *Modernization: The Transformation of American Life, 1600–1865* (New York: Hill and Wang, 1976); Christopher Clark, "Household Economy, Market Exchange, and the Rise of Capitalism in the Connecticut Valley, 1800–1860," *Journal of Social History* 13, no. 2 (Winter 1979): 169–89; Jonathan Prude, *The Coming of Industrial Order: Town and Factory Life in Rural Massachusetts, 1810–1860* (Cambridge: Cambridge University Press, 1983); Winifred Rothenberg, "The Emergence of a Capital Market in Rural Massachusetts, 1730–1838," *Journal of Economic History* 45, no. 4 (Dec. 1985): 781–808; Sellers, *The Market Revolution;* and Wilentz, *Chants Democratic.*

5. Ralph Waldo Emerson, "Self-Reliance" (1836), *Selected Essays,* 185; idem, "The Transcendentalist" (1842), *Selected Essays,* 252.

6. Edgar Allan Poe, "The Daguerreotype," *Alexander's Weekly Messenger,* 15 January 1840, p. 2.

7. Roland Barthes, "Rhetoric of the Image" (1964), *Image-Music-Text,* trans. Stephen Heath (New York: Hill and Wang, 1976), 46.

8. During the course of his lifetime, Whitman posed for over 130 such portraits, a remarkable number for a nineteenth-century artist. See Ed Folsom, *Walt Whitman's Native Representations* (Cambridge: Cambridge University Press, 1994), 99–177.

9. Ibid., 146–47.

10. For similar attempts to read images in this rhetorical and historical manner, see Cara Finnegan, "Social Engineering, Visual Politics and the New Deal: FSA Photography in *Survey Graphic,*" *Rhetoric and Public Affairs* 3 (Fall 2000): 333–62; idem, "The Naturalistic Enthymeme and Visual Argument: Photographic Representation in the 'Skull Controversy,'" *Argumentation and Advocacy* 37

(Winter 2001): 133–49; and Susan Williams, *Confounding Images: Photography and Portraiture in Antebellum American Fiction* (Philadelphia: University of Pennsylvania Press, 1997).

11. Walter Benjamin, "The Work of Art in the Age of Mechanical Reproduction" (1936), *Illuminations*, trans. Harry Zohn (New York: Schocken Books, 1969), 231.

12. Cathy Davidson, "Photographs of the Dead: Sherman, Daguerre, Hawthorne," *South Atlantic Quarterly* 89, no. 4 (Fall 1990): 682. See also Robert Taft, *Photography and the American Scene: A Social History, 1839–1889* (New York: Dover, 1938); Martin Jay, "Scopic Regimes of Modernity," in *Vision and Visuality*, ed. Hal Foster (Seattle: Bay, 1988), 3–23; and Jonathan Crary, "Modernizing Vision," in *Vision and Visuality*, ed. Foster, 29–44.

13. Webster quoted in Folsom, *Whitman's Native Representations*, 107. On the confusions over science versus magic regarding daguerreotypes, see Nathaniel Hawthorne, *The House of the Seven Gables* (New York: Signet, 1981 [1851]).

14. Gustave de Beaumont, *Marie; or, Slavery in the United States*, trans. Barbara Chapman (Baltimore, Md.: Johns Hopkins University Press, 1999 [1835]), 112.

15. Naomi Rosenblum, *A World History of Photography* (New York: Abbeville, 1981), 23.

16. Quoted in William Welling, *Photography in America: The Formative Years, 1839–1900* (Albuquerque: University of New Mexico Press, 1978), 41.

17. David Jaffe, "One of the Primitive Sort: Portrait Makers of the Rural North, 1760–1860," in *The Countryside in the Age of Capitalist Transformation*, ed. Stephen Hahn and Jonathan Prude (Chapel Hill: University of North Carolina Press, 1985), 108.

18. James Thomas Flexner, *America's Old Masters* (New York: Dover, 1967 [1939]), 111.

19. Chandler's portrait of Martha may be seen at the Brookline Historical Museum, Brookline, Mass.; it appears in Jaffe, "One of the Primitive Sort," 107.

20. Flexner, *America's Old Masters*, 129–33. For excellent reproductions and discussions of these portraits, see Theodore Stebbins, Carol Troyen, and Trevor Fairbrother, eds., *A New World: Masterpieces of American Painting, 1760–1910* (Boston: Museum of Fine Arts, 1983), 34–42, 194–200.

21. On earlier forms of American folk art, see *American Naive Paintings from the National Gallery of Art* (Washington D.C.: International Exhibitions Foundation, 1985).

22. James Thomas Flexner, *Nineteenth Century American Painting* (New York: Putnam's, 1970), 112. In "Erastus Salisbury Field," in *American Folk Painters of Three Centuries*, ed. Jean Lipman (New York: Whitney Museum of Art, 1980), Mary Black observes that Field's portrait of Mrs. Moore "strongly resembles" that of her daughter and that the two women are shown wearing "precisely the same comb, collar, gown, pin, and belt buckle" (77).

23. The same pose was used for Field's 1835 portrait of Eleazer Bullard (Jaffe, "One of the Primitive Sort," 121).

24. Jaffe, "One of the Primitive Sort," 120. Prices are taken from *New England Folk Painter: Erastus Salisbury Field*, a 16-mm film directed by Arthur Smith (Colonial Williamsburg, 1968)—I believe the text for this film was written by Mary Black. For additional information on Field's life, see Black, "Rediscovery: Erastus Salisbury Field," *Art in America* 54, no. 1 (Jan.–Feb. 1966): 49–56.

25. See Carl Mitman's entry on Porter in *The Dictionary of American Biogra-*

phy, 20 vols., ed. Dumas Malone (New York: Scribner's, 1935), 15:101. Porter's inclusion in the *Dictionary* indicates his long-standing recognition as an important figure in America's art history. In contrast to Porter, Field languished in relative obscurity until the Springfield Museum of Art offered a retrospective of his work in 1942. Frederick Robinson's review of that show ("Erastus Salisbury Field," *Art in America* 30, no. 4 [Oct. 1942]: 244–53) landed Field's austere portrait of Elizabeth Ashley on the cover of *Art in America,* hence signifying Field's arrival as a luminary in the canon of early American artists.

26. Carol Schloss, *In Visible Light: Photography and the American Writer, 1840–1940* (Oxford: Oxford University Press, 1987), 31. Many daguerreotypists found working with children so difficult that they had separate price ranges for portraits of children under three years old. Thomas Easterly, for example, while charging from one to two dollars for most portrait daguerreotypes in his St. Louis studio, automatically charged four dollars for portraits of children (Dolores Kilgo, *Likeness and Landscape: Thomas M. Easterly and the Art of the Daguerreotype* [St. Louis: Missouri Historical Society, 1994], 53).

27. Flexner, *Nineteenth Century American Painting,* 119; see also Martin Jay, *Downcast Eyes: The Denigration of Vision in Twentieth-Century French Thought* (Berkeley: University of California Press, 1993), 136–37.

28. Beaumont Newhall, *The Daguerreotype in America,* 3d ed. (New York: Dover, 1975), 38, 63.

29. Alan Trachtenberg, "Brady's Portraits," *Yale Review* 73, no. 2 (Winter 1984): 233.

30. Alan Trachtenberg, *Reading American Photography: Images as History, Mathew Brady to Walker Evans* (New York: Hill and Wang, 1989), 294*n*19; Beaumont Newhall, *The History of Photography from 1839 to the Present* (New York: Museum of Modern Art, 1982), 34. For a rebuttal to the democratization thesis, see John Tagg, *The Burden of Representation: Essays on Photographies and Histories* (Minneapolis: University of Minnesota Press, 1994), 34–59.

31. See the discussions in Newhall, *The Daguerreotype in America,* 40–41; and Trachtenberg, "Brady's Portraits."

32. For a description of Gouraud's December 1839 New York tour and the first published responses to the daguerreotype, see Alan Trachtenberg, "American Responses to the Daguerreotype, 1839–1851," in *The Daguerreotype: A Sesquicentennial Celebration,* ed. John Wood (Iowa City: University of Iowa Press, 1989), 60–61. For a discussion of the political intrigue surrounding Gouraud's visit, encompassing the nationalist jockeying of Samuel Morse (American), Dominique François Jean Arago (French), and William Henry Fox Talbot (British)—each seeking credit for having perfected the daguerreotype process—see Floyd Rinhart and Marion Rinhart, *The American Daguerreotype* (Athens: University of Georgia Press, 1981), 3–21. Clarke quoted in Schloss, *In Visible Light,* 33.

33. George Foster's newspaper sketches from 1849 to 1853 are available in the wonderful collection, *New York by Gas-Light and Other Urban Sketches by George Foster,* ed. Stuart Blumin (Berkeley: University of California Press, 1990); the Melville reference is to his brilliant 1857 diatribe *The Confidence Man: His Masquerade;* the Baldwin reference is to his hilarious 1853 collection of stories *The Flush Times of Alabama and Mississippi;* the Lippard reference is to his bitter 1845 indictment of modernity's hypocrisies *The Quaker City; or The Monks of Monk Hall.*

34. Karen Halttunen, *Confidence Men and Painted Women: A Study of Middle-Class Culture in America, 1830–1870* (New Haven, Conn.: Yale University Press, 1982), 188, 189. Also see Stephanie Coontz, *The Social Origins of Private Life: A History of American Families, 1600–1900* (London: Verso, 1988), 176–77.

35. Trachtenberg, "Responses to the Daguerreotype," 64–65.

36. See Douglass North, *The Economic Growth of the United States, 1790–1860* (New York: W. W. Norton, 1966 [1961]), 159–65.

37. Reese Jenkins, *Images as Enterprise: Technology and the American Photographic Industry, 1839 to 1925* (Baltimore, Md.: Johns Hopkins University Press, 1975), 12–25.

38. Ibid., 28. For a sample of the elaborate designs of such union cases, see the collection displayed in Rinhart and Rinhart, *American Daguerreotypes*, 317–49.

39. Richard Rudisill, "Mirror Image: The Influence of the Daguerreotype on American Society," in *Photography in Print: Writings from 1816 to the Present*, ed. Vicki Goldberg (Albuquerque: University of New Mexico Press, 1981), 70–76; Newhall, *The History of Photography*, 35; and Rinhart and Rinhart, *American Daguerreotypes*, 116–29.

40. Regarding the history of images in print journalism, see Michael Carlebach, *The Origins of Photojournalism in America* (Washington, D.C.: Smithsonian Institution, 1992).

41. See Barbara McCandless, "The Portrait Studio and the Celebrity: Promoting the Art," in *Photography in Nineteenth Century America*, ed. Martha Sandweiss (New York: Harry Abrams, 1991), 49–75; Trachtenberg, "Brady's Portraits"; and the gorgeous collection of essays on and daguerreotypes by Brady reproduced in Mary Panzer, *Mathew Brady and the Image of History* (Washington, D.C.: Smithsonian Institution Press, 1997).

42. Mathew Brady, *The Gallery of Illustrious Americans, Containing Portraits and Biographical Sketches of Twenty-Four of the Most Eminent Citizens of the American Republic, since the Death of Washington* (New York: Brady, D'Avignon, and Lester, 1850). Brady's massive text is 15" wide and 21½" high, so the book itself, apart from its contents, is stunning. Given that most consumer daguerreotypes were pocket sized, it is not hard to imagine that Brady's oversized images resonated with citizens as particularly large, sturdy, and important.

43. Roy Meredith, *Mathew Brady's Portrait of an Era* (New York: W. W. Norton, 1982); Alan Trachtenberg, "Photography: The Emergence of a Keyword," in *Photography*, ed. Sandweiss, 17–47.

44. Davidson, "Photographs of the Dead," 669; Oliver Wendell Holmes, "The Stereoscope and the Stereograph," *Atlantic Monthly*, June 1859, in Schloss, *In Visible Light*, 39; see also Folsom, *Whitman's Native Representations*, 153–57.

45. David Rothman, *The Discovery of the Asylum: Social Order and Disorder in the New Republic* (Boston: Little, Brown, 1971), 59.

46. Alan Sekula, "The Body and the Archive," *October* 39 (Winter 1986): 5–7. On the phrenological assumptions driving such arguments, see Stephen Hartnett, "*'It Is Terrible to Possess Such Power!'*: Early Modernity, Phrenology, and Alienated Desire as Class and Gender Warfare in Hawthorne's 'The Birth Mark,'" *Prospero* 5 (1998): 5–26. See also Abigail Solomon-Godeau, *Photography at the Dock: Essays on Photographic History, Institutions, and Practices* (Minneapolis: University of Minnesota Press, 1991).

47. Marmaduke Sampson, *Rationale of Crime and Its Appropriate Treatment;*

Being a Treatise on Criminal Jurisprudence Considered in Relation to Cerebral Organization (New York: Appleton, 1846). For a heartbreaking description of Blackwell's Island, see Fanny Fern, "Blackwell's Island," *New York Ledger*, 14 Aug. 1858, in Fern's *Ruth Hall and Other Writings*, ed. Joyce Warren (New Brunswick, N.J.: Rutgers University Press, 1986), 304–6.

48. For discussions of Sampson's text, see Sekula, "The Body and the Archive," 12–16; and Madeleine Stern, "Mathew Brady and *The Rationale of Crime:* A Discovery in Daguerreotypes," *Quarterly Journal of the Library of Congress* 31, no. 3 (July 1974): 127–35. Regarding the introduction of phrenology into penological debates, see "Observations on Evidence in Favour of Phrenology, afforded by Reports on the Cerebral Development of Executed Criminals, as Indicated by Their Skulls," in *Transactions of the Phrenological Society* (Edinburgh: John Anderson, 1824), 319–79. For similar developments at the turn of the century, see Shawn Michelle Smith, *American Archives: Gender, Race, and Class in Visual Culture* (Princeton, N.J.: Princeton University Press, 1999), 68–93.

49. Mark Haller, *Eugenics: Hereditarian Attitudes in American Thought* (New Brunswick, N.J.: Rutgers University Press, 1984), 16. See also Stephen Jay Gould, *The Mismeasure of Man* (New York: W. W. Norton, 1981); and John Davies, *Phrenology: Fad and Science; A 19th Century Crusade* (New Haven, Conn.: Yale University Press, 1955).

50. These images may be seen at the Peabody Museum of Archaeology and Ethnology, Harvard University, Cambridge, Mass.

51. Robyn Weigman, *American Anatomies: Theorizing Race and Gender* (Durham, N.C.: Duke University Press, 1995), 31.

52. This excerpted quotation/advertisement appears on the final unnumbered page preceding the title page of the American version of *Rationale of Crime.*

53. See Edward Lurie, *Louis Agassiz: A Life in Science* (Baltimore, Md.: Johns Hopkins University Press, 1988 [1960]).

54. Ryder quoted in Schloss, *In Visible Light,* 35; on the Fowler brothers, see Madeleine B. Stern, *Heads and Headlines: The Phrenological Fowlers* (Norman: University of Oklahoma Press, 1971).

55. Ed Folsom, "Appearing in Print: Illustrations of the Self in *Leaves of Grass,*" in *The Cambridge Companion to Walt Whitman,* ed. Ezra Greenspan (Cambridge: Cambridge University Press, 1995), 135. For a catalog of Whitman's use of images throughout his lifetime, see Gay Wilson Allen, "The Iconography of Walt Whitman," in *The Artistic Legacy of Walt Whitman,* ed. Edwin Haviland Miller (New York: New York University Press, 1970), 127–52.

56. Cathy Davidson, *Revolution and the Word: The Rise of the Novel in America* (Oxford: Oxford University Press, 1986), 30. On the publishing history of Jefferson's study, see William Peden's introduction to *Notes on the State of Virginia* (Chapel Hill: University of North Carolina Press, 1982), xi–xxv. David Christy, *Cotton Is King: Or the Culture of Cotton, and Its Relation to Agriculture, Manufactures, and Commerce* (Cincinnati: Moore, Wilstach, Keys, 1855).

57. See Betsy Erkkila, *Whitman the Political Poet* (Oxford: Oxford University Press, 1989); M. Wynn Thomas, *The Lunar Light of Whitman's Poetry* (Cambridge: Cambridge University Press, 1987); Kerry Larson, *Whitman's Drama of Consensus* (Chicago: University of Chicago Press, 1988); Myrth Jimmie Killingsworth, *Whitman's Poetry of the Body: Sexuality, Politics, and the Text* (Chapel Hill: University of North Carolina Press, 1989); and Michael Moon, *Disseminating*

Whitman: Revision and Corporeality in Leaves of Grass (Cambridge, Mass.: Harvard University Press, 1991).

58. Walt Whitman, preface to *Leaves of Grass* (New York: Eakins, 1966 [1855]), vii.

59. Roy Harvey Pearce, introduction to *Whitman: A Collection of Critical Essays,* ed. Pearce (Englewood Cliffs, N.J.: Prentice-Hall, 1962), 1.

60. Kenneth Burke, *A Grammar of Motives* (Berkeley: University of California Press, 1969 [1945]), 503, 506.

61. See David Simpson, "Destiny Made Manifest: The Styles of Whitman's Poetry," in *Nation and Narration,* ed. Homi Bhabha (London: Routledge, 1990): 177–96; James Perrin Warren, "The Real Grammar: Deverbal Style in 'Song of Myself,'" *American Literature* 56, no. 1 (Mar. 1984): 1–16; and Herbert J. Levine, "Union and Disunion in 'Song of Myself,'" *American Literature* 59, no. 4 (Dec. 1987): 570–89.

62. Readers may wish to compare the 1855 facsimile version from which I am working, which has neither the poem names nor section numbers of later versions, with the more commonly cited version of the poem in *Leaves of Grass: A Textual Variorum of the Printed Poems,* ed. Sculley Bradley et al., vol. 1: *Poems, 1855–1856* (New York: New York University Press, 1980), 16–20.

63. See Michael Reed, "First Person Persona and the Catalogue in 'Song of Myself,'" *Walt Whitman Review* 23, no. 4 (Dec. 1977): 147–55; John Mason, "Walt Whitman's Catalogues: Rhetorical Means for Two Journeys in 'Song of Myself,'" *American Literature* 45, no. 1 (Mar. 1973): 34–49; V. K. Chari, "Structure of Whitman's Catalogue Poems," *Walt Whitman Review* 18, no. 1 (Mar. 1972): 3–17; Lawrence Buell, "Transcendentalist Catalogue Rhetoric: Vision versus Form," *American Literature* 40, no. 1 (Mar. 1968): 325–39.

64. D. H. Lawrence, *Studies in Classic American Literature* (New York: Viking, 1961 [1923]), 165, 167; Ruttenburg, *Democratic Personality,* 343; David Reynolds, *Walt Whitman's America: A Cultural Biography* (New York: Knopf, 1995), 235, 286.

65. Whitman's anonymous reviews of himself include "Walt Whitman and His Poems," *United States Review* (5 Sept. 1855); "Walt Whitman, a Brooklyn Boy," *Brooklyn Daily Times* (29 Sept. 1855); and "An English and American Poet," *American Phrenological Journal* (Oct. 1855). These have been collected in *Walt Whitman: The Contemporary Reviews,* ed. Kenneth Price (Cambridge: Cambridge University Press, 1996), 8–14, 21–22, and 23–26, respectively. On Whitman's obsession with his public reception, see Ezra Greenspan, *Walt Whitman and the American Reader* (Cambridge: Cambridge University Press, 1990), 103–52.

66. Graham Clarke, "'To Emanate A Look': Whitman, Photography, and the Spectacle of the Self," in *American Literary Landscapes: The Fiction and the Fact,* ed. Ian F. Bell and D. K. Adams (New York: St. Martin's, 1989), 87.

67. Walt Whitman, "Visit to Plumbe's Gallery," *Brooklyn Daily Eagle,* 2 July 1846, in Whitman's collected newspaper writings, *The Gathering of the Forces,* vol. 2, ed. Cleveland Rodgers and John Black (New York: Knickerbocker, 1920), 113–17 (quotation, 114).

68. For a utopian version of this thesis, see John Wood, "The American Portrait," in *America and the Daguerreotype,* ed. Wood (Iowa City: University of Iowa Press, 1991), 25.

69. Ed Folsom, "Notes on the Major Whitman Photographers," *Walt Whitman Quarterly Review* 4, nos. 2–3 (Fall–Winter 1986–87): 63.

70. Ruth Bohan, "The Gathering of the Forces: Walt Whitman and the Visual Arts in Brooklyn in the 1850s," in *Walt Whitman and the Visual Arts,* ed. Geoffrey Sill and Roberta Tarbell (New Brunswick, N.J.: Rutgers University Press, 1992), 5; Reynolds, *Walt Whitman's America,* 280–86.

71. See Marc Reisch, "Poetry and Portraiture in Whitman's *Leaves of Grass,*" *Walt Whitman Review* 27, no. 3 (Sept. 1981): 113–25; and Miles Orvell, "Whitman's Transfigured Eye," *The Real Thing: Imitations and Authenticity in American Culture, 1880–1940* (Chapel Hill: University of North Carolina Press, 1989): 3–29.

72. See *Contemporary Reviews,* ed. Price, 3–55. Also see James Wallace, "Whitman in *Life Illustrated:* A Forgotten 1855 Review of *Leaves of Grass,*" *Walt Whitman Review* 17, no. 4 (Dec. 1971): 135–58.

73. From the *New York Tribune,* 23 July 1855, in *Critical Essays on Walt Whitman,* ed. James Woodress (Boston: G.K. Hall, 1983), 18.

74. From *Putnam's Monthly* 6 (Sept. 1855), in *Critical Essays,* ed. Woodress, 20.

75. From the *Brooklyn Daily Eagle,* 15 September 1855, in *Contemporary Reviews,* ed. Price, 18.

76. Anonymous, "Notes on New Books," *Washington Daily National Intelligencer,* 18 February 1856, in *Contemporary Reviews,* ed. Price, 37–40.

77. For Madison, Hamilton, and Jay, see *The Federalist,* ed. Jacob Cooke (Middletown, Conn.: Wesleyan University Press, 1961); for Hannah Arendt, see *On Revolution* (New York: Penguin Books, 1963); for Edmund Morgan, see *Inventing the People: The Rise of Popular Sovereignty in England and America* (New York: W. W. Norton, 1988); for James Morone, see *The Democratic Wish: Popular Participation and the Limits of American Government* (New York: Basic Books, 1990); for Robert Hariman, see *Political Style: The Artistry of Power* (Chicago: Chicago University Press, 1995); for Michael Warner, see *The Letters of the Republic: Publication and the Public Sphere in Eighteenth-Century America* (Cambridge, Mass.: Harvard University Press, 1990); for Sacvan Bercovitch, see *The Rites of Assent: Transformations in the Symbolic Construction of America* (London: Routledge, 1993).

78. Warner, *Letters of the Republic,* 73.

79. Hariman, *Political Style,* 121, 102, 121.

80. See Arendt, *On Revolution,* 141–78. Regarding the collapsing of "legitimacy" and "legitimation" in Whitman's poetry, see Larson, *Whitman's Drama of Consensus,* 90.

81. See Ed Folsom, "Whitman and the Visual Democracy of Photography," in *Walt Whitman of Mickle Street: A Centennial Collection,* ed. Geoffrey Sill (Knoxville: University of Tennessee Press, 1994): 80–93.

82. On liberalism, see Benjamin Barber, *Strong Democracy: Participatory Politics for A New Age* (Berkeley: University of California Press, 1984).

83. I came across this notice while examining the 1855 edition held by the New York Historical Society. Greenspan mentions the copyright in *Walt Whitman and the American Reader* (86, 141) but then moves quickly on to other matters. Reynolds mentions the copyright in *Walt Whitman's America* (310) but does not proceed to question how it complicates Whitman's claims in the text itself. The traditional view is summarized by Williams in *Confounding Images,* where she observes that other than the frontispiece, "the book contained no other identifying material about the author" (42).

Conclusion

1. The Honorable Theodore Frelinghuysen, "Study of Our Political Institutions. Essay on the Propriety of Introducing the Study of the Constitution and Political Institutions of the United States, as Subjects of Instruction in Common Schools," *Proceedings of the American Lyceum* 1 (Boston: Carter and Hendree, 1832), 29.

2. Jefferson had presented a similar dilemma, exhibited in his paradoxically elitist populism regarding the relationships between education and democracy; see queries 14 and 15 of his *Notes on the State of Virginia,* ed. William Peden (Chapel Hill: North Carolina University Press, 1982 [1787]), 130–54.

3. See James Ford Rhodes, "Brooks Assaults Sumner," in *History of the United States from the Compromise of 1850,* abridged ed. (Chicago: University of Chicago Press, 1966 [1892]), 171–84. The image's caption is a quotation from a 31 May 1856 speech by Henry Ward Beecher at a rally on Sumner's behalf in New York City. For a collection of such speeches, see Cambridge Citizens, *The Sumner Outrage. A Full Report of the Speeches at the Meeting of Citizens in Cambridge, June 2, 1856, in Reference to the Assault on Senator Sumner* (Cambridge: John Ford, 1856).

4. Gustave de Beaumont, *Marie; or, Slavery in the United States,* trans. Barbara Chapman (Baltimore, Md.: Johns Hopkins University, 1999 [1835]), 114.

5. American Anti-Slavery Society, *The American Anti-Slavery Almanac, for 1839, Being the Third After Leap-Year, and the 63rd of American Independence. Calculated for New York; Adapted to the Northern and Middle States* (New York: S. W. Benedict, 1839). The monthly tables are printed on even-numbered pages, one for each month of the year.

6. Ralph Waldo Emerson, "The Fugitive Slave Law" (speech delivered 7 March 1854), in *Emerson's Antislavery Writings,* ed. Len Gougeon and Joel Myerson (New Haven, Conn.: Yale University Press, 1995), 73–89 (quotation, 73).

7. See Mary Kupiec Cayton, "The Making of an American Prophet: Emerson, His Audiences, and the Rise of the Culture Industry in Nineteenth-Century America," *American Historical Review* 92, no. 3 (June 1987): 597–620; and Donald Scott, "The Popular Lecture and the Creation of a Public in Mid-Nineteenth-Century America," *Journal of American History* 66, no. 4 (Mar. 1980): 791–809. Emerson was topped in terms of public appearances only by some of the religious speakers who burned up the countryside as part of the Second Great Awakening; see Nathan Hatch, *The Democratization of American Christianity* (New Haven, Conn.: Yale University Press, 1989).

8. On Emerson's antislavery activities, see Len Gougeon, *Virtue's Hero: Emerson, Antislavery, and Reform* (Athens: University of Georgia Press, 1990); on Emerson and eloquence, see James Perrin Warren, *Culture of Eloquence: Oratory and Reform in Antebellum America* (University Park: Pennsylvania State University Press, 1999), chap. 2.

Index

STEPHEN JOHN HARTNETT, a historian, rhetoric scholar, and assistant professor of speech communication at the University of Illinois at Urbana-Champaign, is the coauthor, with Robert James Branham, of *Sweet Freedom's Song: "My Country 'Tis of Thee" and Democracy in America* (Oxford University Press, 2002). His essays on rhetorical aspects of American history have appeared in, among others, the *Quarterly Journal of Speech, Philosophy and Rhetoric, American Studies,* and *Text and Performance Quarterly.* His work as a political activist, poet, and critic of the prison-industrial complex has appeared in the *Journal of Applied Communication Research, Journal of Contemporary Justice, Left Curve, The Future of Performance Studies,* and elsewhere. He has taught college in prisons for ten years and, as part of *The Waiting Room,* an interactive work of installation art, has spent three years traveling the country moderating community conversations about the death penalty. His works in progress include "Democracy Is Difficult: Investigative Prison Poems" and "Executing Democracy: The Enlightenment and the Death Penalty in Antebellum America."

The University of Illinois Press
is a founding member of the
Association of American University Presses.

Composed in 9.5/12.5 Trump Mediaeval
with Trump Mediaeval display
by Jim Proefrock
at the University of Illinois Press
Manufactured by Thomson-Shore, Inc.

University of Illinois Press
1325 South Oak Street
Champaign, IL 61820-6903
www.press.uillinois.edu